Frederick Morris Warren

A History of the Novel Previous to the Seventeenth Century

Frederick Morris Warren

A History of the Novel Previous to the Seventeenth Century

ISBN/EAN: 9783337028336

Printed in Europe, USA, Canada, Australia, Japan

Cover: Foto ©ninafisch / pixelio.de

More available books at **www.hansebooks.com**

A HISTORY OF THE NOVEL
PREVIOUS TO THE
SEVENTEENTH CENTURY

BY

F. M. WARREN

Professor in Adelbert College of Western Reserve University

NEW YORK

HENRY HOLT AND COMPANY

1895

PREFACE.

THE idea of writing a general treatise on the early novel was suggested to me by Körting's *History of the French Novel in the Seventeenth Century.* It is hoped that the following chapters may serve as an introduction to that work, and also prove to be, in some measure, an end in themselves. My method in studying into the beginnings of the various kinds of novels was derived from Rohde's *History of the Greek Novel.* This book also furnished the material for the two chapters on Alexandrian fiction, though the theories regarding the development of the Greek romance are not those advanced by Rohde. In the place of a full bibliography of the subject, a few references to leading authorities are appended to the text in the form of notes, under the chapters to which they belong. Occasional citations of more special articles supplement these references, to assist those who may desire to work up the matter from their own standpoint.

F. M. WARREN.

CLEVELAND, *November* 22, 1894.

v

CONTENTS.

CHAPTER I.

PAGES

CHAPTER II.

CHAPTER III.

The Greek Novel. Authors and Works.

CHAPTER IV.

Origins of the Romances of Chivalry.

CHAPTER V.

SPIRIT OF THE ROMANCES OF CHIVALRY. AMADIS OF GAUL.

CHAPTER VI.

SEQUELS TO AMADIS OF GAUL. THE PALMERINS, ETC.

CHAPTER XI.

OTHER KINDS OF SPANISH NOVELS. ENGLISH NOVELS. CHINESE NOVELS.

A HISTORY OF THE NOVEL PREVIOUS TO THE SEVENTEENTH CENTURY.

CHAPTER I.

INTRODUCTION.

THE difficulty in gaining a hearing for a treatise on the novel is apparent at the very start. It is a branch of literature which has become the most popular in depth and breadth, including all classes of writers and readers. Consequently any endeavor to put its history on a scientific basis would excite more general criticism than could befall any other kind of composition. Drama, poetry, letters, essays have been long considered legitimate objects of research, and more recently folk-lore and fiction have received serious attention. But the novel, or the story, or the romance, or whatever other results an analysis of the mass of fiction might give, would either be too trivial to be studied apart from one another, or too closely intertwined to render such a study profitable.

Yet at the present day the novel is fully recognized as an independent species of fiction and has finally received the name by which it is to be known. No one any longer, though a conservative lexicographer, fails to distinguish the novel from the story—possibly also from the romance, though doubts exist on this latter head. Such distinction, however, is not old. Our grandfathers had not formulated it apparently, or if they had their ancestors of the second generation surely had not. Novels they wrote, and they read what we call novels, but they used varied and uncertain terms for our precise and single one. Hence confusion in following out the species, and an unwillingness on the part of writers to discuss it by itself. For should we go back but a century in the history of literature and seek to classify the lighter reading of our forefathers, we find that the names now accepted are no longer guides, that *story* and *romance* are interchangeable terms, while the word *novel* rarely appears.

This statement applies more fittingly to English literature than it does to the fiction of any other people, because novels came into it later than they did elsewhere, and even then rather as imitations or exotics. The same thing is true also of Germany. But the writers of the Renaissance in southern Europe were perfectly well aware of the difference between the romances, the stories, and the novels of their age, though, as all such compositions were unworthy of the consideration of educated men, they did not bother themselves about establishing formally the boundaries between them. These were merely the pastimes of their leisure hours, and were treated as such. And yet the pedigree of even the English novel of the nineteenth century can be traced without any fear of serious mistakes back to its progenitors of the fifteenth and sixteenth. During these dozen generations or more the characteristics and outlines of this particular kind of writing have remained practically the same, and can therefore be plainly recognized at any moment of its intermediate career ; while the inherited resemblance points unmistakably back to the first of the race, the offspring of mediæval fancy.

Since this assertion, if not new, is at least unusual, it behooves its supporter to advance a few proofs that it rests, both in theory and in practice, on a solid foundation, and that the history of literature vouches for its correctness.

To reach this state of assurance, or more properly to lead others to it, a few definitions are necessary.

In the first place the term *fiction* is obvious in its application. It means what is not true, what is feigned. Romances, tales, novels, are *fiction*. So are poetry and drama, and every kind of writing which is not the statement or elucidation of a mental or material fact. But we distinguish poetry from drama, even when the latter is in verse, and mankind has always done so. In the same way these departments of literature have always been held separate from the less aspiring kinds of fiction, and have never been confused with romances or stories. And so to-day, when we say *story*, we do not mean *romance*, any more than when we speak of *romances* we allude entirely to *novels*. Therefore there must be some difference between these words, else they would not be employed in different senses in intelligent social circles.

Consequently for one who undertakes to study the novel it is imperative to determine at the outset what a novel is, and how it differs from the other kinds of fiction. Having first satisfied himself on this essential point, he must then be able to present a reasonable exposition of his views and demonstrate their soundness. But there is always this caution to be borne in mind, there where the forces of nature are at work, either in the evolution of an organism or in the expression of thought: in the process of evolution there is always a point where the separate forms are blended—however far apart may be their general contour—and the line of demarcation cannot be traced with rigid scientific accuracy between the one and the other. French and Provençal are two distinct idioms, yet no student of the Latin dialects can say, without many reservations, where on the soil of France Provençal ceases and French begins. No more can we put our finger on the exact spot where the romance, the story, and the novel diverge.

If we leave aside for the moment the fiction of antiquity, and consider the fiction which belongs to modern times, we can trace it in a very clear and continuous line of descent back to the stories of the Middle Ages. Now, in the Middle Ages the word *romance* was coined as well as the term *novel*. The former of these two expressions was the earlier, and may boast indeed of remote lineage. It was, in a certain sense, a general term, and was used to indicate a division in literature which is not particularly flattering to our national pride. For as all the serious works of mediæval times were written in the only respectable language of those times, in Latin, so the mass of the frivolous, popular, and national literature was expressed in the vernacular of the particular race which produced it. But the Latin races, and especially the Provençal and French, were the first to write extensively in the new tongues, and with a due acknowledgment of their linguistic inheritance from Rome, they called the ballads of the Troubadours and the epic songs of the Northern minstrels productions of the *Roman* tongue—of the *lingua romana*, to speak more learnedly. And afterward they gave to the poem itself—for prose came much later—the name of *romans*, a term which we have borrowed in our English *romance*.

Thus the first literary utterings of the modern speech were *romances*, and were known to their authors and hearers by that title. For some generations they continued to be in verse, so far as the manuscripts show in which they are preserved. But toward the end of the twelfth century the trade of the singers, who alone knew them, and who recited them to the people and the nobles, began to decline in dignity, while together with this passing away of a profession the art of reading became fashionable among the wealthier classes of society. In order to meet this change in taste there arose a new race of literary hacks—though it must be said in their praise that some of them were by no means ignorant of the elements of style—who turned the exploits of Charlemagne and his paladins, of Arthur and the knights of the Round Table, from poetical form into long narratives in prose. Once released from the restraints of rhyme, these story-tellers expanded and modified their traditional material according to the endowments of their own individual talents. To their prose versions of the mediæval epics descended the name *romance*, as a matter of course. Under that title they were made known to the admiring peoples of western Europe, and supplanted in popular favor their plainer poetical forerunners. In this way the term *romance* became fixed in general parlance, and down to the present day we speak of the "Arthurian romances" as a definite section of prose literature, while employing the epithet "metrical" to designate the stories of the cycle which remained in verse.

Still the prose romances were not novels, nor does the past history of the word *novel* aid us in discerning its present meaning ; for its first appearance as a designator of prose fiction was in Italy in the last quarter of the thirteenth century, when it meant what it does now in Italy, Spain, France, or Germany (*novela, nouvelle, novelle*). In England alone has its signification been extended in these six centuries from the title of a tale or story to the name of a much longer prose narrative. But this in comparatively recent years; for though Richardson is often called the "Father of the English Novel," neither he nor Fielding ever speak of their productions under any other title than that of "Histories," while the dictionaries for several decades into the nineteenth century still defined the word according to its original meaning of tale or story. Thus all past historical aid fails us, and we are obliged to define the subject of our study after the conceptions which exist to-day, and to distinguish the novel from its fellows of fiction by the standards which custom at present authorizes.

To return to our mediæval romance which knew itself,
and took its father's name. It was very similar to our
views of a novel. It was in prose, was a narrative, and
fictitious in subject ; though, in order to interest its readers,
it laid claim to the realities of life, and offered to support
its claim by documentary evidence in quantity sufficient to
satisfy the most ardent naturalist of the latest school. An
analysis of one of the kind, as *Lancelot* or *The Holy Grail*,
reveals a series of episodes and adventures which are
either ascribed to one man, and therefore form a kind of
biography, or else cluster around some central idea. A
narrative made up of such material may be said to have a
certain degree of connectedness, and perhaps something
which approaches unity of action. Yet if we look more
closely into the separate deeds, and their setting, we see
that they are not at all peculiar to the hero they laud for
the moment, but by a mere substitution of names they can
be applied to almost any knight of the Round Table.
On the other hand, the loss of many of the episodes would
in no way affect the action of the narrative in which they
appear.

So true to fact are both of these remarks that, with the
exception of Lancelot's love for Guinevere, and Tristan's
for Iseult, you can find hardly a distinguishing essential
characteristic in the whole range of the Breton adventures.
All is indefinite, conventional, and in no way calculated to
satisfy our notion of a novel. For this reason we have
abandoned to them their chosen name, *romance*, and confess
to ourselves that between them and the modern novel there
is a difference which touches the quality of the work, its
plan and its development.

As is well understood to-day, the Arthurian prose
romances are the fountain head of the modern novel.
They supplied its substance, as well as set it a model of prose
composition. They did not, however, furnish it with the

vital spirit, without which it would never have been created.
This shaping force came from another kind of mediæval
literature, and is more directly due to the honest minstrels
of France and to their powers of invention than has been
generally acknowledged. For from them and their songs
the novel received its idea of construction and plot. The
particular kind of poetry in which their talents were exercised was very much in favor during the Middle Ages, with
both French and Provençal writers, and but for the one
shortcoming of being in verse instead of prose it would
easily satisfy all of our modern requirements for a novel.
This kind flourished particularly in the last half of the
twelfth century, and during the thirteenth, and received
from students of mediæval literature the name of *roman
d'aventure*. The title reveals the content. It is almost
superfluous to add that the plot of these *romans*, often
cleverly constructed, was the mutual affection of knight and
lady. Their heroes and heroines comported themselves
like lovers of the present day, and set a worthy, if useless,
example of fidelity to the forgetful swains of Arthur's
household. The surroundings in which their themes were
developed were those of both court and private life, and
the glimpses which they afford of contemporary manners
and sentiments add not a little to their lasting success.
Of all the kinds of mediæval romancing, the *romans
d'aventure* remain the most attractive to readers of all
epochs in history, for they are natural and describe human
emotions.

From the prose stories of the Round Table, then, and
from these poetical accounts in the *romans d'aventure* of
refined life in the Middle Ages, came the first novel of
modern times. The one furnished form and incidents, the
other subject and inspiration. When the gifts were made,
how the two styles were fused, and by whom, we have no
means of knowing. For it was accomplished among the

people, in that stratum of folk legends and traditions which ever underlies the more assuming growth of literary works. And it was undoubtedly a very slow process, a gradual expansion of a simple story of love in castle walls through the addition of details and the insertion of adventures chosen from the favorite chapbooks of the Middle Ages. Two centuries at least must have been consumed by the evolution ; two centuries of humble tales by the fireside, cheering the hard toil of husbandman and shepherd with the pictures of chivalry and royal splendor.

The people gladly eulogized the nobility, for it had no thought of aspiring to the noble's seat. And when the romancers of the crowd had elaborated the praises of the aristocracy to the satisfaction of their clients, authors of higher lineage and better literary training continued their works, refined the crudities of their narratives, diluted the adventures they contained, added others foreign to tradition, and adapted the whole to the taste of a more exacting public. And so the Romance of Chivalry was born into literature.

The name of this universal legatee to the popular fiction of the Middle Ages was *Amadis of Gaul,* and the date of its appearance as a literary product the last half of the fifteenth century. By that time the formative process was completed and the kind had been fixed. As is the fate with all beginners, the rude ancestors of this courtly knight were entirely eclipsed by his greatness. They survived only in rare allusions in the lighter poetry and chronicles of the centuries preceding. Of their career and origins, the families out of which they sprung, and the manner in which they grew, we can learn only from the faint traces which still remain of them in the purified features of their descendant. So, roughly speaking, in the printed *Amadis of Gaul* there is an evident amalgamation, or fusion, of the Arthurian legends with a *roman d'aventure.* From a series of such episodes as composed the epic prose romances, joined together at random and rarely connected intrinsically with the hero or the enterprise they professed to celebrate, the mediæval tradition reappears in *Amadis of Gaul* as one story fairly well put together, consonant in its several parts, and arriving at a definite conclusion. Adventures-at-arms still occupy by far the greater amount of the space of the book, but the adventures had now some motive, some end to serve, and it is this motive which brings in the individual adventure, fashions it, decides its nature, and conducts it to some logical conclusion.

The motive, thus powerful in its action, is love. Out of love for his mistress the knight goes from her presence to win fame for her whose servant he is. And by the fame which thus redounds to her, he hopes to attract to himself her gratitude and her affection. For her sake he takes part in tournaments, fights giants, rescues maidens, befriends the oppressed, destroys the arts of magic, and captures the strongholds of the wicked. And should his lady receive his homage unwillingly, or manifest displeasure at his victories, the conquering hero dares not affront her glance. No solace has he remaining. Deeds of valor are but vanity, and the applause of all Christendom empty noise. He abandons to the admiring world his name and glory, and far away on desert shores he mortifies the flesh in melancholy gloom, until there reaches his ears the tidings of his pardon, and he may take again his sword from the willow and his armor from the altar and return to her feet, once more her invincible champion.

In other words, the presence of this motive for all the the deeds recounted, the motive which guides the entire story and crowns its end, makes a plot. And a plot makes of a prose narrative, such as the epic romances are, a novel. *Amadis of Gaul*, the first epic romance which contains a plot, is therefore our first modern novel. It is this plot which constitutes the essential difference between the romances of chivalry and their ancestors, the Arthurian romances. To their union with the Breton tales the *romans d'aventure* had brought the plot, as their dowry.

It is not to be supposed, however, from the emphasis with which this definition of a novel has been given, that the boundary line between the romance of the Middle Ages and the novel of the Renaissance is so distinct as to be clear at each and every point. Literature, as the expression of thought, must obey the laws which regulate all living organisms. When subject only to natural processes of development, and unobstructed by absolute, arbitrary rules, its various kinds proceed from one another and pass away into one another. So the romance which preceded the novel developed by slow stages into the novel, and at a certain period of this evolution you cannot say whether the story under your eyes is a romance or a novel. Abstract definitions, which under certain conditions should perform for us the same office that his stakes do to a surveyor, and should have no other object than to give us our bearings, apply to completed processes alone.

Having this truism in mind, there is no occasion for surprise at the discovery that we have defined not only the word *novel*, but the term *story* as well. To be sure, it is possible that a *story* may also be in verse, though the present technical application of the word would seem to exclude poetical narrative. But there is, in fact, no difference in quality between the prose story and the novel. It is merely a difference in size, the novel being the larger. Other languages have differentiated between the story and the novel very much as the English has done. In the Latin countries the word for both novel and romance is still the same (*roman*, etc.), while the word for story has its own title (*novela*, etc.), to which English-speaking peoples have now given a wider signification. Consequently the assertion that the difference between novel and story is one of quantity seems to be borne out both by current use elsewhere and by their etymology, with this concession, that the size requisite to a novel is evidently not to be determined by the number of pages it contains. The possibilities of its plot, and the degree to which its episodes might be reasonably expanded, appear to have some weight in the decision. For instance, the first realistic novel of modern times, the Spanish *Lazarillo de Tormes*, is much shorter than many of the self-confessed stories of its own century. And yet it has held its place in the category of novels, possibly on account of its significance in the history of fiction, but also perhaps because it is so greatly condensed. Still, in general, we are quite safe in assuming that a *novel* is a *story* of a larger growth.

Now there is another point which follows the one already made in this discussion. It follows much in the same way as a corollary follows a proposition in geometry. The proposition was that a novel is a fictitious prose narrative which contains a plot. The corollary is that a narrative having these essential features is a novel, whether the scenes it describes and the characters who appear therein are real or imaginary. Of course, if the novelist wishes to hold the attention of his public he must himself mentally share in the life which he pretends to picture. And if he does not choose to relate events, present or past, which really happen, he is bound at least to give to his incidents an air of probability. For no one will continue to delight in deeds and careers which are obtrusively false.

The essential thing, therefore, to be obtained by the novelist is that the reading public of his own day be led to admit that his story is possible. Whether to-morrow's reader believe in it or not, is not necessary to his purpose, though highly desirable for his lasting reputation. As a case in point, no member of this present intellectual generation can force himself to put the least credence in the events narrated by the romances of chivalry. Yet the mass of Spaniards in the sixteenth century not only gave them an existence in fancy, but even an existence in fact, and the immortal parody on them, by which Cervantes endeavored to destroy this belief, remains to-day a monument to the credulity of mankind. He put into current life the supposed actions of the old knight-errantry, and employed the entire range of his talents to demonstrate their absurdity. The pastoral dramas and novels of the Renaissance could also lay claim to numerous dupes in the world of affairs, and many an unfortunate lover and cruel mistress patterned their despair and disdain after their illustrious predecessors of Arcadia, or the shepherds in the less distant valleys of the Tagus and Lignon. Even allegories can be so constructed that their types may become to us living characters, and the experience of the soul take on as much appearance of reality as the vicissitudes of our physical existence. It is hardly necessary to recall in this connection Bunyan's *Pilgrim's Progress.*

The nature of the novel, as distinct from other prose fiction, having been thus assumedly established, the time has come to enter upon a second plane of meditation, and consider the place of the novel in the literature of the various peoples which have given it birth. It has been seen in the foregoing sketch of the development of the modern novel, that it came later than epic, lyric, or narrative poetry, and also later than the drama—at least the drama of the period to which it really belonged. For the romance of chivalry is purely mediæval in its matter and soul, and its plot and substance were derived from the literature of the period immediately preceding it. Consequently it is safe to say that in its first manifestation and form the novel belongs to imitative literature, and not to inventive.

When the time had come for the transformation of mediæval epic poetry into prose fiction, the society of the

Middle Ages was entering upon another phase of being. The years which witnessed the appearance of the prose Arthurian romance—toward the beginning of the thirteenth century—were those which looked upon the rise of the communes also. But the epic poems on Charlemagne's paladins and the knights of the Round Table had been composed on the one hand for the amusement of baronial feasts and princely assemblies, and on the other for the delectation of the crowd in the village market-places, or of the gatherings at the country cross-roads. They were made to be sung, or recited. Consequently when they were worked over into prose, the public for which they were intended must have been an entirely different one. It was a public of readers, and in these good old times the majority of laymen who knew their letters pertained neither to the nobility nor the common people, but to the trading classes, the third estate. So in their new form the epic romances fell in the social scale, and became rather the pastime of plebeians.

Yet this substitution of one body of supporters for another in no way affected the aristocratic tone of the prose romances. The national songs of France, which had their origin in the camps of the Frankish warriors and which were fostered by all the traditions of chivalry, found refuge among the commoners when the lords had tired of them, and had driven from their halls the minstrels who still cherished them. The Celtic legends, which were not of French birth, but which were carried to the French by wandering bards, attracted at first the notice of a new race of court poets, better endowed than the minstrels who had laid claim to the heroic epic. These versifiers were rewarded by Louis VII. and the great vassals of his crown. By them the scattered lays of the Breton singers were joined together into more ambitious poems and dedicated to royal patrons; and when these poems in their turn were made over into prose, they still retained unimpaired their ideals of high-born sentiments and actions.

It is to this last class of epic literature, the Breton stories, that the romances of chivalry are so closely related. The most striking thing about the circumstances of their composition as poems was that they were, with rare exceptions, written at the command of princesses. The *romans d'aventure* coincide with the Breton tales in this respect, being also dedicated to the noble ladies of England and of France. Now, the theme of both these kinds of poetry was love and gallantry, and the stories which celebrated the power of love were the first to find their way into prose. By the middle of the thirteenth century all the important poems on Arthur and his knights had passed into their present form of romances, while the epics on Charlemagne and his warlike followers did not undergo this transformation until full two centuries later, on the eve of the commercial reign of Louis XI. The songs of war and violence were the peculiar property of men. The lays of love and chivalry waited on the pleasure of women. Fortified by these facts, it may not seem too hazardous to conclude that we owe to women the beginnings of the modern novel.

Having these antecedents, tendencies, and patronesses, the stories of chivalry found themselves prepared for a new period of existence, and the history of their development, though often obscure in point of authors and dates, lies near enough to the modern student of literature to furnish sufficient proofs for the theories which may be formed concerning them. But this is not the case when we turn to the novel of antiquity, the one which flourished on African and Asiatic soil in the last epoch of Hellenic literature. Here no references in contemporary writers testify to its origin or popularity. Stories of love and adventure were too trivial to win a place in the works of serious authors, even by mention and in passing, and we have no landmarks to show the road which was followed by the romances of Syrian or Alexandrian narrators. They appear to us only in their final form. Theoretically, it is probable that the evolution of the Greek novel was the same as the growth of its Romance sister. Epic poems passed into epic prose when the Greek traders drove from their kingdoms the monarchs of Argos and Mycenæ, with their retinue of minstrels. But in their new dress they retained the characteristics of the old one, and celebrated still the deeds of Homeric heroes, or their kin, and the loves of a Hector and an Andromache. Yet of these prose narratives, did such exist, there is to-day no sign. One fragment only of a story, aristocratic in tone, whose surroundings are those of noble life, survives the disdain of poet and historian. And this fragment deals partly with historical characters. All the other novels of the Greeks are persistently plebeian (unless *Theagenes and Chariclea* be an exception), and their action is carried on in the midst of merchants and mariners. Between them and the *Iliad* or *Odyssey* were no less than seven centuries of intense mental effort, while between *Tristran* and *Amadis of Gaul* there is a time interval of but three hundred years, years in a period of the world's history notorious for its intellectual inertia and lack of originality.

So we may lay down as we please the laws for the evolution of the novel from the epic song, and conceive that there was in ancient Greece a whole series of gradations through prose romances, in favor with the people, aristocratic in sentiment, traditional or historical in subject, until the era of purely *bourgeois* compositions was reached, the end of the literary creations of the nation. For from its folk-lore and mythology the genius of the Greek race had developed the larger part of the Homeric epic and the drama of an Æschylus. A flowering of lyric verse accompanied the evolution of the stage. Then came the great historians and the most potent philosophers. Afterward, with the decay of public spirit, a decline in literature is visible. The drama loses its vigor, poetry its freshness, and rhetoric comes forward as a substitute for thought. Then the Greek intellect escaped from the narrow confines set by its physical boundaries. It cast its influence over Asia, Africa, and Rome. Alexandria took the place of Athens. Trade engrossed the activity of the members of the Areopagus. The long period of mental growth and poetic imaginings declined into a period of intellectual stagnation. Scholars became compilers, investigators, or critics, such as the nineteenth century sees again. Imitation took the seat which invention had abandoned, while the material accumulated during the centuries of literary production was rehashed, and modified to suit the palates of a less aspiring generation. At the same time the appetite for amusement was stimulated by the increase of riches. The merchants and their families, who now constituted the influential class in society, demanded their portion of the notoriety obtained by letters. And thus to compensate for the weakness of inventiveness in the higher branches of literature, to satisfy the importunity of a set of patrons whose wealth was their chief endowment, and, possibly, to cater to the requirements of a sex debarred from the theater and the forum, the chapbook of the Greek populace was raised, not long after the destruction of Corinth, to the dignity of a well-rounded novel. To be sure, its life was, so far as we know, unimportant and uneventful. Few specimens of its kind have come down to us of modern times, and it seems to have disappeared entirely with the last literary caste of Greece, the rhetoricians, leaving but slight traces of its existence on the subsequent fiction of eastern or western Europe.

From the fifth to the fifteenth century of the Christian era humanity was obliged to do as well as it could without the solace of novels. However, this deprivation was not so serious as it might seem, inasmuch as mankind, in the Dark and Middle Ages, possessed stories and superstitions in abundance. At all events a repose of so long a duration redounded to the benefit of the novel as an influential factor in fiction. For when it came once more to the front, in the Spain of Ferdinand and Isabella, it entered immediately and permanently upon a much wider career of prosperity. Not only did it sum up the traditions of mediæval epic literature in the modern romance of chivalry, but in the sixteenth century it created from the ruins of the popular theater the realistic or *picaresco* novel, and from the rural poetry of Virgil and his Renaissance followers, both Spanish and Italian, the novel of pastoral disguises.

Outside of Spain the sixteenth century saw no especial activity in novel-writing. In Italy the pastoral novel died away without leaving any particular heirs in fiction. In France and England imitation of Spanish writers did not begin until the last quarter of the same century. And only in far-off Cathay, at the very time when the mariners of the Spanish peninsula were seeking for a waterway to its golden shores, was there to be found contemporary with the Spanish romance of chivalry an independent and successful novel of manners.

In the seventeenth century the prospect in Europe somewhat broadens. Cervantes' wit marks in Spain the decline of the whole mass of unreal fiction, but the *picaresco* story continues one generation longer, accompanied by the glorious outburst of the Spanish drama. During this epoch Italy did nothing but follow servilely her Romance neighbor. In England, Shakspere and his successors had absorbed in their plays all the intellectual talents of the island. Germany had not yet awoke to genuine attempts at novelistic writing, and in France alone did the movement which Spain had started in the previous century increase in power. True to their national characteristics the French modified and adapted to their own taste the ideas in fiction which they had received from abroad, and the material which renascent Europe had made available to them was increased by the addition of notable situations chosen from the Greek novels, now widely read, and by the conceptions of the pastoral dramas of Italy. The sentiments of *Amadis of Gaul*, of *Diana*, of *Aminta*, and the *Pastor Fido* were applied by them to actual life, and for more than fifty years the great compilations of D'Urfé, Gomberville, La Calprenède, and Madeleine de Scudéry ruled polite society.

Satirical and *picaresco* novels were also cultivated in France, while various other forms, political, allegorical, fantastic, and religious, united to bear witness to the popular craze for such literature. But the arrival of Molière and Racine put a check on the productiveness of novelists. Dramatists and essayists became for many generations the fashion. Writers of fiction were few, and of the few nearly every one made his story-telling subordinate to his other literary labors. Mme. de La Fayette stood almost alone in the last half of the seventeenth century, while Le Sage, Prévost, Marivaux, Rousseau, and Saint-Pierre make up the short list of successful authors in the eighteenth.

For this latter epoch was reserved all the great revival of fiction which was to arouse the literary men of every nation of Europe, and advance the novelist to a front rank among writers. England was the place of the revival, and the honor of the awakening belongs to Richardson, Fielding, and perhaps also to Smollett. Their inspiration was varied, and their own genius was its wellspring. For Fielding and Smollett the works of Cervantes, Le Sage, and the Spanish *picaresco* writers served as models. Richardson was more individual in his form, and wider reaching also in his influence. It is interesting to see how he applied to his innate fondness for letter-writing the moral sentiments of the *Spectator*, and the ideas of the drama of the generation following. His novels are so many arguments on the reward of virtue and the punishment of vice. If they excel in the delineation of female character, it is to be remembered that, like the compilers of prose fiction in the Middle Ages, their author addressed himself particularly to women.

From England the movement soon returned to France. There, Rousseau fashioned after Richardson his eulogies of sentiment and nature, and passed them on to Germany, where Goethe became his disciple. But the development of this style was broken in upon by the commotions of the Revolution and the campaigns of the Empire. When peace was again restored, and literature was again sought after for its own sake, the historical romances of Walter Scott followed the reactionary idealism begotten of the conflict, while the social changes which pressed hard in the wake of these stormy times received their chroniclers in the persons of Stendhal and Balzac.

In these two parallel streams, romantic and realistic, the currents of the novel of the nineteenth century flowed for more than fifty years, gathering to themselves during that period all the devious outpourings of the human heart, past, present, and to come. And when all the motives of fictitious composition had been explored, and drawn upon to their exhaustion, a great lull in novel-writing came, a calm such as has not existed for perhaps two centuries.

When the present quiet will cease and a new movement begin it is impossible to predict. If the history of the past offers any assistance in the solution of the problem, we may learn from it that the novel, imitative in its material, depends for its inspiration and substance on the more inventive kinds of literature, the poetry and the drama.

Therefore a revival in novel-writing must be preceded by a revival in poetry, or by a renewal of dramatic power. But these highest manifestations of human thought owe their periods of quickening and splendor to great popular commotions and modifications of the social state. Consequently, if these deductions be correct the twentieth century will be well on its way before the world beholds again any considerable flowering of romantic fiction.

CHAPTER II.

THERE may have been novels among the Hindoos and Egyptians, whose civilizations had disappeared before the life of historical antiquity had begun, but so far as records are now extant it is the Greek novel that first made an appearance in literature. It was not a branch of writing much cultivated even in the period of decadence which produced it, if we are to judge from the few specimens preserved and from the absence of contemporary references to it. But it evidently flourished as vulgar reading for many centuries before it was touched up by art, and the rarity of its literary examples may be due to that severity of taste which was the inheritance of the Greek race, rather than to the loss of manuscripts. This same classical taste would also render the composition of the new branch of fiction a difficult task, demanding higher training and more invention than the romancers of the Middle Ages laid claim to, and thus would tend to limit the crowd of aspiring novelists, and permit only the works of the fittest.

The leisure which the average citizen of Athens or Ephesus enjoyed was peculiarly adapted to the refinement and expression of thought, however trivial that thought might be. At no time in the life of the Grecian states do the great authors of their race appear to have been neglected, and this constant intercourse of posterity with their works evidently kept alive the notions of style, long after the inspiration of ideas had passed away. The civilization of the Greeks is a contrast to ours, particularly in the absence of a steady pressure to accumulate facts. Consequently the men of antiquity found time to discuss principles. This feature is especially shown in the management of the Greek drama. The theater-goer knew beforehand all the events which the poet was to relate. There was, therefore, no burden of exposition laid upon the dramatist, but he was free to devote all his energies to the portrayal of the emotion or passion he wished to make prominent in his characters, and his audience could give its undivided attention to his purpose and plan.

Now, this same care for literary polish and clever thinking may have had a repressive influence on the production of prose fiction as well, and the novels which have come down to us may include the larger number of the successful ones known to the ancients. Still, if this supposition be allowed, we may consider it as holding true only for the higher class of fictitious compositions, for what may be called literature, and that beneath this current of fine writing and logical development there ran the broader and more turbid one of popular romances, having its sources even so far back as the period of decline in epic poetry. Such a theory is not only pleasing, but it is also natural, and would be supported by the analogy of the romances of chivalry, as we have seen. Yet we have no proofs of it at hand. No epic romances in prose are known in ancient literature, and even the half-historical one, which might have been patterned on prose versions of Greek feudal legends and foreign wars, cannot be earlier than the first century of the Christian era.

To stick by the facts in the case, therefore, we are obliged to pass from the Homeric epics down over the flourishing centuries of Greek art and learning to that time in the history of the race when Greek genius had well-nigh run out. Long before the appearance of this first remnant of ancient prose fiction, the poetry of the isles and the drama of Attica had ceased to be living forces in the nation's development. The political liberty of the several states, and of the race as a whole, had yielded generations before to the attacks of factions and the inroads of foreign despotisms. The conquests of Alexander in the East had widened the horizon of Greek thought, and had spread Greek culture over a new and immense expanse of territory. So dilution of thought was necessary, and with its dilution its strength and its power of resistance to Oriental fantasies were impaired. The founding of Alexandria midway between the East and the West, and the growth in population which increasing commerce fostered at the mouth of the Nile, soon made that town the intellectual center of the race as it was the center of opulence.

Thus there came about a geographical displacement in Greek civilization, which found itself in an environment unknown to its traditions. With the mixture of peoples the mental conceptions of the new capital became cosmopolitan. Gradually the superstitions of Syria and Egypt were won over by the allurements of Athenian wit, and sought expression in a language whose polish and harmony had made it an almost universal tongue. And when this mingling of ideas and sentiments of widely different peoples had been fully accomplished, the physical strength of the Western barbarian overcame them all and broke down every barrier of race, to the profit of the all-absorbing dominion of Rome.

The first Greek novel known to moderns was written in the midst of these surroundings, and under the influence of these conditions. The elements out of which it was made were partly Greek and partly Oriental. Yet in the fusion of the two civilizations, and in the mingling of the two streams of inspiration, it was the European which maintained its supremacy over the Asiatic. The example of the heroic poetry of ancient Hellas and the power of the epic prose narratives, which undoubtedly kept alive its ideals and incidents among the people, prevailed even when its legends were transported to other lands and were circulated among a heterogeneous population. So we are not surprised to find the first surviving specimen of a Greek novel assimilating, in the land of Egypt, the material drawn from Oriental sources with the traditional conception of a Homeric romance. Unfortunately the novel in question has been preserved only in a fragmentary state, and indeed has but recently been brought to the attention of the modern world. It was written on some rolls of Egyptian papyrus, which were much mutilated by the subsequent uses to which they were put. But still enough of the volume has been kept intact to reveal its subject and afford a fair idea of its style and contents.

The subject is the love of young Nimrod, the fabulous founder of Nineveh, for a maiden whose name is not given, but who is evidently the great Semiramis. The lovers are cousins, and the fragment begins with a petition of the hero to his beloved's mother, Derkeia, not to delay the marriage any longer. He himself had journeyed far over distant countries, and as the ruler of many peoples had been courted everywhere and flattered. Yet faithful to the oath he had taken, he had remained ever true to his loved one, and now, as the captive of his mistress, he longed for the loosing of his bonds in wedlock. To this fervent plea Derkeia replied, that she esteemed his character and wondered at his fidelity, inasmuch as he was but seventeen years of age and already so powerful a prince, but that an ancient custom prevented the marriage of her child until she should reach the prescribed maturity of fifteen. Two years longer they must wait, subject to the will of fate, who might destroy them or keep them alive thus long. Naturally this answer was not pleasing to Nimrod, who entered on another oration, emphasizing the necessities of state that the royal line should be preserved, the uncertainty of a warrior's life, and the purity of his own intentions. To all of which Derkeia answered reservedly, but promised to intercede for him. Now the scene changes, and the maiden comes on in troubled conversation with Thambe, the mother of her sweetheart. Tears and sobs drown her words, in spite of Thambe's consolations. Finally, the older woman takes on herself to answer for the respectful conduct of her son, and restores happiness to the bosom of the girl by the portrayal of Nimrod's matrimonial zeal. With the rapturous gratitude of the girl the interview ends, and the first part of the story abruptly concludes with the meeting of the sisters to take counsel over their children.

The second part of the novel evidently intended to relate the warlike prowess of the hero. But the gaps in the manuscript render uncertain the connection with the first part, and also what has happened since the deliberation of the mothers. Nimrod appears to be sunk in deep despair, at all events, and soon with the approach of spring he summons his host to a campaign against the Armenians. The numbers of his army, their advance over physical obstacles into the country of the enemy, and their wonderful formation in battle order are described most rhetorically. Nimrod himself takes charge of the cavalry, and after a harangue to the soldiers, presses on against the foe. The favorable outcome of the fight and the subsequent happy union of the lovers must be surmised, for at this point the fragment stops, and no sequel to it has as yet been found.

How this tale of love and adventure may be related to supposed epic prose narratives of Greek tradition we can only conjecture. It has certainly forsaken their subject and their locality, and yet there is something in its tone which suggests the spirit of the Homeric age. This tone is not in the sentiment of the work, for such disquisitions on love and on the relations of the sexes were not highly valued in the flourishing period of Greek literature, and here they indicate clearly the effeminacy of a weakling generation. Also tears, unless of anger, did not abound among the heroes of the Trojan war, and the loss of a woman's affection never reduced the feudal chieftains to emotional despair. But the choice of subject in the fragment offers a parallel to the epic themes. Instead of characters which were celebrated by Hellenic legend, our unknown author has availed himself of Babylonian tradition, and has taken from the stories extolling the might of Nimrod and the charms of Semiramis an outline for his narrative familiar to his public. This outline may have even passed among the credulous dwellers of Alexandria as true history. The characters here are also royal personages, like the great names of the Greek epic. The tone is aristocratic, the work is not plebeian, and it professes to narrate the youthful love and prowess of a noble pair, very much as in later times the romances glorified the names of Tristan and Iseult, of Amadis and Oriana, or as before its day the minstrels may have sung of Hector and Andromache. For such tales must have been abundant even in Greece, under the influence of that desire for narratives of love which is common to all times and to all races.

There is a slight analogy between the story of Nimrod and the career of Amadis, the hero of the first romance of chivalry. Both loved at an early age, and were beloved by tender maidens. Each left his love to win fame by prowess at arms, and each kept inviolate, in the face of all temptations, the faith he had sworn to his mistress. Furthermore, both were the sons of kings and succeeded to kingdoms, and the girls they wooed were princesses. Such resemblances, which hold good for but one other Greek novel—and in that case very remotely—are of course merely comparisons, and have very little practical bearing. Yet they might be used to support the conjectural theory that this single specimen of a Greek romance of chivalry—if we may properly give it that title—had the same career as *Palmerin of England;* that its kind descended from the old epic poetry by the intermediary of prose versions; that in these versions, destined wholly for popular use, the element of love played a constantly increasing part, in accordance with the trend of sentiment among the people; and that when one day some literary man of talent looked about for a new theme to introduce into literature he found these traditional narratives awaiting his pleasure. It would be no difficult work to give them a literary finish, to expand certain descriptions in the rhetorical manner of the time, and to add certain details which would make the production more artistic and more vivid. The story of Nimrod would then be an imitation of one of these romances founded on national legends, substituting for them similar traditions of another race. They would, therefore, appeal to the readers of Alexandria and the cities of Syria as an acceptable departure from the time-worn paths of Hellenic story.

When the loves of Nimrod and the maiden were first told is not certain. It was at least as early as the beginning of the first century of the Christian era, and probably preceded that date by a generation or more. Some decades evidently must have elapsed between the appearance of this romance and the composition of the other Greek novels preserved, for the latter differ from the former entirely, both in sentiment and in choice of subject. They break away wholly from past tradition, legendary or historical, and represent only the feeling of their own times. Their tone is plebeian, their descriptions are often realistic, and their actors are almost without exception chosen from the merchant classes. They also lessen notably the part of love in their narratives, and reduce it almost to the office of a mere connecting link, which neither inspires deeds nor rewards them. Love would seem to be the motive power in the story of Nimrod, and his exploits were undertaken to fix on himself more firmly the affection of his mistress. So he confesses himself her slave. But in the Greek novels of the later period Fate, which in *Nimrod* merely cuts short, or prolongs, the lives of mortals, is responsible both for the action of the story and its adventures, while love plays little part in the leave-takings.

The author, however, of the *Nimrod* fragment belongs to the same class of writers to whom the later novels owe their existence. He is a rhetorician, a Sophist, as the schoolmen of antiquity were called. He delights in emotional scenes, in descriptions of passions, in pictures of incidents, and especially in long orations. The Sophists formed the literary class of the Greek decadence. They had in keeping the traditions of the classical past. They were the appointed guardians of the perfected tongue. They dictated the use of words and set the models for composition. They were in fact the academicians of the day, the instructors of the youth, and the professors of eloquence and public speaking.

The Greeks of the Alexandrian age attached an extreme importance to the mode, the manner of literary expression. And this cultivation of style seems rather singular, in view of the decline in the other branches of art, which flourish as a rule contemporaneously with a refined taste in literature. The loss of political independence, and the exhaustion of the native vigor of the Greek mind, had betrayed itself in the domain of the fine arts by the substitution of an allegorical conception of sculpture and painting for the ideal representation of the ancestral gods and national heroes. The migration to Syria and Egypt had gradually introduced a liking for adornment and Oriental picturesqueness. The results of these changes were manifested in art by the use of groups for single figures, of which we have some instances in the later novels of the time, by an imitation of the classical themes of mythology, by the painting of landscapes, and a lavish use of color. Mosaics came into fashion at this epoch.

The Greek artists left the delineation of the ideal for the description of the real, and by thus contributing to dry up the springs of the imagination they quickly descended from realism to crudeness—to what we to-day call naturalism. So poetry in art disappeared and with it poetry in literature. Literature degenerated into rhetoric, and ornamentation of phrase and sentence took the place of classical simplicity and harmony.

Now the period of this exaggerated fondness for rhetoric coincided with the centuries when the Greek novel—as we now know it—flourished. And all internal evidence goes to show that the teachers of rhetoric, the dialecticians of antiquity, were the makers of the literary form of the novel. The themes given out for practice in their schools were on such subjects as are most frequently amplified in the romances, such as descriptions of nature and natural phenomena, verbal reproductions of paintings and statuary, fusions of mythological legends with tales of humble life, dramatic plots, outlines of orations, folk-lore, traditions, and whatever might lend itself to rhetorical ornamentation. As the demand of the public for such diversion increased, the Sophists became a great power in the state. They seem to have considered the whole field of human activity as their possession, and worked it to their own aggrandizement. We can conceive then that when the chapbook of the people first attracted their attention, bowed under the weight of its accumulated traditions gathered since the heroic era of the race, or half hidden by the overflow of Oriental marvels and superstitions, that the vainglorious schoolmen had no scruples at all in relieving it of its burdens, in shaping anew its proportions, and in bestowing on its homely outlines the saving grace of their own art. The result of their zeal was that the Greek novel came forth, a new creation in literature, not at all discreditable to its sponsors.

The Greek novel owes to the Sophists, not its existence, but its reputation and preservation. Besides the many correspondences of manner and subject already pointed out, there may be cited as proofs of their handiwork the pathos of the harangues, and the elaborate expressions of the letters inserted in the narrative. The Sophists also became prominent not many decades before the beginning of the Christian era, and from this period dates our earliest specimen of the novel, the love of Nimrod and the maiden. Probably the predecessors of this story had been prose romances which celebrated more particularly the heroes of old Greece. To substitute for them the royal figures of Asiatic history was comparatively easy. We may also infer that many of these imitations abounded in Antioch and Alexandria, since the original romance of Greek chivalry was the favorite reading in the *penetralia* of Athens and Ephesus. But the *Nimrod* story is the only one of its kind which has outlived the revenge of time. It is the only narrative of court life, aristocratic in its entire feeling, which survives among the novels of Hellenic literature, For though other novels, equally the work of the Sophists have come down to posterity, they differ completely in tone and sentiment from this solitary tale of love among princes.

The main cause for this difference undoubtedly lies in those changes in social conditions which took place between the invention of the story of *Nimrod* and the composition of its rivals. The time interval between the two may have been as much as 150 years. It must have been at least three generations. It would seem that the Roman conquest of the East, which took place at the time when the

Sophists were aspiring to the universal control of literature, had done away with all class distinctions, and had leveled local aristocrats and democrats alike before the paramount privilege of Roman citizenship. With the establishment of this right, which even the most ancient princely houses coveted, had come expansion of commerce, already incited by the rule of an Alexander. When the despotism of the Roman emperors had become assured, and there was no longer any barrier in caste between the sovereign and the people, a social revolution had been accomplished analogous to the transformation of France under Louis XI. The mercantile class became practically the entire nation. And this class was no longer composed of pure Greeks only, but was made up of the various peoples which crowded together in Alexandria, Antioch, Cyprus, Ephesus, or Smyrna.

By their inheritance these new rulers of public thought were not favorably inclined to the maintenance of Hellenic tradition. The aristocrats, whom they had overcome in the municipality, they would naturally antagonize in the domain of literature also. The loss of political liberty would be another element of destruction to the cultivation of the patriotic and national themes which had absorbed the poets and dramatists of ancient Greece. Broader and more general subjects would be required by the mingling of races and customs. So in this period—when the Sophists represented the lovers of the higher literature—erudition, scientific research, the compilation and verification of known facts occupied the time of scholars, while commerce and the pursuit of wealth claimed the attention of the whilom soldiers and statesmen.

It was to be expected that this overturning of the whole economy of the various classes of society, their new relations to one another and to the outside world, would be reflected in the literary production of the times. The increase of riches had surely increased the number of readers and had thus expanded the public tributary to authors. But this very increase on the part of those who had cultivated in the past no literary traditions, and who furthermore were undoubtedly hostile to the old ones, was bound to affect unfavorably the existing standards of taste and style. It must be admitted, too, that the first influence of Christianity contributed to the same end. The new religion was confined for a while almost entirely to the traders and mariners, and to the poorest of these. It therefore would be tinged by their social prejudices and mental attitudes, and, as we know, it displayed in many of its apologists a decided enmity to the rich and powerful. Besides this shadow of worldly taint, the mission of Christianity was to supplant, to banish the old and put forward the new, to destroy the civilization of the ancient world and begin the civilization of the modern. Now the great monuments of Greek literature were based on the mythology of the race, and on the adoration of physical phenomena. All this display of fancy and art must therefore have aroused the twofold hostility of the adherents of a struggling creed, which enjoined on its followers the fraternity of mankind, as well as the worship of one God. Caste and paganism were their natural enemies, and to prepare the way for the new era of peace and love these twin supporters of the old order of things must first be done away with. On the other hand it is an axiom that only by the study of recognized models, bequeathed by the masters of past civilizations, and by a return to nature for fresh material to be cast in the mold furnished by these models, can a revival of literary taste or artistic refinement ever be accomplished. The Greco-Romans, and particularly the Christians, who gloried in a revealed religion, abhorred the teachings of nature and hated the forms of classical culture. Therefore the Sophists, who alone endeavored to oppose the popular will, and to keep alive the memories of the great artists in literature, attracted no earnest body of supporters, and hence their admiration for the past became perfunctory and barren of quickening results.

It is to all these transformations, social, national, political, and religious, that we may very plausibly ascribe the difference in spirit and subject between the *Nimrod* fragment and the surviving novels of the later Alexandrian era. The former still respected the traditions of the race. It was composed before the rise of the one-man power at Rome, before the great extension of Oriental trade, and before the promulgation of the new tenets of religion. Probably when this story was written the Greek emigrants to the Nile Delta still preserved intact their ancestral customs. They still held at bay the inroads of the Eastern peoples which they swayed, and were only beginning to avail themselves of the legends and superstitions of their subjects. When, soon afterward, they too became the vanquished and were arbitrarily classed by the new conquerer with the mass of mankind outside the pale of Roman citizenship, the bulwarks of national prejudice, which they had hitherto defended against the beleaguering barbarians, were also swept away, and Greek mingled freely with Asiatic in the preparation for the new era of the world.

Accordingly, popular literature assumed the characteristics of the new surroundings. The past was ignored. The present became the theme. No longer were the loves of kings and princesses described to arouse the enthusiasm of a loyal public. The patrons of literature, the merchants and traders of the Roman East, demanded that they themselves be eulogized in the works of romantic fiction, and that their adventures and domestic relations furnish the material for the story. And consequently the Greek novel of the four centuries which followed the destruction of Jerusalem is the opposite in exploits and sentiments of the Greek novel which preceded the complete fusion of Greek and Oriental. Its heroes are ordinary characters of the middle class, and its incidents are vulgar happenings to travelers and seafarers. With the exception of Heliodorus, who calls up in the fifth century the ghost of the old romance of chivalry, everything in this new school of fiction is common and plebeian to a degree. No greater change occurred later on in Spanish fiction, when *Amadis of Gaul* yielded to the *picaresco* tales of *Lazarillo de Tormes* and *Guzman de Alfarache.*

Yet in this new age of novelistic effort the same methods of composition prevail as in the former period. Emotions continue to be dramatically portrayed, and orations are still delivered with fulsome eloquence. The fact is, that the Sophist of the earlier epoch—to whose self-consciousness was very likely due the first deviation from the established tradition of the Homeric prose epic—has weathered the social and political storm, and now adapts his pen with praiseworthy flexibility to the new customs and the new requirements. Whether as an idealist or a realist, he retains the manner he had learned in the schools, and connects the romance of chivalry with the plebeian narratives by the links of his peculiar rhetorical phrases. From the standpoint of style the Greek novel of both periods is one and the same. Possibly also there may have been internal evidences of relationship between the two schools, in works which have not come down to us, and the monopoly of the right to manufacture novels which was retained by the Sophists would make such a supposition likely. But there are no existing proofs of such a gradation, and the first novel of the new epoch, of which we have any knowledge, is unfortunately lacking in its original text, thus forcing us to form an idea of its contents by the analysis which a bibliographer of many centuries later has handed down to us.

However, from his summary we can gain a fair notion of the characteristics of the *bourgeois* style of Greek narration.

The bibliographer in question is Photius, the learned patriarch of Constantinople, who lived in the ninth century, and the analysis of the novel is found in his celebrated *Myriobiblion*, which has preserved for posterity so many of the writings of antiquity. In this compilation, Photius quotes quite extensively from the book of a certain Antonius Diogenes, who seems to have been an author of the beginning of the second century. His narrative is called by Photius *The Marvelous Things beyond Thule*. It was in twenty-four books, and its author claims to have borrowed his material from preceding writers. The story is told, in the first person, by Dinias, the leading character, and who is an Arcadian settled in Tyre, to Cymba one of his former compatriots.

Dinias, with his son Demochares, had left Arcadia with the object of improving their minds by travel. But instead of visiting the centers of civilization they voyaged over the seas of Greece to the northward, and journeyed through savage tribes to the shores of the Scythian ocean, and thence to the island of Thule, which lies toward the sunset. There Dinias met a maiden of Tyre, Dercyllis, who with her brother, Mantinias, had fallen prey to the cunning of an Egyptian priest, Paapis. They had been induced by him to give to their parents a healing draught, as they supposed, but which turned out to be a sleep potion of the strongest sort. Unable to arouse the victims from their lethargy, and fearing punishment for their mistake, the children had fled from Tyre. Over the Mediterranean they wandered to Italy. There Dercyllis descended into Hades and explored its mysteries under the guidance of Myrto, one of her servants, who had died some time before. Coming again at length into the light of day she loses her brother, but finds other companions, with whom she visits Spain and the remoter Celts. After long stages, in which many wonders are seen and much magic is practiced, she returns to Italy and finds there Paapis, and also her brother, who has himself undergone wonderful experiences in the sun and moon and in distant islands. The two now unite to rob the priest of his implements of magic and flee to Thrace, where an oracle foretells their excursion to Thule and their ultimate return to Tyre, after undergoing many hardships.

Mutual adventures of so thrilling a sort awakened of course the tender passion in the breasts of both Dinias and Dercyllis. But their true love has many courses yet to run, of strange perils, incantations, occasional suicides, resurrections, and murders, until it finally triumphs over all obstacles, and Dercyllis, whom a robust constitution and much exercise in the open air have kept alive in spite of everything, returns to Tyre with her brother, while Dinias joins an expedition to the North Pole and eventually does the tour of the moon. His sight-seeing propensities are dulled at last, and by availing himself of a magic wish granted him he is transported to Tyre, where he meets his true love and all her relatives, who have by this time slept off their potion. In order to preserve to mankind the account of their journeyings they now hire an Athenian orator to inscribe them on two tablets, one for Cymba, as a reward for his auditory endurance, the other for Dercyllis to place in Dinias' tomb. This latter copy was found in after years by one of Alexander's soldiers, at the capture of Tyre, and passing through many hands came at length into the possession of Antonius. He did not delay in giving it to the public, with a dedication to his sister Isidora.

This abstract of *The Marvelous Things beyond Thule* must be the barest outline of the original work. Yet it is sufficient to show plainly the spirit of the story, and the principal elements which entered into its composition. It is clearly a tale of erotic adventure, inclining more to the adventurous side than the amorous, though its dedication to a woman might suggest the inference that the complete novel contained a stronger dose of love than appears in Photius' summary. Still, as we get it, the love story seems to be a device for introducing new adventures by repeated descriptions of what befell both hero and heroine. In this respect, as well as in the social standing of the characters, Antonius diverges entirely from such romances as the *Nimrod* fragment. In the good old times the woman stayed at home, and had no experience in wandering. The hero performed all that. But here, and in the novels which follow, the heroine is subject to the same conditions of life as the hero, and undergoes her full share of adventures by sea and land. Such a transformation of the female part in the action reveals an entirely different class of readers, and a wholly different conception of the place of woman in society, and this intrinsic change proves of itself a descent of the novel in the social scale. It had passed from the nobility to the commoners.

The subject chosen by Antonius partakes largely of the marvelous, dealing in incantations and magic, as well as in fantastic adventures, such as the journey to Hades—a favorite excursion with the ancient authors—expeditions to the North Pole, and round-trips to the heavenly bodies. These were undoubtedly among the notions which our novelist borrowed from his predecessors, and in certain places they appear to be results of his sympathy with the doctrines of Pythagoras. Now the subsequent Greco-Roman novels accepted the element of magic, but rejected these fanciful adventures. They were more matter-of-fact and realistic, and could hardly be expected to indulge in such extravagant episodes. So in this striking characteristic Antonius stands alone, and his work may perhaps be an example of the transition stage between the imaginary narrative of vulgar life and the presentation of actual events which take place in current existence.   Possibly the imaginary tale may have served also for a parody on the exploits of the noble heroes of the old novels, just as in modern times *Don Quixote* was a parody on *Amadis of Gaul.*   But our later stories of fantastic or satirical adventures, beloved of Swift, Poe, or Verne, do not proceed directly from *The Marvelous Things beyond Thule.*   The models for these were the novels of Cyrano de Bergerac, that witty Frenchman of the seventeenth century, and his great predecessor was Lucian, who may perhaps have parodied Antonius, but who certainly found his ultimate inspirations in the teachings of the Pythagoreans.

The other elements of Antonius' narrative remain in the works of his rivals.   All the Greek novelists of the *bourgeois* school delight in murders and suicides, perhaps because of the opportunity thus afforded them for highly colored delineations, and certainly because of the terror and interest such events are supposed to excite.   The solutions of their various plots likewise imitate his melodramatic ending.   Vice is always punished and virtue rewarded.   The heavy villain is foiled, and persecuted innocence repeatedly escapes from the many snares set for its unwary feet, until at last it finds safety and peace in the arms of Hymen.   Cruel stratagems and violence may for a time postpone the desired conclusion, but it comes at last, as inevitably in the fiction of the Alexandrian age as in the popular novels of the nineteenth century.

Apart from the divergence in sentiment between the Greek romances of chivalry and the later plebeian novels, there is a notable difference in the motive to the action. It would seem as though the former introduced adventures into its narrative through a certain psychological impulse, arising from the love of the hero for the heroine, and his desire to win his spurs in order to be more worthy of her hand. In the novels of Antonius and his successors this motive is lost. Far from being an incentive to the action of the story, love might now be rightly considered a hindrance to it, for the loving pair never willingly take leave of each other, and sometimes the separation is brought about even after their happy marriage. This passing away of the natural motive to the action must have taken place at some point in the transition from the later epic romance, of which the *Nimrod* fragment would be a fair example, to the vulgar stories of ordinary life. And its disappearance would seem to indicate that this period of transition was an era of parody on the prose epics rather than of serious novelistic construction. For a parody would not require a plot, but would put all its stress on ridiculing different episodes, as Cervantes has clearly demonstrated. So when the time for genuine fiction came again, and it was necessary to create the novel of every-day life, the authors who had gone so far astray from the natural method of construction were hard pressed for a means of starting their stories, and of continuing them when the leading episode was exhausted. Instead of returning to nature and finding there an impelling force, their artificial conception of conventional literature sought for springs of action outside of the assumed relationship of their characters. The methods of the dramatists were constantly before their eyes, offering devices ready to hand, and so we find that a *deus ex machina* is the main reliance of Alexandrian fiction. But still true to the received tradition, this external agent took the form of some command from an oracle, which the lovers and their parents were bound to obey unquestioningly ; or it became even a genuine personification of Tyche, the goddess of fate or chance, whom we call by her Latin name of Fortuna. She it was who especially delighted in separating the hero from his loved one, and in disarranging the best-laid plans of mortals who were subject to her caprice. And when the Greek novelist had once admitted the efficacy of these supernatural powers, he had no further need to bother about inherent motives of action. When situations could be suddenly transformed with a stroke of the pen, all the labor of plotting and planning the various turns of his narrative was labor ill-spent.

There is no need of insisting on the two chief elements of these novels of antiquity, epic or plebeian. Love and adventure are the constant ingredients of the most simple kinds of fiction in all periods of the world's literature. They are as old as mankind, and reappear, after each decadence of the human race, endowed with all the vigor of the regenerated people. To be sure, the literature of ancient Greece had kept the element of love in the background, and had thereby confessed its fear of that absorbing passion. The early epics were in their nature warlike and foreign to the tender emotion, and the drama which succeeded them was based on the national mythology and shared its prejudices. The undue absence of love in the higher literature reveals a deliberate and formal resolve against its employment, and leads to the surmise that it must have been the great theme of the intimate poetry and legend. It is possible, for instance, that in the popular tradition the alienation of Achilles from the Grecian interest may have been based on something which would appeal more to common sympathy than his Homeric attitude of offended dignity. And who knows to what an idyl the relations of Hector and Andromache may have given birth, with the story-tellers of the domestic fireside? So, while no important work of the classical literature may be said to have chosen love for its theme, yet allusions to the passion are plentiful enough, and hints at erotic folk-tales are not wanting. After the decline of the great epics the elegiac poetry, which to some extent succeeded them in popular favor, seems to have depended for much of its interest on the portrayal of affairs of the heart. Through these elegies, and through the later stories of mythology and folk-lore, we have gained an insight into such legends as the loves of Cupid and Psyche, the wooing of Daphne by Apollo, and the never-dying affection of that god for the metamorphosed image of his mistress, or the punishment of Arsinoe, who for her harshness was changed to stone before the corpse of her departed suitor. Out of such material as this Ovid fashioned many of his most winning stories ; and whatever was their outward disguise, religious or allegorical, at the bottom of these legends of the Greek people lay something most tenderly human, which has outlived in the sympathy of mankind all the enmity manifested toward them by the defenders of classical art.

When the higher literature of the nation passed away into tradition, these pathetic tales of love and disappointment increased in influence. The poets of the decadence sought through them to gain the attention of the public, and to their efforts we owe our knowledge of the calm fidelity of Pyramus and Thisbe, as well as the tragic courtship of Hero and Leander. Not only did they keep alive the love plots which they took from the bards of the people, but they gave them an artistic form, modified their contents, and adapted them to the taste of the age by adding many rhetorical features, which descended later to the love story of the Greek novel. Among these are such standard episodes as the meeting of a couple in a temple and their sudden change, by a single glance, from enemies of Eros into his worshipers, the subsequent progress of the erotic malady, its torments by night and day, the laments of its victims poured forth to groves and rocks, the consolation afforded by plucking the petals of flowers, and the satisfaction given by carving the name of the beloved in the bark of sympathetic trees. The constant use of these incidents by the erotic poems of the Greek decadence and by the later novels of the Greco-Roman period, would point to a fairly intimate connection between these two forms of fanciful narration.

But the element of adventure—if Antonius' story and the novels which followed his are good representatives—was much stronger in the prose fiction of the Alexandrian age than the element of love. Possibly this is the case among all peoples, that the telling of deeds is a more inexhaustible mine of interest than the account of an abstract emotion. Still the Greeks, owing to their location on both sides of the Ægean, and in the islands studding that sea, were particularly open to the allurements of travel. Their earliest traditions are those of voyages—Jason and the Argonauts, Ulysses, and Hercules. The colonies which they founded in every part of the Mediterranean attracted the merchants and mariners of the mother country long after the freebooting, adventurous spirit of the race had calmed down with the development of a stable civilization. Yet discoveries were still made, and the more restless souls, pushing ever beyond the confines of the known world, were constantly bringing back to the metropolis fresh tales of wonderful experiences. The sum total of these narratives of adventure, accumulating in the legends of the people from the time of the first half-mythological expeditions to the latest explorations beyond the Spanish straits, can only be conjectured. The epic poems of Greece, the chronicles of her historians, and the dreams of her philosophers bear witness to their multiplicity and their extent.

The Marvelous Things beyond Thule, even in its fragmentary state, is therefore a very good example of the fusion and the relative proportion of the two elements which made up the Greek novels of the more vulgar type. It also gives a fair idea of the locality where they were produced, and of the composite character of the peoples which favored them. It is no longer Athens and the Peloponnesus which are described; but Asia Minor and its outlying islands, Syria and Egypt are to be the homes of the actors and the chosen setting for their wanderings. Antonius, whose desire for the marvelous is unrestrained by the later discipline of the school, transgresses, to be sure, these boundaries and leads his heroes on an endless chase throughout our planetary system. But he takes care to make Tyre the central point of his story, and though it is incidentally connected with Greece proper, this is evidently done only in obedience to the requirements of previous tradition. The social position of Antonius' characters is as significant as the change in geographical location. The romances of chivalry must have entirely died out among the reading public for the novelist to presume to celebrate only actors of common birth. The third estate had gathered to itself all the emoluments of existence, and the rule of the aristocrat was never to be restored in the civilization of antiquity. And the trading class was neither refined nor high-principled, if we are to believe its eulogists in fiction.

Antonius dedicated his work to his sister. It is possible that this notion was suggested to him by the prominence of the heroine in the adventures he narrates, for she claims in them a share almost equal to the quota of the hero. The appearance of a woman in a leading part was nothing new to fiction. In the epic prose narratives, and in such stories of high life as the *Nimrod* fragment, she must have already occupied a place, second in importance to that of the hero only. But in these aristocratic stories her demeanor was more retiring. The girl of high birth in all Greek and Latin countries was always secluded, both before and after marriage, from public gaze and public interest. Among the Athenians, down to their absorption by Macedonia, we know that the same customs in regard to women were observed. And it does not seem credible that when the scene of action was transferred to the cities of Asia Minor and Syria, this attitude of the ruling classes toward their wives and daughters could have been seriously modified. Only the women of the lowest grades in family and social standing could have frequented the streets of Antioch and Ephesus. That the novelists were aware of these restrictions is clear from the conventional way in which they first bring their couples together. The meeting takes place generally in a temple, as the only spot where both sexes could properly meet. And when the wanderings begin, it is almost always by violence or accident that the girl is exposed to the adventures she undergoes. Antonius' heroine fled because she supposed herself in danger of condemnation by law, and thus of being enrolled among criminals. But the proprieties being once satisfied, and the heroines safely embarked on their wanderings, the novelist gives free rein to his fancy and puts their reputation as travelers on the same plane as the fame of his heroes.

But these continued peregrinations must have been unnatural except with women of degraded life, and they must have been kept up to satisfy a particular demand on the part of the readers of fiction. For there are many instances in the novels where the heroine is reduced to slavery, or at best to a kind of servitude, and she is held in very light esteem by her captors and persecutors, escaping the common consequences of their contempt only by the display of extraordinary talents, or by the sudden appearance of the hero. So it is quite plausible to suppose that in this reduplication of dangers surmounted by members of the gentler sex, there is a deliberate purpose on the part of the novelist to cater to the prejudices of his public, and that as the romances of the preceding period celebrated the beauty and purity of noble maidens, and showed how the very memory of their charms swayed in his absence the most powerful of princes, these historians of a lower social caste had in mind the cloistered families of the great merchants, and indulged the secluded readers of their times with the tales of woman's freedom—though in danger—and her reliance on her own talents and energy. It was not a life of ideal liberty which they thus portrayed to the wives of the Greco-Romans, but it was at least an improvement over an every-day existence shut up within four walls. And the tyranny of Tyche was very likely preferable in their minds to the lordship of an irresponsible husband.

Here we have doubtless the real audience of the Greco-Roman novelist. He wrote for the women of his time, as the romancer of the preceding period had written for the aristocratic families of the classical era, and as the story-teller of the Middle Ages invented for the benefit of the gentle ladies of France. Nor does it appear that this appeal to woman corresponds to any change in her condition. The royal mistresses of the epics were flattered by the pictures of the power they exerted over man from the midst of their calm retirement. The wives of the commercial princes of Syria and Egypt delighted in the freedom which their fictitious adventures granted them in common with their seafaring masters. The writers of each school responded to the leading passion of his public, and endeavored to beguile its forced inactivity with a delineation of the desired influence and career. We must not be surprised, then, that Antonius dedicated his fantastic tale to his sister, for he probably knew, as Sir Philip Sidney with his *Arcadia*, what best suited the temperament of his dearest relative.

The lack of a psychological motive for the action of the Greek novel, and the centering of all its events on the caprice of destiny, naturally deprived its characters of any particular traits which would make them interesting to modern readers. Hero and heroine were marionettes, puppets who danced on the wires which Fortune pulled. As they were devoid of any individuality, so their emotions of sorrow or joy were conventional and gesticulatory, like those of the average actor. Together with this uniformity of personal attributes went a rhetorical conception of nature. For physical phenomena were by no means disregarded by these artists of the schools, and in the description of storms at sea they especially attained quite a remarkable degree of pictorial excellence. Yet whatever may have been these deficiencies in the creation of living people, we must concede to the Greek novelist a considerable amount of observation and a ready adaptation to the taste of his readers. His narrative is often vivacious, in spite of his academic training, and his style, even if it was a kind of mosaic made up out of the fragments of classical art, is not to be dismissed without commendation. Could the Sophist have broken loose from the precepts of his class, he might easily have handed down to posterity enduring and interesting studies of contemporary manners. But with the traditions that girt him about, and the demands for fine writing to which he felt obliged to respond, his productions are wholly unsympathetic in their subject-matter, and seemed designed entirely for such excitations of transitory emotions and displays of literary art as could have deceived in their purpose only the most credulous among his readers.

CHAPTER III.

THE account of *The Marvelous Things beyond Thule* is fantastic and improbable, but the narratives which followed it are limited to known occurrences and possible happenings. The majority of the novelists of the new school rather emphasized the realistic part of their work. A favorite proceeding with them was to compose detailed descriptions of places and things which were familiar to their readers, and to turn contemporary fashions and customs to good use. In this way their most extraordinary incidents acquired a striking actuality. They also refused to follow Antonius in the scope of his adventures. While he knew no limits to the climates and worlds visited by his characters, his successors confined their topography to the boundaries of civilization, and in fact rarely departed from the countries which border the eastern shores of the Mediterranean.

This decided transference of the action, from the realms of fancy to those of fact, reveals a great difference in theory between the later novelists and Antonius. If we may judge by Photius' analysis of his book his interest lay mainly in the number and strangeness of the incidents he could relate. In this respect he seems to be at variance with the general method of the Sophists, and perhaps was in fact not an adherent of that school, but a free lance who wrote for the delectation of his own immediate circle. Of his style and composition we can of course gain no idea from Photius' summary, but all available evidence would go to show that he thought mainly of what he should write, while his artistic successors laid their chief stress on the manner in which they wrote.   And possibly if we had the facts in the case placed plainly before us, we might discover that Antonius was a story-teller of the people ; that *The Marvelous Things beyond Thule* was intended for popular consumption ; and that Antonius' talent and powers of invention may have contributed much to bring these vulgar accounts of wonderful adventures to the attention of the more refined and cultivated schoolmen.   They, in their search for something new, would then have abandoned the old romances of chivalry for the fresher tales of popular tradition and superstition.

The six novels of the later school in Greek fiction which have been preserved in their original form are all productions of the Sophists.   In date they must have followed Antonius, being composed between the beginning of the second and the end of the fifth century of our era.   On general principles we cannot say that these few stories are all the novels which were written during the Greco-Roman period, though according to the law of the survival of the fittest they may very well have been the best of their kind. But we must remember that the great destruction of manuscripts, during the many centuries which elapsed between the reign of Constantine and the rule of the Medici, involved the loss of records of a far greater importance than was attached to the literature of mere amusement. Thus we are left almost entirely in the dark as to the extent and interest of the love stories of antiquity.   That they must have been many and excellent may be inferred from the fragments of novels—clearly due to Sophist influence—which reappear among the legends of the Middle Ages.   One of the most favorite stories with the clerks and warriors of the twelfth century, *Apollonius of Tyre*, is a genuine Greek novel, which can be traced no further back than to a Latin version, while others, less complete, furnished plots and episodes to the writers of mediæval Greece and Italy.

Of the six novels of the Alexandrian epoch which have come down to modern times in the original Greek, five are stories of erotic adventure, like the narrative of Antonius, and one is the pastoral, *Daphnis and Chloe.* The earliest of the novels of erotic adventure has been saved for us by the same Photius of *Myriobiblion* fame, and we also know that manuscripts of it, now lost, were extant in the Renaissance. It is the *Babylonica* of Jamblichus, a Syrian writer, who lived in the second century, in the time of the Antonines. He wrote in Greek, evidently regarding it as the universal language, but his subject, as the title indicates, was suggested by a Babylonian tutor, and the work pretends to be made up from Babylonian traditions and to describe the customs of that capital. Jamblichus chooses as a heroine Sinonis, who with her husband, Rhodanes, flies from the unwelcome suit of Garmus, king of Babylon. The king sends eunuchs in their pursuit, and the story enters at once upon a series of strange performances. A demon-goat drives the lovers from their first shelter to a cave, which bees then successfully defend against the king's guards. But Sinonis and Rhodanes eat the honey, are thrown into a trance by it, and again elude their enemies' vengeance by this seeming death. They soon awake, but only to witness a brother poison a brother. They are accused of this crime, are acquitted by the suicide of the guilty one, and find shelter afterward with a robber, whose house is straightway burned by the royal troops. The pair escape by claiming to be ghosts, occupy a newly made tomb, and are again supposed to be corpses. Captured at last, they attempt suicide by poison, but swallow only a sleeping potion. Sinonis then stabs herself with a sword. Her despair moves their captor to pity, and he sends them to the island of Aphrodite in the Euphrates, where Sinonis' wound is healed, and where Rhodanes is befriended by the priestess, to whose son, killed by a poisonous fly hidden in a rose, he bears a close resemblance.   But pursued once more, they leave the island, kill one of the king's guards, and other people are by mistake made prisoners in their place.

Sinonis now becomes jealous, and leaves Rhodanes, kills a man, is arrested, but is set free by a general pardon of prisoners.   All kinds of murders, suicides, and buryings-alive now for a time give a zest to the fortunes of the minor characters.   A daughter of the priestess of Aphrodite is taken for Sinonis and sent to Garmus.   Sinonis' father comes upon Rhodanes' dog, which has just made a partial meal of one whole man and the half of a woman. The other half Sinonis' father buries for his daughter and so inscribes on the tombstone.   Rhodanes now comes up and is about to kill himself on the grave, when he learns of his error from Sinonis' rival.   Sinonis next appears and proceeds to exterminate the rival, but Rhodanes seizes the sword she wields, and Sinonis rushes away again in anger. All the actors finally fall into Garmus' power—save Sinonis, who marries the King of Syria—and a general execution is ordered.   But in the midst of the latter festivity, Garmus is informed of Sinonis' doings, and invites Rhodanes to leave his own execution and lead the king's army into Syria.   Our hero naturally accepts the proposition, defeats the Syrian king, regains Sinonis, and ends by becoming king in Babylon, as a little bird had once indeed foretold.   So virtue is rewarded at the end, vice is punished, and all is well.

It will no doubt be conceded on all sides that the reward of the virtuous in the *Babylonica* came none too early. And it may also be subject to debate whether those are indeed the truly good, who indulge their higher natures in thefts of the sneak variety—we omitted to mention that Sinonis was first arrested for offering grave clothes in the markets of Mesopotamia—in highway robberies, murders of the guileless, and general devastation of an unhappy country. But it is evident that Jamblichus considered his hero and heroine as examples of persecuted virtue, and it is also plain that they really were persecuted. Hence, admitting the persecution, we will also allow the virtue, and rejoice in the final ruin of the rascally Garmus, and the occasional destruction of the satellites whom he commissioned to hunt our lovers, and whom he executed in the good old Oriental way when they returned without any fruits of their labors. It is also possible that public morality in Syria of the second century is not the morality professed in the Europe of the nineteenth. As for the hero, Rhodanes, he surely merited a throne, if for nothing else than for having gone through a wilderness of adventures, which must have become extremely monotonous from their resemblance to one another, and for having been endowed with the strength of mind not to commit suicide, when he had so many examples of that mild sin before his eyes. Still we must not forget that we do not possess the original of the *Babylonica*, but only an abridgment of its most interesting parts—interesting at least to Photius—and that the learned Byzantine may have suppressed a few scenes of tenderness and charity. For all he gives us is gore, and hate, and jealousy, and man leaping at the throat of his brother man. Jamblichus confesses his indebtedness to Asiatic sources for his material, a civilization where refinement was but a veneer on barbarism, and where luxury seems rather to have intensified the brute in humanity. So after all Photius may have interpreted his author rightly, who in all his characteristics is a genuine Greek novelist, and shows many of the ordinary traits of his class, though too one-sided to fairly represent it. One or two of his episodes, the bees defending the fugitives, or the dog mangling the unrecognizable carcass, have survived in literature, and re-appear many centuries later in the poets of the Italian decadence, where they are most faithfully copied by the father of Marinism, the Cavalier Marino.

Let us delay no longer with this writer, whom we know only at second hand, but proceed to examine the work of another who has come down to us in the original text, and concerning whose talents and methods there is no room for doubt. This author is a certain Xenophon, and he comes from Ephesus in Asia Minor. He may have written at the beginning of the third century. Possibly in imitation of Jamblichus, he calls his production *Ephesiaca*, after his native town. With Xenophon we find ourselves in the usual locality of the Greek novel, the shores and islands of the eastern Mediterranean. He gives also the conventional account of the meeting, separation, and perils of his favorite characters, and in all other respects may be considered a fair sample of the novelist of his day. But there is one reservation to be made in regard to him, and to our judgment on his work: The text of the *Ephesiaca* is very concise, dry, and devoted to the bare statement of facts, so that we must wonder again whether it is not an abstract of a novel rather than the novel itself.

The lovely Anthia and the stalwart Habrocomas, whose youthful pastime it had been to scoff at Eros and to despise the power of that god, meet one day by chance in the temple of Diana at Ephesus. In one quick mutual glance the offended deity finds himself avenged, for most violent love immediately inflames the heart of damsel and swain. Perplexed by the strangeness of their children's new mode of life, subjected to the sway of the passion, the anxious parents consult Apollo's dread oracle, and by it are informed that the pair are to be married, and then sent off to suffer and endure until the god of love shall be appeased. The oracle is obeyed. Habrocomas weds Anthia, and they start on their obligatory wedding journey.

They first visit Rhodes. On leaving that island, however, they are captured by pirates, and carried to Tyre. Now trouble begins in earnest. The charms of both hero and heroine are such as to excite undesirable affections in the breasts of their captors. They are separated from each other and, apart, undergo many hardships on land and sea. The number of their hairbreadth escapes is to be placed at no small figure. Anthia, seized by a fresh supply of pirates, is offered matrimony by their leader, but curiously enough she prefers suicide. The poison she takes for that end fortunately proves to be a sleeping draught, and Anthia, supposed to be dead and buried, awakes in her tomb, deserts it, and after many hardships reaches Alexandria.

Meanwhile Habrocomas has been in his turn tormented by suitors. One of them, whom he firmly refuses, accuses him falsely of a murder, and the authorities crucify him in due season on the banks of the Nile. But the sun god, moved to succor, stirs up a great wind, which blows the cross into the river and saves the victim. The governor next tries a funeral pyre on our hero, but the Nile itself comes to the rescue and extinguishes the fire. These physical phenomena induce sufficient delay in the execution to enable Habrocomas to prove at last his innocence. He is set at liberty and begins a search for Anthia, who by this time is also on his track. A mutual pursuit ensues, which is not only enlivened by many perils, but also proves an excellent exercise in geography. Italy, Sicily, and the larger part of the Mediterranean are visited by one after the other. Finally both come once more to Rhodes, where they are separately recognized by their old and trusty servants, and are reunited in the temple of Apollo. They now return to Ephesus, erect tombs to the memory of their parents, whom their prolonged absence had driven to suicide, and, having been faithful to each other through all their perils, live happy ever after.

This summary of Xenophon's pleasing tale does not by any means exhaust its contents. For with amiable thoughtfulness our novelist has supplemented the story of the trials and triumphs of Habrocomas and Anthia, which form what we may call his principal plot, with a subplot in which the fortunes of their domestics, Leukon and Rhode, are epitomized. He has done even better. The most attractive episode of his novel is the autobiography of an old fisherman, whom Habrocomas finds in Sicily. The former was a native of Lacedæmon, and there had fallen in love with a maiden and had fled with her, dressed as a boy, on the very night her parents were to marry her to another. Many blissful years had the lovers passed in Sicily, though ever exposed to poverty and want; and when the wife died her body, preserved by the skill of Egyptian art, remained in the hut which had so long been her dwelling, to recall to her lover the happy days of youth. To the eyes of Habrocomas the body was old, shriveled, and no better than a mummy, but in the sight of the husband it was ever the blushing maiden who had forsaken all for him so many years ago. There is no more graceful idyl in classical literature. Apart from this digression, however, the *Ephesiaca* makes but slight allusions to the tender side of human nature. Its adventures are thoroughly commonplace, and center around Habrocomas' experience with robbers and Anthia's stratagem to preserve her good name. The style of the book is also plain and concise, and on the whole it would seem as though Xenophon held his material in greater esteem than the manner in which he presented it.

The *Ephesiaca*, however, proved to be a popular story, and subsequent novels borrowed many of its inventions. Among their imitations the mediæval tale of *Apollonius of Tyre* holds a prominent place. The lost Greek version of this novel may be placed shortly after the *Ephesiaca*, or as far back as the third century, while the Latin translation, by which we may trace the second step in its history, is undoubtedly as early as the fifth. Gower, in his *Confessio Amantis*, and Shakspere, in the play often assigned to him, *Pericles, Prince of Tyre*, have made the substance of *Apollonius* so familiar to English readers that we would gladly be rid of an analysis of it at this time.

But in its passage from Greek into Latin, and on its way from antiquity to the Renaissance, this old novel of the Sophists naturally borrowed something from the new surroundings in which it found itself. One evidence of this modification is the Christian coloring it has assumed, instead of the conventional paganism which was a feature of the kind in the Alexandrian epoch. The addition of all that concerns King Antiochus and his daughter, an episode having no real connection with the rest of the story, is also a device of some later reviser; and should it be argued that these adaptations are not external, but essential, and that *Apollonius* may never have had a Greek original of the period to which it is commonly referred, we may call to witness the real plot of the legend. There you see a fisherman, who befriends the hero, as his colleague befriended the hero of the *Ephesiaca*. There you read of the triumph of the innocence of Apollonius' daughter, which resembles the triumph of Anthia, of the attempt on her life by a slave, and of her rescue from a tomb by pirates, experiences undergone by Xenophon's heroine, while many other adventures in *Apollonius* are the stock ones of the Greek novel.

If *Apollonius of Tyre* is truly an Alexandrian story, it brings up a point of considerable literary importance. For, so far as we have any knowledge, this legend is the only complete novel of antiquity which was known to mediæval Christendom, where it was exceedingly popular, as may be inferred from the number of manuscripts in which it is preserved, and the translations which turned it from Latin into the vernacular of the new peoples.   In France it was made over in the twelfth century into an epic, *Jourdain de Blaie*, and connected with the heroic cycle of Charlemagne.   In Spain, the poem *Apollonio*, of the thirteenth century, seems to be based on another French version, now lost ; while in England, where it was destined to take on so many literary forms, it exists in an Anglo-Saxon translation which is supposed to have been made before the Norman conquest.   The popularity which *Apollonius* enjoyed, being so great and so general—it even returned into Greek in the fifteenth century and revisited at last the land of its birth—it could hardly have failed to exert by its plan and composition, so superior to the art of the Middle Ages, a most notable influence on the budding novelists of the time, and may have even served to shape the order and arrangement of the prose fiction of those centuries.   While this influence is necessarily conjectural, though wholly in the ordinary run of things, it is not a conjecture, but a fact, that the *romans d'aventure* began with a subject borrowed from the East, and from a degenerate descendant of the Greco-Roman novels; and the part which the *romans d'aventure* played in the make-up of the modern novel has been already more than hinted at here.   There is in the particular version of *Apollonius* found in the *Gesta Romanorum*, a genuine survival of the Sophists' art in the description of the swooning heroine, though this scene was no doubt eclipsed in the eyes of mediæval spectators by the fabulous treasures of the hero, and the great natural gifts of Tharsia, additions of a more childish age than that of the falling Empire.   But the fact that even one carefully detailed episode is still retained in the tale, after so many vicissitudes of time, goes far toward proving the authority which a well-proportioned story, containing an elaborate plot, must have exercised over the untrained compilers of early European literature.   Perhaps the

Greek novel, through this extant member of unknown authorship, sustained the same relation to mediæval fiction as Aristotle did to mediæval philosophy. And this may be suggested without any intention of flattering the sons of Hellas in either case.

The attitude of *Apollonius of Tyre* toward the fiction of the Middle Ages was repeated in the literature of the Renaissance by another Greek novel, the most celebrated of its race, Heliodorus' *Theagenes and Chariclea*, or (to keep the same form of title which has obtained among those already mentioned) the *Ethiopica*, after the native country of the heroine. The author of this best of Greek romances states that he is a Phœnician, an inhabitant of Emesa, in Syria. He has been often confounded with the bishop, Heliodorus. But the whole trend of his novel is rather pagan than Christian, and, like the *Ephesiaca*, it seems to be written in praise of the sun god, Helios. Still the writer may have been the pious bishop, for all that we know to the contrary, and his work may have been the offspring of a youthful indulgence in romantic notions, for which after years beheld a bitter repentance. Not that there is anything to be ashamed of in its make-up or plan. The episodes are higher in tone than the events of the average Greek novel, though primitive Christian zeal might rigidly condemn the favor in which the gods are held and the magic arts which enter so largely into the action. As for plan, it follows the approved method of the rhetoricians, plunging the reader at once into the middle of the story and explaining the situation later. Also its parts are well arranged and proportioned ; and though the romance is by far the longest of its class, the author's art in the disposition of his matter and the development of his plot is such as to keep up the interest in his narrative and justify the reputation he gained among his countrymen, and which he held down to the end of the Eastern Empire.

Therefore we are not surprised when the revival of Greek learning in western Europe reached, as the last subject of interest, the Alexandrian novel, that the fame of *Theagenes and Chariclea* passed beyond the educated classes and penetrated to the people. It furnished Amyot with his pioneer translation into French in 1547, and was done not much later into the other important modern vernaculars.

The curtain rises on Theagenes and Chariclea seated by the strand of the sea, near the Nile Delta, in the midst of corpses. They had been shipwrecked and Theagenes had afterward been wounded in a conflict with the pirates who had worsted his companions. While Chariclea, thus desolate but in sound physical condition, is lamenting his injuries, the two are seized by a fresh band of robbers and carried away. They pass the following night in listening to the woful account of Cnemon, an Athenian, who tells how his step-mother, when he refused her proferred favors, persecuted him, and how she committed suicide when her villainy was made known. The following day our hero and heroine—who pretend to the robbers, for their greater safety, that they are brother and sister—are separated from each other, and start on the conventional round of adventures.

Having thus safely launched his story, Heliodorus brings in the previous history of his pair by introducing an aged priest, Calasiris, who relates to Cnemon how he had brought up Chariclea from infancy, how when a maiden grown she had met Theagenes at a festival, how mutual love with all its joys and its longings had taken possession of them, and how they had finally started on their wanderings in obedience to Apollo's oracle. In the description of the festival where the lovers met, and where Theagenes won a race and received the palm of victory from Chariclea, as well as in the delineation of the ravages of love on the maiden, our author has passed by far all his rivals. His

.skill also in the dialogues between his characters, and his devices to keep alive the interest of the narration, reveal an artistic and practical sense, which makes the novel a readable one even at the present day. In his whole exposition it is clear that he has studied the stage to good purpose. He has chosen from among the writers of tragedy many apt similes and metaphors, while Homer comes in for a share in his admiration, and the Greek historians, especially Herodotus. Finally Calasiris' account is interrupted by the arrival of Chariclea, and thus the first part of the novel is brought to a close.

In the second part the lovers journey along by the banks of the Nile, sometimes together, more often apart, and are exposed to many dangers, all of which they surmount in the optimistic manner to which we have by this time become accustomed. Magic is introduced to add a new incentive to our curiosity, and further material is furnished to the narrative by the recital of the fortunes of Calasiris and his family. At last, after many hardships, the persecuted pair reach Ethiopia, and are made prisoners by its inhabitants. Being spoils of war they are condemned to death, but the Gymnosophists, who in that region formed a sect opposed to human sacrifices, contrive to delay the offering until the sovereigns of the land have time to recognize in Chariclea their own daughter. Although of black parents she was born white through the influence of a marble statue, and her mother, the queen, fearing her husband's jealousy should this fact be known, had consigned her in the good old-fashioned way to the care of nature. From this care a diplomat had rescued her and had handed her over to Calasiris, at the lucky age of seven. Theagenes is also set free on the entreaty of his bride, the omens are interpreted to be unfavorable to human sacrifices, and these are finally abolished throughout the realm of Ethiopia. So not only is the happy union of the lovers the culmination of the story, but also a moral reform has been accomplished through them, and the name of the Gymnosophists is magnified.

Aside from its lively narration and its well-drawn descriptions, *Theagenes and Chariclea* merits, for many reasons, a permanent place in the history of novel-writing. It will be noticed from the abstract given above, and which presents only the leading features of the work, that Heliodorus, unlike his fellow-novelists, is not melodramatic in his plot, and does not insist in his happy ending on the punishment of the heavy villain as well as the triumph of the innocent. In this respect he shows his reliance on the incidents of his work to excite the interest of his readers, and does not merely contrast virtue with vice. This attitude alone is a marked advance over what had preceded him, but it is not the only merit of the book. For there is, running quietly through the novel, and becoming prominent in the final scenes, the eulogy of a sect whose cause the author had espoused, and the justification of their doctrine by the abolition, in Ethiopia, of human sacrifices. It would be unwise to lay too much stress on this extraneous matter, which has very little to do with the real plot, but it deserves at least a passing mention, since it is the first example in fiction of a moral argument made agreeable by a tale. In later times we have been quite familiarized with such side purposes of novelists, and many romances have, indeed, no other excuse for existence than that they are the traditional sugar which coats the pill of some moral reform. Heliodorus does not make his plot subservient in any way to his doctrinal teaching, but inasmuch as he alone of the Greek writers of fiction has any idea other than that of pleasing his audience this beginning of dogmatic story-telling is interesting to note.

Heliodorus was not content with being a literary artist and a defender of morality; he also endeavored to give to his narrative an air of probability. In spite of the wonderful adventures and deeds of superhuman daring which he relates, he succeeds oftentimes in making his episodes lifelike and actual. For instance, Calasiris' long rehearsal of past events to Cnemon is constantly broken in upon by the latter's questions, which, in turn, give rise to many explanations and descriptions. Thus one has the feeling of participating in the action. Frequently, in depicting his scenes, the author gives them a finish of detail which would not put to shame the most sensitive modern realist. When Cnemon—to cite an illustration of this point—supposes that Thisbe, the tool of his step-mother in his condemnation, and whose murdered body he had just found, has come to life again, he hastens in terror to regain his own room. And the novelist thus describes his mishaps while a prey to fear : " Now his foot stumbled ; now he fell against the wall, and now against the lintels of the door ; sometimes he struck his head against utensils hanging from the ceiling ; at last, with much difficulty and after many wanderings, he reached his own apartment and threw himself upon the bed. His body trembled and his teeth chattered. . ."

We have not yet done with the good qualities of the greatest of Greek novelists. We have already spoken of his knowledge of classical literature. He was also a romanticist as well and believed in local color. Whether he makes Delphi, the Nile Delta, Memphis, ancient Thebes, or Ethiopia the setting for the events he narrates, he preserves admirably the characteristic features of each place, and portrays with careful hand the customs of the various peoples, the games of Greece, or the heathen sacrifices of the Upper Nile. He further justifies his title to romanticism by a genuine love of nature both on sea and land, and in his descriptions of scenery he forsakes the conventionalism of his class for the teachings of his own observation. So his language is quite brilliant and poetical, especially in the last half of his work.   He also displays a fondness for folk-lore, which he ingeniously mingles with book learning. Best of all, his incidents are clean and lacking in the customary coarseness of the age.

Heliodorus' exposition of the action, and the skill with which he delays the solution of the plot, and keeps up our interest in it, have already been remarked upon.   But we have not said that he sometimes jests, a rare thing in the dry and sober times of Greco-Roman literature, and that he also betrays a great fondness for popular etymologies, as Homer from $o^{'}\ \mu\eta\rho\acute{o}\varsigma$ (*the thigh*), and the Nile from $\nu\acute{\epsilon}\eta\ \iota\lambda\acute{\upsilon}\varsigma$ (*new soil*), brought down by that river in its inundations.   His device of causing Chariclea to be born white on account of the statue of Andromeda, which was placed in the queen's apartments, is another striking evidence of his simple delight in received traditions, while her royal parentage, like the aristocratic origin of the heroes of the epic stories, may show that such legends still lingered among the people.

But Heliodorus is by no means perfect as a writer, nor is he to be taken as a model for moderns.   Though he is readable to-day, he is so on account of his own originality and variety, and in spite of his likeness to the other writers of the Sophist school.   For he resembles them in many particulars : in the introduction of episodes foreign to the plot, in the unnecessary obstacles to the progress of the action, in the long-winded descriptions, in the orations, letters, rhetorical phrases, dreams and visions, in the monstrous crimes, in the perils suddenly overcome, and above all in the absence of any psychological analysis of character.   To be sure the bearing of Chariclea throughout the story, and particularly at the end when she deliberates on how to rescue Theagenes from immolation, gives her the attributes of courage, skill, and refinement of feeling, which are not sufficient, however, to make up a character in the modern sense of the word. Theagenes, on the other hand, is a poor stick in what he does, and far inferior to his sweetheart in even the supposed manly qualities. Therefore, in summing up our author's merits and defects it is only necessary to say, that so long as he adhered to his own talent he rose above his class. When he yielded to the fashion of the times, he fell back into the commonplace. And at no point is this weakness to be more regretted than in connection with his heroine. For a few more touches of detail and a slight development of the traits he seems to have given her in his own mind, would have created for posterity a sympathetic and lovable type of generous womanhood.

But we have long rung the changes on Heliodorus and his contribution to our favorite kind of literature, and the fleeting hour and lengthening chapter warn us to hurry on to the mighty men who follow him in Sophistic story. For he had many imitators in his own day as well as at the time of the Renaissance. Foremost among the former was Achilles Tatius of Alexandria, who flourished not far from the middle of the fifth century, and who was the author of *Clitophon and Leucippe.* Nothing else is known about him, though from his few allusions to the gods, which had become a stock feature in the Greek novels, it is surmised that he may have been a Christian.

Clitophon and Leucippe begins with a description of a painting of the rape of Europa, which the author finds frescoed on the walls of Sidon. As he stands admiring the picture and meditating on the might of Eros, he is accosted by a youth who proceeds to unfold his sorrows to him. This youth is Clitophon. He tells how he, a native of Tyre, had been affianced by his father Hippias to his step-sister, Calligone, and how at the same time a vision had forewarned him of future ills. Soon after, his cousin Leucippe takes ship from Byzantium, and no sooner reaches Tyre than she inflames Clitophon with love's fires. She likewise burns to a considerable extent. Their imprudence soon reveals to their family the state of their affections, and they fly from punishment by eloping over the sea. But they suffer shipwreck on the coast of Egypt, and are there captured by pirates and separated.

Now the real adventures begin, and Achilles exerts himself to supply novelties to his audience. He makes Clitophon a distant witness of the murder of Leucippe by the robbers, and her burial. Coming up to the place where her grave is made he is on the point of killing himself, when the ever ready slave interferes, draws Leucippe alive from the pit, and they then discover that she had put on as protection a sack of false intestines, and that the pirates had used, without knowing it, a theatrical dagger, which they had found in an actor's wardrobe cast up in the wreckage. Soldiers now arrive on the scene. Their chief becomes enamored of Leucippe, but she is made insane by a love draught.

Pirates finally steal her and put to sea with her. Clitophon follows after and sees them behead a woman, whose body they throw overboard. This he picks up and mourns over as the body of his mistress. He then returns to Alexandria, where a rich widow from Ephesus falls in love with him, and persuades him to accompany her home. At her country house near Ephesus he finds Leucippe employed as a domestic. Their meeting is not of the most joyful nature, and to add to the gloom Thersander, the widow's former husband, comes back from the dead, bullies Clitophon, and makes love to Leucippe. He also attempts to obtain legal redress for his marital wrongs and commences a long trial, which is not without amusing incidents. The suit ends in the application of the common test of chastity to the lovers. They both survive it and, certain of each other's innocence, are reconciled at last.

Clitophon and Leucippe contains some redeeming features, even if it is not remarkable for its originality. The mistaken likenesses had already been employed in the *Babylonica*, and the majority of the episodes it presents existed before Achilles soldered them together. But if he is not to be mentioned for his powers of invention he at least may lay claim to a facility for adaptation—as in his borrowings from the drama—and to a faculty for description. He cleverly divides his story into three parts by means of the locality where the scene of each is laid, Tyre, the Nile Delta, and Ephesus. But his machinery for introducing these changes of place is the artificial one of the whim of the goddess of fate, Tyche. Achilles imitated Heliodorus in many details, yet he did not present the morality of the great novelist's incidents, and often was coarse and broad. His story is really an autobiography, but the hero, who tells it, gives himself by no means an attractive character. Like Theagenes he is weak and irresolute, and allows himself to be cuffed about at will by the rough Thersander, who is a kind of braggart, ruling his household like a despot. Leucippe is also uninteresting, and only the lovesick widow, Melitta, seems to possess any personality at all.

But while Achilles thus neglects to emphasize the traits of his heroes, he shows great fondness for the traditional speeches and letters, a genuine zeal for discussions on love and woman, also for monologues and soliloquies. He delights in displaying his erudition, quotes frequently from Homer, tells stories taken from mythology and from the fables of Æsop, is familiar with the fortunes of Hero and Leander, and can interest the student of folk-lore with his account of the trial of chastity and his versions of popular tales. In scientific statements, pure and simple, he is to be placed among the fantastic zoölogists, as in his descriptions of the phœnix and hippopotamus.

Still we shall not forget his praiseworthy effort to delineate the gradual growth of love in Clitophon, instead of relying on the sudden eruptions of the hitherto sleeping volcanic desires by which his predecessors saved themselves so much bother. On all occasions he is on the alert for descriptions, and in developing them he practices all kinds of style, from the most simple and direct to the most redundant. A good specimen of Euphuistic art is his picture of Leucippe's grief on meeting with Thersander : " Upon hearing his voice, Leucippe burst into tears, and appeared even more charming than before, for tears give permanency and increased expression to the eyes, either rendering them more disagreeable, or improving them if pleasing, for in that case the dark iris, fading into a lighter hue, resembles, when moistened with tears, the head of a gently bubbling fount ; the white and black, growing in brilliancy from the moisture which floats over the surface, assume the mingled shades of the violet and narcissus, and the eye appears as smiling through the tears which are confined within its lids."

A passage like this fairly bursts with the pride of word pictures, and we can vibrate in reading it with the self-satisfaction of the honest Achilles in penning it. In the same manner he admires his own acquaintance with the Greek and Oriental traditions, with which he filled out his somewhat meager plot, and beams with ecstatic joy when he hits on a good invention, as he sometimes does. For he is not lacking in observation, and some of his scenes have justified the labor he spent on them. In *Clitophon and Leucippe* appears that stratagem which Shakspere has made familiar to us, of concealing an army by the branches of trees, which the soldiers carry with them. The book furnished also that episode, which Tasso has made famous by his *Aminta,* where Clitophon succeeds in stealing a kiss from his mistress by pretending that a bee had stung his lips, and entreating her to heal them by murmuring incantations over them. Achilles also excels in descriptions of the works of art his hero runs across, in analyses of the senses, and in the stock exercises of the Sophist school, particularly in the storm at sea. Consequently when his work reappeared in the Renaissance it met with a flattering reception, was translated from a Latin version into both Italian and French, in the third quarter of the sixteenth century, while its more exciting episodes were appropriated by the Spaniard Nuñez de Reinoso to form the substance of his story, *Clareo y Florisea*, which saw the light in 1552.

There remains to be mentioned but one more novel of erotic adventure belonging to the Sophist school of the Greco-Roman period. It is the story of *Chæreas and Callirrhoe*, and was written by a certain Chariton, a rhetorician of Aphrodisia, in Caria, who perhaps was a contemporary of Achilles Tatius. His work, however, is much more in sympathy with our modern feeling, and differs in essential respects quite decidedly from the other fictitious narratives of the time. Chariton begins in the usual way by placing the first meeting of his couple in a temple, during the festival of Aphrodite at Syracuse, in Sicily. Love straightway ensues and marriage. But before many days have passed the demon of jealousy gains access to the husband's heart. In a fit of madness he tramples on the prostrate body of his wife and flees from the house, leaving her for dead. She is carried to a tomb, which robbers soon break into, and finding her alive steal her away to Miletus, where she is sold into slavery. She wins her master's love and marries him in order to save her husband's son from a slave's fate. Meanwhile, Chæreas, discovering the theft, has set out for Miletus also, but has been captured by the Persians. Callirrhoe, however, supposes him to have been killed by his captors, and accordingly celebrates his funeral. At this ceremony the satrap of Caria, Mithridates, first sees her and falls violently in love with her. Some time afterward the satrap finds Chæreas held as a slave in Caria, discovers his relation to Callirrhoe, and unites with him in sending letters and presents to her. Her new husband, Dionysius—who throughout the whole narrative is seen to be an honorable, upright man—complains of the satrap to the king. All parties are summoned to Babylon to appear before the great Artaxerxes, who no sooner sees the heroine than he too yields to Cupid's shafts. He therefore delays his decision in the case until a revolt in Egypt calls away his army, and with it the ladies of the court. Chæreas, hearing a false report that his wife has been ceded to her second husband, now joins the Egyptian army, leads it against Tyre, conquers the Persian fleet, and takes the island of Ardo, where he finds Callirrhoe and learns from her all that has passed. Overcome by the generosity and highmindedness of Dionysius, the first husband acknowledges in an eloquent epistle the magnanimity of the second, dismisses his followers, and returns with Callirrhoe to Syracuse, where the whole city comes out in festal array to meet them.

Thus the Greek novels of erotic adventure end with a story, which is more natural, more definite, more modern in a word, than any of its companions. With the retention of much of the old mechanism—apparent death of the heroine, pirates, a storm at sea, slavery, power of a divinity, which is here Aphrodite and not Eros or Tyche— we find many new springs of action in the plot. Jealousy, which had already appeared, to be sure, in other novels, particularly in the *Babylonica*, takes on here the brutal shape of a criminal court case, while it is the point of departure for the adventures. In the development of his plan Chariton takes especial pains to have it proceed simply and logically, without dallying with delaying episodes, though he is very partial to monologues and dialogues, which indeed form the best part of his composition. The interest in the fortunes of his lovers increases steadily up to the happy ending, and this improvement has been brought about by merely making the writer's art subservient to his plan. In the delineation of character he differs widely from his colleagues, not in defining the attributes of his central figures, but in developing the traits of Dionysius. This prince is shown to be a kind, noble, and just man, far above the egoists by whom he is surrounded, and his deeds of charity and self-forgetfulness cast in the shade the deceit, violence, and sensuality which stamp the average hero of the school.

But Chariton's greatest originality lies in his pictures of court life, under a sovereign known to history. His historical exactness is, of course, not to be taken seriously ; still in his introduction of real personages, and in the citation of actual events in their lives, he can claim the merit of having fixed the time of his plot, which the other Greek novelists had no notion of doing. The whole tendency of the last half of his work is in fact towards the generation of the historical novel. This bent is further emphasized by his fondness for the historians, Xenophon and Thucydides, who rival Homer in the number and importance of allusions which he makes to them. How potently to the development of an historical school in fiction the story of *Chæreas and Callirrhoe* might have contributed, had Tyche so ordered, we have no means of judging. For the circumstances which had been favorable to the rise and growth of the Greek novel were now passing away, and Chariton, instead of occupying the enviable position of the head of a new school in romance, was condemned by fate to be content with closing the old one. The remaining novel of the Alexandrian period was begotten by a sentiment entirely different from the idea which prevailed in the tales of erotic adventure.

There can be no reasonable doubt, when we consider the taste of the Greco-Romans, as to which of the two classes of novels they produced was most in favor among them. The proportion among the survivals, six on erotic adventure to one pastoral, is a sufficiently plain guide in this respect, though the destruction of manuscripts, already alluded to, deprives any conclusion of absolute certainty. The novels of adventure corresponded more to the trading, mercantile spirit of the age and manifestly appealed to the class of merchants and traders. Their flavor is decidedly *bourgeois*, even with Chariton, who tries to acquaint his readers with that life of royal courts, which no longer was known within the limits of the Roman Empire. Also in the rise of the novel of adventure we may discover a period of preparation, and in its development a variety of scene and plot which clearly point to a wide constituency. And the manners it portrays cannot be alien to the age, even if they are not wholly representative of it.

On the other hand the sole pastoral novel of antiquity possesses but few features which may be regarded as typical of its time and place. In its sentiment and feeling it appeals entirely to the views of a select few who held themselves aloof from the stirring world of trade. The existence it sketches is thoroughly artificial. Furthermore it has neither antecedents nor successors. Not that the pastoral idea was unknown to the ancients, for from the midst of their luxury and refinement they looked back to a Golden Age, in which no crime dwelt, whence toil was absent, and where all thoughts were pure and innocent. This longing for an ideal state often affected ancient literature. Inasmuch as the men of the Golden Age were pastoral in their occupations, watered their cattle and tended their flocks, it was a literary vein worth working to transfer their ideas and attributes to the shepherds of the Greek decadence and the herdsmen of an Augustan era. So

Theocritus sang in Sicily of rural delights and rustic pastimes, and Virgil on the banks of the Po extolled the blessings of country simplicity and peace, when contrasted with the cares and turmoils of him who dwells in the great centers of human activity. Thus the pastoral idea had received an artificial quickening and had become perhaps a fashionable theme in the more elegant and doubting classes of society.

To such a social caste the one pastoral novel of the Greeks belongs. It calls away from the world's corruption and complex civilization to the purity of nature. It illustrates this purity by the infancy and youth of two beings, whose vocations are pastoral and whose interests are wholly in each other, free from all notion of worldly gain or ambition. The scenery is placed on an island, Lesbos, in the blue Ægean. The landscapes are the rural pictures of the great poets. But in its setting alone does *Daphnis and Chloe* remind one of Virgil, or Theocritus; nor can any connection be traced from it to them. The novel stands by itself without sponsor and without apologist. The notion of absolute innocence, both mental and physical, which is its theme, is peculiar to itself, and in the constant insistence on this notion there is a lack of freshness, a dryness, an effort which smacks of the school and the study. Its elaborate composition and its anxiety for harmonious and flowing periods disclose beyond a question the rhetorician's art.

So when we examine closely into its substance we find there the conventional episodes of the novels of adventure, while occasional glimpses of the real life of these enervated generations of antiquity jar by their ugly contrast with the attempted artlessness of the primitive guilelessness assumed. We read of spring brooks, of summer flowers, autumn's vintage, and winter snows. In this framework of nature stand a boy and girl, young man and maiden, lovers at times, friends always. And the story of their growing affection is told so simply! But suddenly, without warning, the ideal purity is violated, the peaceful narrative reflects shameless things as innocently as it did the features of unsuspecting virtue, the cloven foot of nature's god, the merry Pan, becomes the sign of the arch-enemy of man, and into this Eden crawls the serpent of human iniquity. Our pastoral life exists only in words, and nature's joys are but a pretext for a Sophist's declamation.

The one thing certain about the origin of *Daphnis and Chloe* is that it is to be traced to the same source as the novels of erotic adventure. Though undoubtedly addressed to a more refined public than they were, it contains some of their material and shows many of the ear-marks of the Sophists. Very likely it is an aggregation of themes in use in their schools, which some more talented orator undertook, under the influence of the stories of adventure, to connect together and to expand into a narrative. For Longus—a name which has been applied to the author of the work— may indeed be no name at all, but merely a wrong reading for λόγος in the manuscript, and the date of the novel is no less uncertain than its author, being limited for no evident reason to the second century as the earliest and the fifth as the latest. The book, however, shows considerable familiarity with the island of Lesbos, and may be therefore called, after the analogy of the novels of erotic adventure, the *Lesbiaca.*

The popularity of this pastoral novel has always been so great that one more analysis of its contents may hardly be welcome. The author begins with a preface, in which he first gives a hasty description of a picture which represents the episodes of the book, and then proceeds to dedicate his work to the " God of Love, to the Nymphs, and to Pan." Thus relieved of his burden, he tells how Daphnis and Chloe, both foundlings, were brought up by rustics, who taught them how to tend their flocks. The life they led together, from childhood on, developed in them mutual affection and the truest friendship. As they increased in years this affection ripened into love, a passion which, in their state of innocence, thoroughly bewildered them. Daphnis had rivals, and Chloe also, but each repelled the new suitors. One of Chloe's swains, the cowherd Dorco, plans to carry away his mistress by force, and to that end disguises himself in a wolf's skin ; but dogs fall upon him and nearly kill him before Daphnis can come to his rescue. Some months after this adventure a boat-load of pirates from Tyre steal Dorco's oxen—mortally wounding him— and carry away Daphnis with them to their ship. But Dorco, before expiring, gives Chloe his rustic pipe. She hurries to the strand and plays upon it. The oxen rush to the side of the vessel, leap overboard, and thus capsize it. The pirates are drowned by the weight of their armor, but Daphnis swims to shore. Other events follow, the most important of which is the capture of Chloe by some enemies of Daphnis, and her release through the intervention of Pan himself. The unsuccessful efforts of the lovers to gratify their physical love forms now the main theme of the story, while winter and autumn come and go, and land-scapes, rural scenes, and gardens are described, until finally the wealthy parents of the young shepherds appear, and recognize in them their own offspring through the tokens they had exposed with them at their birth. A wedding festival marks the happy ending of this rural courtship.

Besides its eulogy of natural scenery and the glorifica-tion of absolute innocence, *Daphnis and Chloe* differs both in plan and make-up from the novels of erotic adventure. In the first place, the author tells the story himself and re-peats his dialogue, or what may pass for dialogue, at second hand and in a narrative way. Consequently we lose the directness and sense of participation in the events, which

Heliodorus, for instance, imparts to us.   Again, the author of the pastoral has weakened his pastoral sentiment by his borrowings from the episodes of the other school.   The fortunes of his lovers he has placed under the control of Eros instead of a rustic divinity, though Pan does appear at times to guard his worshipers.   The introduction of pirates clashes with the quiet serenity of the fields and groves, and brings in a scene of bloodshed which is not at all consonant with the idea of rural emancipation from crime and violence.   The same criticism may be made regarding the scenes of sensuality and corruption, which are peculiar to a people who studied how to violate nature rather than to conform to her laws.

When all these discordant elements are put together the artificiality of *Daphnis and Chloe* is strikingly manifest. Still, to insist on them to the exclusion of the other senti‑ ments, which, indeed, make up the main body of the novel, would be doing it injustice.   For the pastoral idea, when all deductions have been allowed, is still the overshadowing principle with Longus, and the only one by which he has exercised any influence on modern fiction.   The bucolics of Theocritus and Virgil, who did not preach such astounding innocence as the Alexandrian Sophist conceived, are far removed from the rusticity of the Greek idyl.   Yet the degree of development which the new views have here attained would seem to indicate a long series of eulogies on country life antecedent to the composition of *Daphnis and Chloe.*   These eulogies may have been perfected, and the verbal pictures of natural scenery outlined, either in the public schools of rhetoric or within the narrower confines of pastoral poetry.   Ever since the time of Aristophanes and Plato Greek literature had delighted in extolling the charm of rural existence as contrasted with the complexity of urban life, and among the poets of the Alexandrian epoch many stories of shepherds had been celebrated in verse.   One of these tales concerns the shepherd Daphnis, to whom the invention of bucolic poetry is often ascribed, and who was himself a foundling, brought up by shepherds, and hating cities. It was widespread, and evidently furnished our author with the name of his hero and some of his details. Chloe was also a word long connected with the pastoral idea, and had attained common use as the surname of Demeter, the goddess of the fruitful field. So there was plenty of material at hand awaiting Longus' choice.

As regards the manner of the novel, we have already cited the tendency of the Sophists to exercise the ingenuity of their scholars by giving them subjects for elaboration in rhetorical exercises. An unusually good description is the picture of winter in *Daphnis and Chloe*: "On a sudden heavy falls of snow blocked up the roads and shut up the cottagers within doors. Impetuous torrents rushed down from the mountains, the ice thickened, the trees seemed as though their branches were broken down beneath the weight of snow, and the whole face of the earth had disappeared except about the brinks of the fountains and the borders of the rivers." This last touch of reality indicates, by its observation of actual facts, something more than the artificial ornateness of an academic oration.

And yet we know that the rhetoricians dealt gladly in these scenes, for Dion Chrysostom, the celebrated orator of Domitian's and Trajan's reigns, extolled in one of his elaborate harangues the simplicity and innocence of rural life in the island of Eubœa, and related the story of a huntsman whom he had once met on the coast of that country. In this oration there is the nucleus of a genuine pastoral novel, and Longus—if Longus it was—can hardly have been ignorant of it.

Though there is much in *Daphnis and Chloe* which might seem to reveal a deep love of nature for herself alone, yet we are always in a state of uncertainty regarding the sincerity of the author.   The question whether he really feels the force of his own delineations of her changing moods and phases, or whether these pictures are the product of a perfect art concealing itself, has not been solved to our satisfaction.   The winter's landscape is both natural and rhetorical, and in most of the other descriptions the balance hangs even between nature and art.   But in one of his most careful sketches—the plan of a pleasure garden—the writer clearly shows his fondness for the work of man's hands. In the geometrical lines of this retreat, in its regular flower-beds, and its studied glimpses of landscape, Longus might well have belonged to the age of Louis XIV, and have given to Le Nôtre the idea which the latter carried out so success-fully in the arrangement of the famous park at Versailles.

But the blemishes of *Daphnis and Chloe* disappear in the contemplation of its attractions.   So simple a plan and so excellent a composition have, perhaps, never been known in the history of pastoral writings.   For this reason it is all the more strange that Longus had no successors in his own time, when his defects in taste and morals would be less apparent than they are to-day.   If his success incited the ambition of rivals, their names and even the very men-tion of their works have been lost to posterity ; and Longus himself experienced but a slightly better fate in the cen-turies immediately following.   Certain Byzantine authors of the Middle Ages would appear to have come under his influence, but it was not until the Renaissance, when good Bishop Amyot had taken him under his protection, through his translation of *Daphnis and Chloe* in 1559, that our Sophist's view of pastoral love and life was restored to pastoral writers.   And even then the current of rural description, which looked to Virgil as its fountain head, was flowing too swiftly to receive any noticeable additions from this newly reopened source.   Some of the episodes of *Daphnis and Chloe* were incorporated into the pastoral poetry of Italy, but they brought no particular inspiration. Not until the eve of the French Revolution, when the thoughts of mankind were reverting to an age untrammeled by social conventionalities, did the idea of this Greek novel of bygone times live again in St. Pierre's immortal idyl of *Paul and Virginia.* For whether the two stories bear any actual relation to each other or not, they surely represent similar views, and by their likenesses and contrasts they reveal the great changes of sentiment and feeling which differentiate the thought-standards of the modern world from the ideals of the ancient.

To the Sophists we undoubtedly owe the existence in literature of the various kinds of the Greek novel, and with the decline of their sect it seems to have passed away. The causes for this death by sympathy are not hard to ascertain. The old Greek novel must have had, while it was among the people, a vigorous life. When the Sophists took it up, they dried up its sources of tradition and legend, and refined it to their own false views of sentiment and action. They gave it its literary form and involved it in their fall. Its representations of life at their hands had been too distorted, and its field of action too narrow, to raise up successors to their work. Besides, the end of the Alexandrian period saw in full possession of civil and social power the various sects of Christians, whose rules of conduct, whatever may have been their actual practice, were directly antagonized by the cruelty and sensuality which formed a large proportion of these stories. The dedication also of the novels—however conventional and unmeaning it may have been—to some pagan deity was especially calculated to call out the opposition of the new religion with its increasing number of adherents. So we find that the Church at first forbade novels to its members, and afterward, when their hold was felt to be too tenacious for mere prohibition to have much effect, it tried to turn their influence into moral and religious channels. The same opposition, and the same attempt to appropriate to religion's ends the weapons of the adversary of souls, we shall find again in the case of the romances of chivalry in Spain of the sixteenth century. Therefore, we are not surprised that, after several centuries of vain attempts to suppress this pestilential literature, the Greco-Roman novel should reappear as the work of Christian hands. *Clitophon and Leucippe*, which had divided with *Theagenes and Chariclea* the admiration of the Byzantine readers of fiction, took then to itself a sequel, where, maliciously enough, the unhappiness of the married life of the lovers is related, and in contrast with that the felicity of a son, whose birth came about through the repentance and baptism of his mother, and whose marital continence offered a stinging rebuke to the earthly passions of his father. This model of all virtues was at last translated through a martyr's death.

Photius' liking for these condemned volumes has been sufficiently commented upon, though Longus and Chariton find no place in his *Myriobiblion*. Many other officers of the Church besides Photius used to read the Alexandrian tales of adventure, and adapt them to their doctrinal aims. An instance of this is found in a sermon of the tenth century on "Abraham the Jew and the merchant Theodore," in which many adventures are related, love is replaced by superstition, and the moral is reached by the conversion of the Jew through the faith which the merchant has in the protecting power of the image of Christ, set up in the market-place of Constantinople.

From the seventh to the tenth centuries, Byzantine literature was entirely under the control of the Church. But in the eleventh century there began a short revival of learning, extending to the capture of Constantinople by the companions of Villehardouin early in the thirteenth, in which serious efforts were put forth to restore the artistic side of fiction. Among the products of this Greek Renaissance are four works which in plot may be called novels, though three of the four are in metrical verse. One of these three, *Dosicles and Rhodantes*, by Theodorus Prodromus, a monk of the twelfth century and a prolific writer, is modeled on Heliodorus. Fables, of a probable Oriental origin, fill out his meager plot. Another is by a disciple of Prodromus, Nicetas Eugenianus, whose *Charicles and Drosilla*—less violent in its episodes than his master's poem—is made up from lyric and bucolic poets, the Anthology, and Greco-Roman novels. The erotic digressions of this example of composite fiction are almost limitless. Fortunately the third romance in verse, *Aristander and Callithea*, by Constantine Manasses, a contemporary of Prodromus, has come down to us only in a few moral and sententious extracts. Their evidence points to the usual series of extravagant and ever-recurring episodes.

More important than these romances is the prose "drama," *Hysmenias and Hysmene*, in eleven books, by the philosopher Eustathius, whose uncertain date may be fixed somewhere within the twelfth century. An analysis of the contents of his story would not redound to any considerable edification of the reader, and it is enough that to say that the work is an imitation of *Clitophon and Leucippe*, though degenerating often to a perhaps unconscious parody of that favorite novel. For the merits of Achilles are here much diluted and his defects very decidedly concentrated. Paintings, dreams, and persistent love-making by the heroine to the hero form a large part of the material. Yet in spite of all these insipidities, Eustathius was not only popular in his own day but also received early attention at the Renaissance, as an Italian translation of his " drama " dating from 1550, a French version of 1559, and passages in Montemayor's *Diana* conclusively prove.

From the Eastern Empire and the scrolls of Byzantine

literature the Greek novel, with its imitations and ramifications, early found its way to the peoples of western Europe. Not, however, in the examples we have hitherto chronicled—exception being made for *Apollonius of Tyre*—but in plots of novels unknown to us in the original, and in episodes of others, which cannot be traced to any definite ancestry. To their transmission and diffusion not only the learned, in their eagerness for novelty, contributed with copies of manuscripts still extant, but also the oral interchanges of traders, pilgrims, and crusaders were even of greater assistance. Of undoubted Greek origin is the subject of *Éracle*, versified in French, about 1169, by Gautier of Arras, whose hero rises at last to the dignity of Emperor. The source of *Flore and Blanchefleur*, so popular in all mediæval literatures, must have been some novel of erotic adventure. But more important than either of these, *Florimont* (dated 1188), by Aimon of Varennes, will doubtless prove, since its theme, the career of Philip of Macedonia, was found by the author in Greek territory, and may have been the echo of some lost romance of chivalry, similar in many particulars to the unique story of Nimrod.

Italy gathered up gladly the wreckage of the Greco-Roman fiction, loaning it afterward to her northern neighbors or keeping it for herself. These borrowings may be easily recognized in some of Boccaccio's tales, where the heroes are persecuted, undergo perils by land and sea, are cast away, or captured by pirates. The first story of the fifth day of the *Decameron* tells how Cimon, denied the hand of his mistress Iphigenia, carries her off, is himself overcome and thrown into prison, but escapes and regains his bride. The action is placed among the islands of the eastern Mediterranean, and Boccaccio himself cites the annals of Cyprus for his authority. The seventh story of the second day, where the power of fate, the familiar Tyche, is extolled, may be regarded as a caricature of such constancy as Anthia showed in the *Babylonica.* Crete and Rhodes are the scene of the events related, and the standard attraction of murders is not at all despised. A Greek novel may have also been the ultimate source of the third story of the fourth day of the *Decameron.*

Mediæval Europe, then, knew the novel of the East in its mutilations and abridgments, and welcomed it with the same hospitality with which it greeted the literary fragments of all times and all peoples. But it was not until the revival of learning, beginning in Italy with Petrarch and Boccaccio, had nearly run its course, that the greater writers of Alexandrian fiction, who had for centuries lain neglected in their manuscripts, were revealed to the modern world. The works of Photius first called attention to them; next the humanists rendered them from Greek into Latin, and from Latin they were translated finally into the modern vernaculars. But the most literary form which they received at the Renaissance was the French version of Bishop Amyot, made directly from the original. Not all, however, were thus favored with the notice of the sixteenth century, for the stories of Xenophon and Chariton did not come to light until the eighteenth was well under way. So that the influence which the novels, as a whole, exerted on modern fiction is to be limited to the specimens in the hands of the humanists. Though the most important part of their contributions to the fiction of Spain and France consisted in their more striking incidents, yet the indirect force of their plan and composition was not without beneficial results to modern novelists, as witness the influence of *Theagenes and Chariclea* on Cervantes' *Persiles y Sigismunda.* And through the popularity which their episodes and style had gained, the makers of the heroic-gallant novel of the seventeenth century were led to imitate from them some of the leading features of their plots and to repeat to some extent the excellences of their methods.

CHAPTER IV.

THE mediæval romance of chivalry resembles more closely the historical novel of Walter Scott than any other style of fiction with which we are now acquainted. This resemblance is not, indeed, in the material or plan. For the romance of chivalry deals wholly with fanciful personages and realms, and has no more plan than *The Three Musketeers.* But the sentiment and the ideals of the two kinds of narrative are practically the same. They both eulogize a social condition which is ceasing to be, or perhaps has been, and they have to do with the exploits and affections of nobles or princes alone, while the common herd neither toils nor suffers in the background, but rejoices in its ability to add to the glory and power of the master. And the master always prospers in his affairs, with these ancestors of Scott, for the romance of chivalry is persistently optimistic.

We claim nowadays that we are the inheritors of the ages, an assertion which is no doubt true, and if we should specify " Middle Ages " the claim might meet with even less contradiction. For in that era of the world our family tree first appeared above the ground, and its trunk has since been fed from the roots twining among the ruins of ancient civilization. And so the soil made of the dust of its own monuments has nurtured the grafts of antiquity set so repeatedly on our parent stock. Socially and politically we are confessedly mediæval in origin, but not so evidently mediæval in our literature. Poetry, the drama especially, essay-writing, history, philosophy, have each and all experienced at many points in their evolution the power of Greek and Roman thought, and felt the influence of classical taste and forms. Fiction alone has been comparatively unhindered in its development during these centuries of continuous change, so that if we except the pastoral novels, and allow a strain of Greek blood in the heroic-gallant novel of the seventeenth century, we may quite safely assume that the romances of our ancestors have descended to us unmixed in lineage. To be sure they profited by their relations with the East, whose stories, legends, or superstitions, brought overland through Persia and Constantinople, or taking ship from Arabia to Italy or Granada, had entered into the material available for modern fiction, even before the formation of the modern tongues.

But the novel by itself has not shared so largely in this gift of Eastern lore and fancy as the other classes of fiction. Its substance is more indigenous, and its growth has been more independent of external and foreign influences. The explanation of this fact is readily seen, when we stop to consider that the longer narratives of imaginative happenings, which form the main body of our novels, are connected with the legendary past of the nation's history. They thus are interwoven with its national life, they are cherished the more fondly in the popular heart, are kept more rigidly in their primitive shape, and are defended more jealously against the invasion of events and incidents which the people instinctively recognize to be alien to their ancestral heritage. And to this wide-reaching national antipathy to all innovation from sources foreign to the national spirit, we must add the disdain which the educated classes, down to comparatively recent times, felt for that branch of writing which was intended for popular amusement. In the Middle Ages and during the early Renaissance particularly, they avoided even the higher grades of vernacular literature.

How much more, then, the recitals composed for the pleasure of the rude nobles or the delectation of the unpolished burghers! Dante is the only author who seems certain of the immortality of his compositions in the popular tongue. Petrarch, on the contrary, reveals the true conception of the scholars of his time, when he considers his lyrics the amusement of his leisure hours, and bases his reputation with posterity on his epic poem in Latin, the forgotten *Africa.* Taking these attitudes and feelings into consideration, there should be no surprise at the purely national and modern character of the early novel.

Between the Greek novel of antiquity and the modern romance of chivalry are many points of correspondence. Their essential resemblance is nowhere shown more strongly than in their actual make-up. Both arose from the fusion of a love story with a narrative of exciting adventures. The spirit of both was undoubtedly the same at the start, aristocratic in tone. The purpose of each was the same, to amuse the nobles and the people. And when the tales of court life had run their course, both were succeeded by plebeian stories of a more or less realistic cast. The material, out of which the Greek novel of the aristocratic school and the romance of chivalry were fashioned, is also the same, relatively speaking, and the time of the appearance of each in their respective literatures corresponds also in a striking manner. We had only theory and the one example of the *Nimrod* fragment to support this view of the formation of the Greek novel; but for the development of the Spanish, abundant evidence is at hand. It was born when the flowering period of mediæval literature had passed, when the heroic songs of the paladins and the lyric strains of the Trouvères had been stifled under the weight of a garrulous prose and the burden of linguistic resonance. The mediæval drama had reached its height in the mysteries of the *Nativity* and *Passion*, the *Miracles of the*

Virgin, and the plays of Corpus Christi day. Then, like his colleague of ancient Greece, the ambitious author of the later fifteenth century abandoned the repetition of themes long worn out, and exercised his talents in giving shape to a new aspirant to literary distinction, by adapting to the taste of the cultivated classes the favorite legends of the common people.

Unfortunately for the excellence of this new branch of composition, its literary sponsor was himself of no great mental force, and had not the backing of a school of rhetoricians or of a group of humanists. For one of the greatest drawbacks to the whole vernacular literature of western Europe previous to the Renaissance lies in this, that very few authors, whether poets, dramatists, or novelists, had the gift of self-correction or the notion of literary style. After the originality of their first inspiration had departed they wrote hopelessly on and on, turning over and over and diluting the same matter, varied only by the most elementary methods of artistic composition. The consequence was that there is hardly a piece of work produced in the whole mediæval workshop—if we leave aside the university-educated Italians—which in its plan or form appeals to the literary public of to-day, or indeed of any generation subsequent to the contemporaries of its first fashioner. We may not then expect to find pre-Renaissance literature of absorbing interest, either in thought or style. In thought it repeats with a few variations the ideas of the Middle Ages. In style it does not at all foreshadow the classical criticism of the Renaissance. The fourteenth and fifteenth centuries employed their slight literary activity in the modern vernaculars with summing up the results of the previous three centuries, and in placing them within the reach of all classes of society. It was the period of preparation, which was to make the modern nations ready for the reception of ancient art and learning. So the romance of chivalry, the only literary creation of that period, reflects most faithfully its traits and characteristics. And in all the 150 years of its favor, from the invention of printing to the publication of *Don Quixote*, it never was able to attain, in spite of the most labored inventions, the force and directness of its first production. Rather it went farther and farther astray from nature, until it finally disappeared in the region of the unreal and fantastic.

As would probably be the case with the Greek novel, did we possess that part of it which must have had its origin in the prose form of the national epic, the romance of chivalry may be regarded as the epitome of the Middle Ages. If we look at its substance alone we see in it a mixture of the Breton epic, in large proportion, of the national epic, in small proportion, and of the *roman d'aventure*, the recipient flask—to carry out our simile to the bitter end.

The *roman d'aventure* gave the rambling epic narrative a plot, which, however, is of no more importance here than it was in the novel of the Greco-Romans. To be sure, the incentive to adventure arises from the relation of the hero to the heroine, instead of from some offended deity, although in the *Nimrod* fragment the absence of Nimrod from his lady-love seems to be occasioned by almost the same cause as brought about the separation of Amadis and Oriana, in *Amadis of Gaul*. But from whatever reason the adventures are entered upon, it is they, and not the mutual affection of the leading characters, which are the main subject of the narrative. The reader is carried on from one peril and combat of the hero to another, and can scarcely hear, amid the breaking of lances and the clashing of swords, the plaintive murmur of the solitary maiden pining within the castle walls. She is brought again to our attention only when it is necessary to give an excuse for a new series of wanderings. In this predominance of adventure the romancer showed beyond mistaking his rude conception of his art. By catering to the desire for the marvelous and the appetite for excitement, which are liable to fluctuations from age to age, he left to one side those traits of human life and action that are ever true, and that extend the fame of their faithful delineators throughout all time. It is apparent, therefore, why the poetical *roman d'aventure* has enjoyed a longer term of popularity, in its brevity and simplicity, than all the long-winded prose narratives with which the fifteenth century endeavored to supplant them.

But the *roman d'aventure* is itself an evolution from something more simple and shorter, and, consequently (owing to the lack of taste among the mediæval poets), from something more perfect and pleasing in form and style. This forerunner is the *romance* or *chanson d'histoire*, a lyric-epic poem of but few strophes, which presents to us an adventure, or an episode of love, pure and simple. More often love and adventure are combined in these charming miniatures in verse. When they first appeared in French literature—for the *romances* are peculiar to northern France—the feudal system was already solidly established. Their province was to depict the courtly side of that system. Their tone is thoroughly aristocratic, and their surroundings are clearly the same as those of the heroic epic.

How great the popularity of these gems of early poetry may have been we can only conjecture from their theme, and from the name sometimes given them of *chansons de toile*, because they were sung by the noble ladies while sitting at their embroidery. Their numbers are now few, and those preserved may not be the most interesting of their kind. A good example of what have come down to us is afforded by the poem called *Rainaud*, after its hero. It tells us how that knight, returning from the court, passes before the castle of his sweetheart Arembour, who is embroidering at the window, but from unfounded jealousy does not look up at her. She laments to him the former times, when he had hung on her words and been grieved at the idea of her indifference. In answer he replies that she had been false to him ; but when she offers to swear to the contrary he believes her and they are reconciled. All this scene of love and repentance, its setting and its dialogue, is expressed in thirty lines of ten syllables each. It is true miniature painting of the great world of life and action.

Another of these poems, *Orior*, is not so long even as *Rainaud*. Two sisters are seen bathing in a fountain which gleams white in the valley among the trees, where "the winds blow and the branches crackle." Back from a jousting comes Gerard. He spies out the sisters, makes love to Gay and carries her away with him, while Orior, abandoned by her playmate, sadly returns to her lonely home.

The pastoral scenery of *Orior* and the melancholy tinge to the tale become urban and tragic in another romance of *Belle Doette*, which is later in date and longer, but still simple and straightforward. Doette sits at her window with a scroll in her hand, but she sees not the words before her and is thinking of Doon, her lover, who has gone to win fame at a tournament. Suddenly a messenger arrives without. Doette hastens down the steps to meet him. Tears are the only answer to her first question. She trembles, sinks, swoons, yet revives with great effort and asks again. It is too true. Doon has fallen dead in the lists. Her self-command returns. Calm and resigned to the decree of Heaven she makes ready her robe of mourning and renounces the world, while she desires that her dower may go to build an abbey into which no faithless lover may enter.

There is a charm about these poems of princely love in the eleventh and twelfth centuries, which might well delay us on our barren way from fact to fact. In their few lines they give all the essentials of their surroundings and plot, with words direct and full of meaning, and phrases luminous in the dawn of poetry's morning. The spirit of the three we have cited warrants us in going still further than their actual contents allow, and finding in them the germ of longer, but not less delicate, tales of love. *Rainaud* is heroic in its tone. Pride and jealousy animate it. *Orior* is full of the joys of nature, which are at last diminished by the desires of the human heart. *Belle Doette* is a complete picture of longing, disappointment, and resignation, and is like the erotic poems of Greece in these first two attributes. But where, in the solution of the stories of the heathen world, the loss of the lover is generally followed by the suicide of the one who is left behind, in the drama of mediæval sorrow a new element has entered, which is to change the whole spirit of modern literature. The Christian maiden of France does not attempt her own life in blind despair of happiness and hope, but has learned to find in religion and its promise of immortality a solace for the present and a comfort for the future. Trusting in Providence she submits to its mysterious ways.

The French *romance* presented to its listeners—for these poems were intended to be sung—details of actual existence, not at all fanciful, but real, and for this reason it may be well compared to the Greek love story. But there is another kind of French erotic poetry of the Middle Ages, which approaches much nearer to the elegies of antiquity, not only in its melancholy strain and tragic ending, but also in the partially mythological nature of its plot. This is the narrative *lai*, the original of which is the musical *lai* of the Celtic bards. Wandering minstrels had brought the traditions and legends of the vanquished British tribes into French and Norman territory, where the popular curiosity they excited soon demanded local renderings. These versions were made either directly from the Celtic, or indirectly from an Anglo-Saxon translation of the Celtic.

They relate events out of which grew the stories of King Arthur and his knights. They tell of heroes beloved by fairies, of magic castles containing enchanted maidens, of combats with monsters, and of victories crowned by love. Many of them are more particularly devoted to the passion of Tristan and Iseult and the vengeance of Mark, the king. Later, in the course of their increasing popularity, these *lais* of Celtic origin attracted to themselves stories of strange adventures from other sources, especially from tales of the East.

The best known writer of the narrative *lai* is Marie, "de France"—as she always signs herself—who lived at the English court, probably under Henry II., and who preferred to translate into French, Anglo-Saxon versions of the Celtic legends. A good specimen of the kind of poem she thus worked over is the *lai* called by her *Guigemar*. The hero of that name, while hunting in the forest, shoots at a white hind, but the arrow rebounds and wounds the knight himself. Now the hind speaks and tells him that to be healed of the wound he must find a woman who has suffered more than any other woman has ever suffered, and for whose sake he shall have done deeds at which all lovers shall marvel. Unable to think how all this may be accomplished, Guigemar wanders off in deep despair, until he reaches a bay of the sea, where he finds a boat moored. He enters the boat and is astonished at the richness and luxury of its appointments. While he thus lingers in mute admiration invisible hands are pushing the boat from the shore, and Guigemar looks up at last only to find himself on the open sea. Soon sleep overcomes and binds fast his senses. Toward evening he arrives in the harbor of an ancient city. There, in a castle facing on the deep, a young wife, attended by her niece and an aged priest, is strictly guarded by her jealous husband. To the castle landing comes the boat. The inmates of the tower go to meet it, find the knight, bring him within the walls, and the pitying lady dresses his wounds. His gratitude for her tender care awakens her affection, and he tarries until the coming of her lord counsels flight. Then the boat returns for him and bears him back over the waves to Brittany, where by many deeds of valor he wins great renown. The lady thus deserted, after many weary months of waiting for tidings from her absent lover, resolves to end her burdensome existence. She goes to the sea-wall to throw herself from it, but the boat comes before her, receives her on board, and carries her safely to Brittany, where after many perils and disappointments she is finally united in marriage to her knight.

Guigemar is a good example of the *lai*, and does not present any more incidents than many others of its class, which in common with it contain certain episodes that are to be found in the later romances of chivalry. Among these are the boat moved by unseen forces, which transports the hero to strange lands, the magic of the wound and its healing, the tower of the stronghold unbarred to the coming knight alone, and the necessity of undergoing adventures in which the fidelity of the lovers is tested by many suitors of the opposite sex before their happiness can be complete. This last mentioned device was a favorite incident in the Greek novels. All these traits of the *lais* appear again in every romance of chivalry.

At this point in the evolution of the modern novel, on the boundary between the *romance* and *lai* on the one hand, and the *roman d'aventure* on the other, there arises a problem of literary history, interesting to contemplate, but most difficult to solve. The romance of chivalry, like the Greek novel, is made up of adventures combined with a love story, and the former very much exceeds the latter in importance as well as in extent. The question, therefore, naturally presents itself, as to whether this proportion was always observed, and whether the relative position of the two elements was established at the very origin of the novels. To pretend to give an answer to this question, based on the study of the ancient novel alone, is not possible, inasmuch as we do not possess any other than its completed form. But the case is different with the romance of chivalry.

For the first of the kind, *Amadis of Gaul*, is already an expansion of a much shorter narrative, as can be seen on its surface. This expansion was brought about by the insertion of episodes of dangers and wanderings, and not in the multiplication of love scenes between the leading characters. The proof of this statement is in the reading of the book. Now *Amadis of Gaul* received its final expanding in the last third of the fifteenth century. But many of its essential features may be found in stories of love and adventure before the end of the twelfth. Consequently it is probable that the development of our romance occupied all this interval, or at the very least two centuries of it, and judging from what we know of its definite form, we may assume that the tendency of its evolution was always along the line of the addition of new adventures.

Now the earliest type of French erotic poetry known to us, the *romance*, is a union of love and adventure. But its interest lies wholly in the sketch of the passion and in the meeting of the lovers, while the element of adventure furnishes merely the environment, the frame. The jealousy and repentance of Rainaud is what fixes the poet's attention, and it is only to give his scornful passing-by a suitable pretext that the knight's connection with the royal court is mentioned. So in *Belle Doette* no importance is attached to the fact that Doon was killed in a tournament. It is the domestic, intimate side of the hero's life which is the object of the artist's portrayal.

But in the next step in the evolution of mediæval erotic

poetry, the *lai*, we see the beginning of the desire to gain the reader's attention by laying stress on the events themselves, rather than on their influence over the people who participate in them. Hunting scenes are introduced, magic spells are cited, superstitions are evoked, and combats with hostile warriors are described. All of which is so much extraneous material, and has only an arbitrary connection with the actual plot of the story. Yet the main theme of the *lai* is still the love of the hero and the heroine, and to this theme the adventures, though numerous, are still subordinate. When, however, we descend a little farther in the order of time and take up the successor of the *romance* and the *lai*, the *roman d'aventure*, we find that the balance inclines away from the side of the love story.

There is another argument available for the point at issue, an argument derived from analogy. The first evolution of which we have any knowledge in French mediæval literature is in the field of heroic poetry, the national epic. It has been proven beyond any doubt, from references in contemporaneous authorities and from the actual testimony of successive manuscripts of the same poem, that the long recitals existing in the twelfth century of the fabulous and historical deeds of the peers of Charlemagne began, as far back as the eighth, with short songs celebrating the prowess of some favorite leader, or the popular emotion caused by some unusual occurrence. These songs were at first almost wholly lyric, being composed by the retainers of the hero for the edification of his countrymen. They were also historical and abode by facts, even while magnifying them. But as time wore on, and the generation which had seen the exploits thus proclaimed gave way to one which knew of them only by hearsay, the minstrel, who had received these songs as his poetical inheritance, found it necessary to give them an introduction and a running commentary. In other words, as the event and the hero receded in time, more and more explanation was required in the poems of which they were the theme. So that the song from a purely lyric composition became more and more narrative, until finally, all historical connection being forgotten, it incorporated, without protest, the inventions with which ambitious bards sought to adorn it, and suffered the annexation of poetical recitals based on incidents which had happened in other times and in distant places. In such a way was the first manuscript of the *Chanson de Roland* made up, and it was afterward lengthened by the same methods. Thus from a simple eulogy of some one exploit in the great hero's career the song developed, under the successive revisions of five centuries, into a complete biography not only of Roland, but of his friends and his enemies as well, and finally ended in a regular chronicle of all the real and imaginary events which took place in the lifetime of the great emperor. Other epic poems of France have the same history. Their original statements of fact and praise have been expanded and increased, until the interest in the subject, which they were written to commemorate, has been completely engulfed in the multiplicity of details which preceded and followed it.

The *romans d'aventure*, which are the next step in the assumed development of the romance of chivalry, appear to have been the chosen literature of the nobility of France. Their vogue lasted from the middle of the twelfth century to the last quarter of the thirteenth. Some sixty of them have been preserved in manuscript, and these vary from a few hundred to several thousand lines in length. At their beginning they seem to have been expanded *romances* or *lais.* But later they drew upon a great variety of sources, both native and foreign, and adopted any subject, historical or legendary, which they could turn to good account. The earliest *roman d'aventure* known to modern scholars is *Ille et Galeron* (about 1168), written for Beatrice, wife of

Frederick Barbarossa, by the same Gautier of Arras who versified *Éracle.* A Breton *lai*, the story of *Éludic*, supplied Gautier with a part of his material. He tells how a knight of Brittany, Ille by name, an orphan and abused by his relatives, regained his estate at last with the aid of the king of France, and married Galeron, the daughter of his feudal suzerain. Afterward, while jousting, he loses the sight of one eye. In despair he forsakes his wife, and makes the pilgrimage to Rome. There he finally becomes the emperor's seneschal, and the imperial princess falls in love with him. But like his prototypes of the Alexandrian period he remains constant to his bride. She in her turn reaches Rome, finds her husband, but does not acquaint him with her presence, and for some time she supports herself with the work of her own hands. But at last she reveals herself to Ille and returns with him to Brittany, where they live happily for many years, until Galeron retires to a convent, and Ille is at liberty to wed the love-lorn princess. Thus after all virtue is rewarded, even in the twelfth century.

Something like this reward is the recompense of another hero, whose life is the subject of the French *Guillaume de Palerme*, better known to us by its English version. The action begins in Sicily, where a Spanish prince, changed into a wolf by the arts of his step-mother, rescues young William from an uncle's cruelty and carries him away to the vicinity of Rome. The emperor soon finds him and makes him page to his daughter, Melior. Mutual love in due time kindles both mistress and attendant. They escape together from court, disguised in bearskins, and after enduring perils and adventures of every kind, finally reach Palermo, where all comes to a happy end, including the disenchanting of the good were-wolf, who has stood by the lovers nobly and rescued them often from the greatest dangers.

Elements of plot and episodes for the future novel are here in abundance.   Like William, Amadis, too, was a castaway.   He met Oriana in the same way as the Sicilian hero met Melior.   A fairy also protected them both in their trials and smoothed the way to their future happiness. Many other *romans d'aventure* might be cited which would offer numerous resemblances to the details of the romances of chivalry, some of which even are true to real life.   *Guillaume de Dole*, for instance, which was written in the first quarter of the thirteenth century for a male patron, is a genuine historical novel in verse.   The action takes place mainly at the court of Conrad, Emperor of Germany, located by the poem at Mayence, and in the various cities and castles of the Rhineland.   The subject is based on the friendly intercourse of French and German knights, their banquets and tournaments.   The story is the love of Conrad for Lienor, William's sister, the unjust accusation brought against her by an envious seneschal, her own defense at the imperial court, and her marriage with the emperor.   Descriptions of court and baronial life are many and varied, the reality of the events is accentuated by the detail of manners and fashions, even to the introduction of many well-known songs into the narrative, and the whole design and carrying-out of the plan reveal a talent which in its veracity and force is curiously like the manner of the great historical novelist of the nineteenth century.

Even the modern realistic novel has a predecessor among these charming poems.   *La Châtelaine de Vergi*, written in the last quarter of the thirteenth century, contains the ever recurring tale of love, jealousy, and death.   The Lady of Vergi loves a Burgundian knight and admits him to her chamber by night, on a certain signal given to identify him.   But the knight is summoned later to the ducal court, where the duchess falls violently in love with him, is rebuffed, and, in revenge, accuses him to her husband of attempted injury to her honor.   The duke, who admires his courtier, is about to punish him with banishment only, when the latter, unwilling to leave his mistress, reveals his secret love to his lord.   The duchess, seeing that her husband has become, after all, rather the firmer friend of the knight than his enemy, questions him about the case, and by repeated assaults finally worries the whole affair out of him. Pentecost comes, and with it all the vassals, including the Lady of Vergi, arrive at court.   A great banquet is held, and when the ladies have withdrawn from the table, and are presumably gossiping among themselves, the duchess twits her attendant about her lover's signal.   The Lady feels that her knight is false and has betrayed her honor.   When the others go to the court ball she retires alone to a darkened chamber, and there, in the hearing of a maid whom she does not see, breaks out into sad bewailings over her desolate lot.   Her pathetic expressions of grief are suddenly checked by death, the result of excessive emotion.

Now the knight, missing his beloved from the dance, comes in search of her.   He finds the chamber, enters it, and the lifeless body meets his gaze.   From the maid he learns what has passed.   Full of reproaches for his own weakness in surrendering her secret, he seizes a sword which hangs near-by on the wall, and buries it in his own breast.   The duke then appears, finds the lover lying near his mistress, hears the sad story, takes the dripping sword and bears it to the ballroom.   The trail of blood and the countenance of the duke stop short the affrighted guests in the midst of their merriment.   He slowly tells them of the fidelity of the lovers and the perfidy of the duchess, and their tears mingle with his, while the duchess droops and dies before the light of morning.   The next day the duke oversees the interment of all three.   Joy has now fled from his life, he crosses himself, and dies fighting for the faith in Palestine.

But our partiality for the *roman d'aventure*, certainly the most attractive, lifelike, and interesting production of mediæval literature, is leading us somewhat astray from the point at issue, with which *La Châtelaine de Vergi* has really nothing to do, since it exercised no influence on the romances of chivalry nor on any other kind of mediæval fiction. For its keen observation of human sentiment and the dramatic exposition of its narrative either passed unnoticed by its contemporaries, or were repugnant to their longing for the marvelous. Four centuries passed away before the psychological novel repeated in France this brilliant beginning, and Mme. de La Fayette published *La Princesse de Clèves.* We must also confess that the historical novel, whose prototype might have been *Guillaume de Dole*, did not fare much better. A few short stories in prose of the fifteenth century, like *Pierre de Provence*, or the more alluring *Jean de Paris*, may be taken for weak followers of such a vigorous predecessor. But its action on the romances of chivalry is vague at the best, if indeed the pictures of court life and notions of geography found in the latter are not drawn from a more epic source than springs from *Guillaume de Dole* and its kind. And in only one feature of their construction are the later prose romances like the *romans d'aventure.* This is in the diminishing proportion of love relative to the share of adventure.

It is quite certain that the romances of chivalry take their subject from a *romance* or a *roman d'aventure* as well as the general features of their plot. But their substance they obtained from the prose versions of another style of mediæval poetry, akin in form and length to the *romans d'aventure*, contemporaneous in date and partly similar in origin. This kind is seen in the poems which celebrated the deeds of Arthur and the Round Table, the love of Tristan, and the mystery of the Holy Grail. The forerunners of these stories in their turn—excepting those relating to the religious part of the Grail legend—were Celtic *lais*, which toward the middle of the twelfth century had been joined together more or less artistically, and thus formed a connected poetical narrative. This welding took place in England at first, at the Anglo-Norman court, and the stories thus formed were soon exported to France, either orally or in writing. Fashionable poets received them there and tried to put together more perfectly their incongruous parts, enlarged this episode, rejected that, interpreted at haphazard legend and symbol, and strove to substitute reason for mysticism. They modified the primitive savagery and strange manners of the Celtic traditions, refined their sentiment, polished their verse, and in due time presented them to their royal patrons as models of chivalry and honor. No point in literary history is more obscure than the record of the passage of the wild, rough, and undisciplined Celtic *lai* into the courtly French poem which has come down to us. But it now seems probable that the trimming and refining process began under the Henrys of England, and was continued and completed in the literary circles of the Continent.

The great center of the final revision of the Arthurian cycle of poems was the court of the province of Champagne. The Countess Mary, the daughter of Louis VII. of France and the celebrated Eleanor of Poitou—who carried the spirit of Provençal poetry and the freedom of Provençal manners, first to the knights of France and afterwards to the nobility of England—held sway there from 1164 to 1198, and her vassals, both high-born and plebeian, brought the art of French lyric verse to its full development. The favorite author of Mary's reign was Chrétien, from the town of Troyes, an admirer and translator of Ovid, an imitator of the Provençal forms of lyric poetry, and the most unwearying revisor of the Breton legends that ever lived. In fact, through him we derive a large share of our knowledge of those legends. They came to him from across the water in prose or rhyme, by word of mouth or in manuscript, and at the command of his countess Chrétien adapted them to the fashion of his age. Yet notwithstanding their indebtedness to him it is a great misfortune for the Celtic traditions that Chrétien very rarely understood what he received, and did not bother to cast about for an explanation. He distorted their sense and twisted their application to the profit of the idea of gallantry which the Troubadours of the South had conveyed to him. So that, between the veritable chasms he would leave in his narratives and the delight he took in postponing the solution of what he did comprehend, modern scholars have almost renounced further efforts to arrive at the unraveling of this most enticing literary snarl.

The poems of Chrétien comprise the stories of the Round Table, properly speaking, and the search for the Holy Grail. His revision of Tristan's career is lost in the original form but is preserved in a later prose version. Nearly all of these poems are of a biographical nature. They are made up of adventures which are undergone by some leading character, but which are not sufficiently connected by cause and effect to be called a plot. The element of love in them is very slight, since their whole purpose is to present a model of gallantry. Therefore we can hardly call them novels in verse, and cannot look to them, as we did to the *romans d'aventure*, for any ideas of construction. But the material out of which they are made, and which they transmitted to their prose successors, is plainly the substance of the romances of chivalry, and was openly borrowed by the authors of these romances to fill out the skeleton of their plot—to give it shape and attractiveness. An excellent illustration of the likeness of matter between the romances of chivalry and the poems of the Breton cycle is afforded by one of the most famous of Chrétien's works, *Iwain*, better known to scholars as *Le Chevalier au lion.*

The poet tells how one day, at Arthur's court, the knight Calogrenanz was relating his experience in the forest near an enchanted fountain, and bewailing his overthrow by a giant of most hideous aspect, armed with a mace. Among the listeners was Iwain. Stirred up by his friend's recital he resolves to avenge him, leaves the court, journeys though the forest and comes at length to the fountain, gleaming white beneath a majestic pine. Around the fountain is a beautiful marble balustrade, and near by stands a chapel. On the pine a golden basin is hanging. This basin Iwain takes and with it he dips water from the fountain, and pours it out on the balustrade. Suddenly from all corners of the heavens rush mighty thunderbolts, and from the sky the clouds fall in rain, snow, and hail. But the sudden storm is followed by as sudden a calm. Birds gather and settle on the tree in such vast numbers as to hide its branches, while they sing most sweetly, but each a different song. In the distance next appears a hardy knight who, on his approach, assails Iwain with abusive words and rebukes him for having desolated his country by the storm. But our hero, nothing daunted, rides stoutly at him, puts him to flight, and pursues him hotly to his castle. On reaching it the fugitive disappears and Iwain, pushing on his horse into an open room of the stronghold, feels a raised door suddenly falling behind him, which cuts off the horse's hind-quarters and blocks all egress from the place.

Iwain is now a prisoner. But a maiden comes who gives him a ring which shall render him invisible. Armed with this talisman he remains in the room and escapes detection, even though the body of the knight, who has been done to death by Iwain, bleeds from its wounds when it is borne through the chamber. Then when the danger has passed he reveals himself to the weeping widow, becomes enamored of her and she, mindful of his prowess, with true worldly wisdom, elects him to be her lord. Now Iwain is in duty bound to defend the magic of the fountain. This he does valiantly even against Arthur's knights, to whom, when he has unhorsed the braggart Kay, he makes himself known, invites them to his castle and entertains them most royally.

But a change comes over the spirit of Iwain. The sight of his old companions awakens in him his slumbering love for adventures. He asks his lady for a year's leave of absence, obtains it, and, along with her permission, a ring which is to keep him mindful of her love. Now, with Gawayne, his dearest friend, he roams the world as a knight-errant. So absorbing are the perils and combats they undergo that the twelve months pass as one day, the furlough is unwittingly exceeded, and the lady in anger sends to Iwain, demanding her ring. By the same messenger she forbids him to appear in her presence again. Sorrow, and shame, and unavailing repentance torment forthwith our hero's heart. His grief robs him of his senses. Abandoned and frenzied he wanders in the forest until he meets with a pious hermit. By him Iwain is befriended until a balm can be brought to him from the fairy Morgan and he is cured of his malady. Though his mind is healed, the anger of his lady is unappeased. So he seeks oblivion in fresh adventures. He defends innocence, punishes guilt, and protects the unfortunate even among animals. In this way he frees a lion from a serpent's folds and wins the lasting affection of the beast. Attended by him, Iwain comes once more to the enchanted fountain, hears there a sound of lamentation in the chapel hard-by, and going into it finds the maiden who had given him the magic ring, now condemned to be burned at the stake. Iwain promises to be her champion and rescue her from her enemies. He then retires to a neighboring castle for the night. But there he learns that a giant, Harpyns of the Mountain, had demanded the daughter of the house in marriage, and was holding as pledges for her hand four of her brothers, having already killed two others. Early the next morning the giant comes in sight, attended by a dwarf and driving on before him his four prisoners. Iwain sallies forth from the castle, meets the giant, overcomes him, and sends him and his dwarf to Gawayne at Arthur's court, bidding them say that they were sent by the Knight of the Lion. But this incident has deferred too long the aid pledged to the imprisoned maiden, and Iwain hurries now from the grateful master of the castle to the fountain. There he finds the girl already bound to the stake. He loses no time in challenging her three accusers, and with the help of his lion worsts them all. The fight takes place before his mistress' eyes, but, under his new title and in his new dress, she does not recognize him. Disheartened once more, Iwain withdraws to a castle to be healed of his wounds.

Here a fresh adventure awaits him. The elder of two sisters is trying to disinherit the younger, and has secured Gawayne for her champion. The younger, who has gone to Arthur's court for a defender, hears there of the prowess of the Knight of the Lion, and sends for him to help her. Iwain sets out with her messenger to obey the summons, but on their way to court they meet with evil greeting from a castle's battlements, and Iwain resolves to avenge the insult then and there. He enters the walls of the fortress and comes into a courtyard, where are sitting many maidens, wan and wasted, who are busily working on cloths. Once within the gate the porter roughly refuses an exit to the strangers, and Iwain is forced to pass on through the inclosure, into a meadow. There some one answers his questions, and tells him that the girls he saw in the court had come from Maiden Island, the king of which, having been conquered by two sons of the Devil, is compelled to send thirty girls to the victors as an annual tribute. Their rescue had already been tried by many knights, all of whom had failed. That night Iwain is hospitably entertained by the owner of the castle. The next morning, however, his host tells him he must fight these two sons of the demon. Soon after this unwelcome announcement the two devils, in the shape of black and hideous giants, come in sight, attack Iwain and are beaten after a long and bloody fight. Though a victor, our hero modestly declines the hand of his host's daughter—the reward pledged to the successful champion—and contents himself with setting the captive maidens free, after which he hastens to the assistance of the younger sister. In defending her he necessarily is pitted against Gawayne, who champions the elder girl. But as neither of the knights knows who is to be his antagonist, and as neither of them recognizes the other, they fight, when they meet, with no advantage until evening falls, when each names himself, the combat ends, and with true friendship they submit their quarrel to the decision of the blameless king. This duty done Iwain is thrown back upon his own cares once more, and presents himself again at the fountain. But this time there appears no defender of its enchantments. For the lady is without a knight, and sorrow oppresses her because of her disgrace. Here is an opportunity for the maiden of the magic ring to reconcile the two lovers. First she persuades her mistress to accept the Knight of the Lion as her champion. Next she brings Iwain before her, he makes himself known, and is pardoned at last.

So long an analysis of this poem would demand, perhaps, an apology, if its own story, which in the Middle Ages was so popular with the nobility of Germany and England, as well as with the knights of France, did not possess sufficient interest to justify its repetition in these latter days. The account of the adventures of the Knight of the Lion ranks among Chrétien's best works. But it is independent of the great subjects which perpetuated the fame of the Arthurian legends, and having no bearing on the love of Lancelot for the Queen on the one hand, or on the quest of the Holy Grail on the other, it was never incorporated into the long prose narratives of the cycle, and so has not come down to posterity with them. But though we know it only through the original poem, or by means of the translations of this original into foreign tongues, and though no prose form of it appears to have existed, which would be an intermediary between Chrétien's verse and the romances of chivalry of the fifteenth century, yet there are so many points of resemblance between the two that the former may be well considered as one of the models for the latter. Or it might be better to say that *Iwain* would offer a type of the models of *Amadis of Gaul.*

In giving credence to this statement we are obliged to face the objection that a dozen generations of writers separate the model from its copy. But invention in the Middle Ages, at least in the vernacular literature, was wofully poor. The poets of the people repeated blindly one after another the traditions and superstitions which were current before their day, and modified them only in the direction of the unnatural and incredible. They had no idea of a return to nature, to freshen literary ideals and correct poetical images. Thus taste degenerated rather than improved, and mediæval literature, lacking truth in thought as well as comeliness in form, possessed no defenses which were able to resist the inroads of Renaissance style and learning. Only in the present century, by the discovery of the old manuscripts, has the educated world become aware of the many excellences of imagination and expression which, in the twelfth and thirteenth centuries, characterized the ambitious writers, whose works were so crudely parodied in the vulgar compilations of the fifteenth. And no kind of literature shows the marks of this decadence so strongly as those universally popular narratives which were based on the stories of the Round Table.

But generalities must be upheld by details, and we must point out the particular features of plot or description which justify this view of a connection, whether strong or weak, between *Amadis* and *Iwain*. First, in regard to the plot, we find in both stories the leave of absence granted by the mistress to allow the knight to win fame by exploits; the ring which she gives him to keep him mindful of his allegiance to her; her dismissal of him, through a messenger, for his apparent faithlessness; his despair in consequence, and the reception he meets with from a benevolent hermit; his reappearance in the world under a descriptive title, and in an armor which conceals his identity, both from his friends, who may fight with him and he with them, each in ignorance of his opponent until the end of the combat, and from his mistress before whom he does mighty deeds; finally his pardon by her and their happy union. Also in the episodes which concern the minor characters, as well as the leading ones, there is some likeness. Such are the imprisonment of knights through force or magic and their release by enamored maidens, attendants of the mistress of the castle, or by the mistress herself; the enmity which always exists between knights and giants; the sending of prisoners to court with messages from their captor, and the release of girls and knights by the prowess of the hero, who overthrows their jailer and breaks down the enchantments which bind them. Descriptions in *Iwain*, which are repeated in *Amadis*, include the location of fountains under pines; the appearance and arms of the giants; the deadly combats, beginning with the lance and continuing with the sword; the insults hurled at the hero from castle walls, and his reception when he has entered them. All these resemblances in material, and actors—among whom the beneficent fairy is not to be overlooked—emphasize the near relationship of the romances of chivalry to the poems of the Breton cycle. To go further and endeavor to establish a definite line of descent from *Iwain* to *Amadis* is not possible, inasmuch as the circumstances and birth of the hero, in the latter, point to some particular story unknown to the present day, and which very likely may have been told in a *romance* that has forever disappeared.

Though the story of *Iwain* always remained, so far as we now know, in the form it received from the poet of Champagne, many other accounts of the deeds of Arthur's knights have been handed down to posterity in prose as well as verse. It was these prose versions—which seem to have been composed in the first five decades of the thirteenth century—that attracted the attention and admiration of contemporary readers. While their freedom from the restraints of verse and rhyme allowed their compilers to exercise their wits by the invention of new exploits and more wonderful adventures, yet in taking this liberty, their narrative, which appealed all the more to the sympathy of their audience, lost nothing in interest, but gained in connectedness and even in taste and style. With the vogue of French literature the enthusiasm for these, its best examples of prose writing, spread beyond the limits of French territory, and caused them to be looked upon in foreign lands as models of elegant composition, while foreign translations followed close on this introduction of the originals.

In the Spanish peninsula the stories of Tristan and Merlin won especial favor among the nobility and the people, and no doubt aroused ambitious scribes to gain glory and profit for themselves by imitating them in the romances of chivalry. At least the latter borrowed freely from the Breton tales at every turn of the narrative, and had no scruple in appropriating the most characteristic features of their predecessors, as a comparison of *Iwain* and *Amadis* clearly shows. Furthermore it is possible that the incidents in the early career of the knights-errant were suggested by the youthful experiences of the Breton heroes. *Amadis* and his successors were royal foundlings, like Arthur, and castaways, like Merlin. Then, too, the topography of the romances of chivalry possesses that charming indefiniteness which distinguishes the localities of the Round Table's valorous deeds, though their subject and its working-out reveal an unmistakable desire in their authors to be looked upon almost as historical novelists, even if they do place their courts and realms under the sway of fanciful rulers.

But the tales of the Breton cycle did not provide the romances of chivalry with all their material. Or if they did at first, later expansions of the story drew on other sources besides these. It would indeed be strange if all the epic poems relating to Charlemagne, his race, and his vassals, and the many versions which they received in prose, had passed away without leaving a trace of their influence on the heirs of mediæval fiction. The national epic, to be sure, was popular, outside of France, in Italy alone. In Spain and England it was the court of King Arthur which overshadowed the imperial household at the head of the Western Empire. The glory of the twelve paladins was probably too exclusive, too patriotic, to prove of much interest to other nations. At all events they had no particular reason to praise them, and it is chiefly those works of the Carolingian cycle, which transport the scene of action beyond the limits of Europe, and summon united Christendom against the infidel, that were incorporated into the literature of foreign peoples.

It is curious to see how this selection from the various traditions of the mediæval French poems affected the romances of chivalry. From what we know of the first specimens among them, and of *Amadis of Gaul* in particular, it would seem that the romancer began his work with the influence of the Arthurian legends strong upon him. Then, after the interest in adventures from this source had subsided, he would turn to the tales of Eastern marvels, and join the fabulous history of Constantinople and Syria to the accounts of feudal Europe and the magic of the Celtic mysteries.

Not all of these stories of the East, however, are to be charged to the credit of the Carolingian epic. Already in the first years of the twelfth century there had appeared in French verse strange recitals of the deeds and daring of the great hero of antiquity, Alexander. These vernacular versions were based on Latin narratives and forged accounts of his life and career, which had been invented at Alexandria. Magic and superstition occupied by far the larger place in them, while the facts of history formed merely the outline. But they suited the times. Hardly had these stories found their way into French when they became one of the favorite themes of mediæval literature. Successive generations of poets tried their hand at them, translators carried them into foreign lands, and by the end of the thirteenth century the series of poems on Alexander had grown to epic proportions, and had become domesticated among the household traditions of all the nations of western Europe. As a consequence of this universal adoption they became common property, and could be taken out of their original setting and placed in any new one, according to the momentary fancy of the borrower.

The trace of this Eastern addition to the literature of the West is easily followed from its very beginning. At first it is to be recognized by the elaborate descriptions of rooms, furniture, and buildings, whose luxury and magnificence had appealed to the Frankish pilgrims and Crusaders. Later, in the adventures of Christian heroes among the infidels who had conquered Palestine and were threatening Constantinople, the imprisonment and suffering which the Knights of the Cross endured, their prowess in single combat, and the talent which they possessed—to their worldly advantage—of setting fire to the combustible substances, already prepared for love's torch, in the hearts of the bewitching Saracen princesses. So when the romancers of chivalry succeeded the poets of gallantry, and started on their prose narratives, which were to develop into the future novels, they found their material all mixed to their use. A striking instance in support of this view of the mediæval mingling of ideas, is furnished by a French poem of the twelfth century, *Huon de Bordeaux*. Its author is unknown, but his work, which is a singular compound of French heroic poetry, of Celtic tales, and of Eastern superstitions, has been always popular in all its changing forms. The beginning of the story is in true epic style. Huon, a knight of Charlemagne's court, has won renown by his warlike deeds, and has received from the emperor an absurd commission, which is to be performed in the Orient. To reach the region of his task Huon must pass through an enchanted forest, where his arms are of no avail. From its perils, however, he is rescued by the sorcery of the dwarf, Oberon, well known to literary fame. Passing through one trial of magic art after another, Huon, led by his cunning guide, finally emerges from the dangerous wood and eventually arrives in Babylon. He is welcomed at the sultan's court, wins the love of the imperial princess, Esclarmonde, repays her affection by converting her to Christianity, and gives effective aid to the sultan in subduing that monarch's enemies. Later, on his return to France, Huon recovers, through Oberon's assistance, his ancestral inheritance, confiscated during his absence.

The advent of stories of Eastern adventure into the national epic of France is seen—as in this example of *Huon de Bordeaux*—to be prompted both by a desire to describe the marvelous and luxurious for the benefit of the rough warriors of Gaul, and by the desire of the poet to gain a larger circle of readers with the account of a love affair—in his time a novelty, so far as the Carolingian cycle of poems was concerned. Love had held hitherto but a very small place in the careers of the vassals of Charlemagne ; and whether this new departure in expanding the erotic element of the cycle was original with the author of *Huon de Bordeaux* or not, it is certain that it entered into high favor not long afterward, and rivaled in extent, and perhaps surpassed in interest, the conventional recitals of conquests and joustings. We are not surprised, then, to find in a poem of the fourteenth century, written on Italian soil, where the warlike tradition might be supposed to have less vitality and less power of resistance than in France, that this story of love in the East, and the adventures which accompany it, are ascribed to no other than the great national hero, to Roland himself. In the poem in question, the *Entrée de Spagne*, written by a certain Niccolo of Verona, Roland claims some of the attributes of the knights-errant of the later novels. His birth, like that of Amadis, takes place before the marriage of his parents. He grows up at the court of the great emperor, follows him in his wars, and accompanies him to Spain. But during the campaign he quarrels with his sovereign, leaves the French camp, and, coming to the sea, embarks on a merchant vessel. A storm drives his craft on the coast of Arabia. Roland, nothing daunted, journeys overland and reaches at last the court of Persia, whose king he rescues from his enemies. By this act he naturally attracts the gratitude and love of the Saracen princess, which he declines out of sheer fidelity to his first love in France, the tender-hearted Alda. Yet he takes some slight interest in the lady's brother, Samson, converts him speedily, knights him as a Christian, and takes ship with him for the West. On their way, which is by land as well as by sea, they are challenged to mortal combat by two of Roland's friends, who have been sent in search of him, and who do not recognize him until the fight is ended without loss to either side. When they reach Spain they meet a hermit who kindly tells Roland of his approaching death at Roncesvalles, and the poem returns to the normal epic tradition.

Similar digressions from the beaten track of exploits which were confined to western Europe enliven the narrative of many poems subsequent to the *Entrée de Spagne*, and were probably not without influence on the later books of *Amadis* and the other romances of chivalry. There is, in fact, another version of this journey of Roland and Samson from the East to the West, which may be of too late a date to have entered into the composition of the romances, but which is none the less worth citing as an indication of the popularity of such adventures. It tells how the two knights, in ship on their way to Spain, are wrecked on a desert island, where they are forced to encounter monsters and enchantments, which only their unwavering faith in the true belief dispels. Corresponding episodes occupy a good share of the romances of chivalry, and very likely could be traced—were the intermediate links at hand—either to this variant of the *Entrée de Spagne*, or perhaps to a story which is the source of both accounts.

It will be noticed that the scene of the poems last cited as predecessors of the romances of chivalry is laid in the actual territory which gave birth to the latter, Spain. And now that we are once on Castilian soil it may be well to see whether any other poem of the French epic has made the peninsula the theater of its action. Long before the Italian poet wrote out the *Entrée de Spagne*, two centuries earlier at least, an unknown rhymer of France composed a long account of French exploits in Italy, and the overthrow by Roland's friend, Oliver, of a pagan champion, the giant

Fierabras. This episode afterward became separated from the rest of the narrative, the place of action was transferred to Spain, and the combat and its results were revised and expanded, about the year 1170, into an independent poem, *Fierabras*, named after the Saracen hero. In its new form the story tells how Oliver, advancing to fight the giant, was taunted by many boasts and insults, and how, after the battle was joined, the horses of the champions had a jousting on their own account. Fierabras is, of course, worsted, but instead of being by that event only hardened in his sins, he repents, accepts Christianity, and joins the escort of his conqueror.

Oliver and his friends continue the course of their adventures and prosper in them until they are surprised by the Saracens, made prisoners, and thrown into a dungeon, which is below sea-level and is flooded by the tide. Aid reaches them, however, in the shape of the emir's daughter, the sister of Fierabras, who is in love with one of the French knights. Meanwhile Charlemagne, anxious about their fate, sends ambassadors to the emir to treat with him. To reach the castle the embassy must pass over the high and strong bridge of Mantrible, which is defended by a huge giantess armed with a heavy mace. The diplomats, however, are too wily for this guard. They elude her, pass the bridge, and come to the castle, where the princess leads them to their friends. Thus united they fall on the infidels at dinner, slay them, and make themselves masters of the castle, in which they are besieged later by the whole Saracen army. Many exploits and brave deeds while away the weary hours. But the emperor hears of their plight and advances to their relief with the whole strength of the Christian host. Again the defenders of the faith are stopped by the bridge and its champion, who is no longer of the gentler sex, but a fierce and terrible giant. Below the bridge the stream runs deep and fast. There is no place to ford it, and no way to navigate it. No resource remains to the French leader but to force the passage. A furious fight ensues at the first onslaught. Long does victory hang in the balance, but at length the giant weakens, falters, is beaten down, and after him his wife, an enormous giantess, who signalizes her discomfiture by emitting, as she expires, a blinding cloud of smoke.

These are the main incidents in *Fierabras* that connect it with the romances of chivalry. Whether the poem appealed to the Spaniards through it own intrinsic merits, or whether they welcomed it because the deeds it narrated were located in Spain, it is certain that it became very popular among them, and influenced the formation of the later novels. For these reproduced bridge fights, giants, and giantesses, so akin to those of *Fierabras*, even down to the descriptions of details, that one can hardly believe three centuries had passed between the appearance of the model and the date of its imitations. And in this respect they illustrate the extraordinary hold of successful invention on the popular fancy, and the great lack of originality, characteristic of all the vernacular work of mediæval literature.

Besides monsters which may be said to be related to human beings, there are, in the romances of chivalry, animals and wild beasts which perhaps go back for suggestions of their presence to the heroic epic of France, where the founder of the imperial dynasty, Pippin, is seen in a hand-to-hand struggle with a lion. A lion protects Octavian, another of the Carolingian heroes, as the lion guarded Iwain. In the dreams of the emperor and of his paladins, portents are foreboded and personified by the likenesses of savage beasts. Yet it would be straining the point beyond what is reasonable to claim that the romances borrowed this part of their material from such minor instances, and it is more likely that stories resembling the account of Iwain's career offered all the examples necessary to the romancers' purpose. But in the case of another and more important auxiliary in exciting interest in the developments of the novels, the intervention of magic and the magician, the poems relating to the peers of Charlemagne may have been equally productive with the stories of Celtic adventure. The former may indeed have borrowed from the latter, yet, if this were so, they expanded and defined their loans and lent them in turn to the romances of chivalry. One of the most famous poems in the whole national cycle, second in reputation to *Roland* alone, is *Renaud de Montauban*, and one of the leading characters in this poem is a necromancer, Maugis by name. His part in the action of the story is to help by his art his cousin Renaud, and his three brothers, against Charlemagne, whose rebellious vassals they are. Maugis is also, in his leisure moments, a pious hermit, and for that reason, perhaps, his sorcery is impregnated with benevolence, and harmless in its results. Instead of bringing ruin and despair on the enemies of his house, he mildly rids himself of them, when they become too pressing, by sinking them into a deep sleep from which a certain herb from over the sea can alone awaken them. Or when the necessities of the case may be satisfied with a weaker dose of magic, Maugis prefers to envelop the emperor's champions in a dense cloud, which deprives them, for the moment, of the power to follow the fleeing knights. Besides these innocuous gifts of enchantment, Maugis is a master of the knowledge of healing plants and ointments, and is also able to disguise himself beyond recognition with the juice of peculiar grasses.

The author of *Renaud de Montauban* proposed to himself to write a narrative of war and ruse, and he brings in Maugis—who, outside of his slight endowments from the domain of the supernatural, is a true and blameless knight— as an additional, but very subordinate, element of interest.

The idea of sorcery and magic took, however, with a public which had been half initiated into the mysteries of the Druidical religion by their blundering reproductions in the Arthurian cycle of poems, and which was superstitious and fearful from its dense ignorance of man and nature.

Among the credulous readers of the Middle Ages the character of Maugis soon became famous. Poets found it worth while to multiply his exploits, and half a century after the appearance of *Renaud de Montauban*, the occasional magician of the Aymon family finds himself and his deeds the subject of an entire poem, *Maugis a'Aigremont.* There the days of his youth and his career as a man are related in detail. Like Lancelot, whose education may have been in the poet's mind, Maugis is stolen from his parents and reared by a fairy. But he is taken from her in turn by a Saracen who escapes with him to Sicily, and who there sits down under a thorn tree to rest from the fatigue of his adventure. Wild beasts come up as he reposes. A lion and a leopard fall upon him and tear him to pieces, then turn and rend each other. So the child is left without any protector, though he is soon found by the fairy Orianda, who adopts him and brings him up as her own son. Her brother Baudry, who had studied at the famous school of Toledo, teaches the youth the arts of magic ; and when he is grown to man's stature Maugis disguises himself and sets out for the volcanic island of Bocan. Here a huge serpent stands on guard against all comers. But Maugis succeeds in despatching him, and afterward in catching and mastering the horse Bayard, the object of his quest. With Bayard he returns to Sicily and puts to flight an army of Saracens which is besieging Orianda. Then, attended by Baudry and Bayard he visits Toledo, runs across Charlemagne's army, which was at that time in Spain, and employs in its favor the power of the enchantments he had learned.

But it was tit-for-tat in the old epic, and no sooner do

the infidels discover the harm which Maugis does them than they oppose to him a sorcerer of their own creed, and many and frequent are the attempts of each to outwit the other. The poet fairly revels in the invention of puerile magic, and impartially divides the spells between the two sides. The inhabitants of a beleaguered city fancy that it is on fire, and that they are surrounded by flames. Maugis himself is led to believe that he is attacked by a dragon, and his followers think he has gone mad when they see him beating the empty air—incidents which are fair samples of the methods used to please the mediæval public. The Christian, of course, gets the better in the long run, and Maugis' arts triumph finally over the stratagems of his rival. But though in this poem the gifts of necromancy are the principal theme, still the poet does not depart from the beaten track of the epic, and when Maugis is not busy with the display of his peculiar powers he fights and makes love in the good old way of the Carolingian heroes. He is still a feudal knight, and is not the out-and-out magician, who became later on the delight of the romances of chivalry.

Perhaps enough has now been said to satisfy all demands and indicate the probable sources of the romances of chivalry in the literature of the Middle Ages. It is not possible to prove absolutely that these pioneer novels of modern times are the direct heirs of the poems and prose narratives which formed the body of fiction dear to the generations that preceded them. The evidence in the case must be wholly circumstantial. Too great a lapse of time separated the one set of stories from the other, and we have in the intervening literature but vague hints at the growth and development of the first and best of the romances, *Amadis of Gaul.* Other currents of mediæval tradition may easily be traced, in spite of serious breaks, by the continuity of the leading characters in them. But the romances of chivalry introduce names entirely new to fiction, both of heroes and heroines, of giants and necromancers, of relatives and friends.   Consequently we have no clew at all to lead us through the maze of adventures and enchantments back to the original story, and are compelled, therefore, to select from out of the mass of available material whose history is known to us, typical deeds and striking likenesses of plot and action.

With him who reads the first books of *Amadis* there can be little doubt that they arose from some such model as the poem of *Iwain* would furnish.   The adventures of the later books would require but little alteration to point back to the *Entrée de Spagne, Fierabras,* and the series of poems on Alexander, while the supernatural element in them may be considered as a legitimate expansion of the magic arts attributed to Maugis, Orianda, or their great prototype, the fairy Morgan.   The relation of knight and mistress is such as might be found among the *romances,* the Breton *lais,* or the longer poems of the Round Table.   From these similarities we may draw conclusions which seem at least fairly tenable, and affirm with a good degree of confidence that in the ideas of love, of knightly exploits, and the supernatural, the romances of chivalry are the true descendants of the poems of the mediæval epic and the court lyric of France.

It is perhaps due to the fact that the romances of chivalry grew up in the Spanish peninsula, far away from the locality of the adventures they pretend to narrate, that no light at all is thrown on them by the writers of France, Italy, or England.   Nor can any conjectures, regarding their development or authorship, be gained from like fiction in other countries.   Indeed, but one single prose narrative written outside the peninsula (before 1390), which, like the romances of chivalry, is independent of the various epic series, while deriving its contents from them, has come down to the readers of to-day.   This is the strange compound which goes under the name, or nickname, of one of its heroes, *Perceforest*. It is not a novel, for it has no plot, nor does it possess even an apparent unity of action. Its author was not endowed with any constructive sense, and his literary merit depends mainly on his talent for good description. He was influenced in his undertaking by the evident desire to give to the reading public something that was new, and in carrying out this desire he jumbled together fact and fancy, erudition and superstition, in the most ridiculous way.

He starts out with an itinerary of Great Britain, comes soon to its fabulous history, told many times and many generations before him, and finally branches out on his poetical idea (if we may call it by that name), which con-sists in transporting Alexander and his victorious troops from India to England. On arriving at the island the first care of the king is to give rulers to both England and Scot-land. The monarch of the former country, Betis, is soon engaged in subduing the enchantments of the forest of Glar, inhabited by the magician, Darnant, and a long war ensues between the Orientals and the race of the magician. Betis, before this, had acquired, by his conquest of the wood, his title of Perceforest. His brother, Gaddiffer, the ruler of Scotland, moved to emulation by Betis' fame, endeavors to overcome the sorcerers of his realm also, and his vassals wage with them a never-ending war. Under the reign of Gaddiffer's grandson, Julius Cæsar invades Britain, and after the Romans have withdrawn Christianity is intro-duced, in order that a converted member of the Scottish royal family may close the list of his house's exploits, by preaching the gospel to his ancestors who had departed this transitory existence, and were dwelling peacefully heathenish in the Island of Life.

There is not much in *Perceforest* which concerns the sub-ject of this chapter. Its artificial compound of the traditions about Arthur and Alexander is only too apparent, and unlike the romances of chivalry it underwent no long elaboration, which would make of it a new creation in literature. *Perceforest* is merely a literary crazy-quilt, and only bewilders its readers, who cannot readily take the sudden leaps with which its author spans his numerous chasms of time and place. But in certain of its incidents and details, and in a portion of its episodes, it shows that there was active in northern Europe the same fanciful tendency which the romances of chivalry reveal in the South. The place which magic and witchcraft occupy in its pages far exceeds the space given up to them in the lines of epic poetry, or in the epic prose narratives, and forms its most noticeable resemblance to the later books of *Amadis*. The transference of the scene of action to Scotland suggests also the topography of the romances of chivalry, and this feature is emphasized by a steadfast indefiniteness concerning the world's surface and territorial divisions. And finally in the idea of the Island of Life, where the spirits of the great departed hold sweet communion, we have a compromise between the Avalon of the Arthurian legends and Firm Island of *Amadis of Gaul*.

Yet all these notions combined show no real progress in the art of story writing, and are hardly worth citing, when compared with the elaborate episodes of a like nature which abound in the completed romances. The latter were the product of a steady, systematic effort, supported by the favor of a whole nation, and extending over a formative period of some two centuries, while *Perceforest* is evidently a work of individual initiative, by an author of no especial talent. It had no successors so far as is known. The North continued to abide by its old traditions of epic story. Its prose narratives repeated with unwearying patience the deeds of the paladins of Charlemagne and the marvels of Celtic Britain, and it was left for the South to inspire the mass of inventions it had received from abroad with another spirit and a higher life, so that it might give to the world in the fullness of time that union of new ideas and old exploits, which is the characteristic of the first novels of modern literature, the romances of chivalry.

CHAPTER V.

ONE of the most striking features of the romances of chivalry is this origin of theirs from matter which was wholly foreign, in its antecedents, to the land where they came into being. The chief among them, *Amadis of Gaul*, the undoubted creation in its final form of the Spanish peoples, and the faithful mirror of their sentiments and aspirations, at the time when they were struggling for national existence and race unity, contains hardly a mention, even in its concluding pages, of a place or a name which can be assigned to the Spanish peninsula. Such an entire absence of local pride among native authors would be indeed incredible at any other stage in the history of the world's literature. Some allusions, at least, to their surroundings, or, at best, occasional expressions of loyalty toward their rulers, would not be lacking in the popular stories of any other period.

But in the Middle Ages and in the centuries following the position of writer and reader was different. Excepting in court poetry, or in works written to order for some patron, there was no thought of time or place in literature. The world of fact disappeared before the allurements of romancing. On this account it is difficult to determine the date and locality of so many productions of mediæval fancy.

Nor does the subject-matter of the mediæval poem or narrative help us out of this uncertainty. An episode or a description which was started by some rhymer of talent in the tenth century may be found intact, or embellished with further details of the same sort, in the fifteenth. Repetition and imitation mark deeply this whole age of compilation. The vernacular literature, abandoned as it was to the keeping of the uneducated, came rarely into the hands of a man of any originality in invention or vigor in expression.

And having this condition of literary production in mind, we cannot be surprised to find that Spanish topography and genealogy play no part in the favorite prose compositions of the Spanish nation.

Naturally, then, this extreme example of mediæval indifference would lead us to look for the early career of the hero, the knight Amadis, among those nations, the English and French, which furnished the romance *Amadis* with its material and story. From the beginning of the redemption of Spain and Portugal from the Moors, the influence of French literature had been widely felt in the rising states of the frontier. It was Burgundian nobles who delivered the western coast in the eleventh century, and founded the throne of Portugal. French knights fought also for Castile and Leon, and married even into the royal families. With the warriors of the North came the singers of their exploits, and French minstrels and Provençal troubadours were soon the official poets of Galicia and Aragon.

Later than the poets, and when the emigration of Crusaders from France to Spain grew less notable in numbers and rank, the longer stories of French fiction found their way in manuscript, or by word of mouth, into the peninsula. In the thirteenth century *Apollonius of Tyre* was translated from a French original into Spanish, while the adventures of Alexander received a southern version, after a Latin poem composed in France. By the end of the thirteenth century those models of fine writing, the prose romances of the Arthurian legends, had been done into Spanish and Portuguese, and some decades before them the more attractive *romans d'aventure*, such as *Floire et Blanchefleur*, had reached the South. The themes of the Breton *lais* inspired the poets at the court of King Diniz of Portugal, whose reign ended in 1325, while the very ballads of the Moorish conquest, and the romances of feudal rivalries among the Christians themselves, bear many marks of the presence of those epic poems of France which recounted events that took place on Spanish soil. And in the midst of this foreign importation, which was very likely fully naturalized before the idea of *Amadis of Gaul* had acquired any definiteness, it is most significant, for the future development of the romances of chivalry, to notice that the testimony of contemporaneous literature affirms that the stories of the love and death of Tristan and of Lancelot of the Lake were the favorites above all others.

So the ground had been prepared for many generations for the introduction of the marvelous legends of France, and the curiosity of the Spanish race had come to look for its gratification in fictions invented on foreign soil. The Christians of the peninsula were too busy in wresting their patrimony from Moorish dominion to allow themselves that leisure from action and from contact with disturbing elements, which is imperative for the formation of folk tradition. Not that the Spanish genius was in its nature averse to story-telling. The legends of Bernardio del Carpio, or of the Seven Lords of Lara, and the mystery which enveloped the Cid, and made of him an epic hero barely half a century after his death, prove rather the contrary. But wars and invasions followed one another too quickly for any considerable development of the national literature. Even ballad poetry, that first form of the epic, which has become so typical of feudal and crusading Spain, was shut up within the poet's breast so long as the minstrel was forced to be a warrior. Still national tradition watched for every opportunity to escape from its confinement. It stole into the eulogies of Charlemagne and his paladins, it transformed the freebooters of the southern frontier into loyal knights of the Cross, and it even bewitched the recording quills of the sober historians. For the romancing spirit of the Spanish people sported with the very dates and names of the nation's genealogy, and enlivened the great *Cronica general* of Alphonso the Wise with the valiant and dramatic exploits of Pelayo and Fernan Gonzalez. It was also from France, from a half-historical, half-legendary Provençal poem on the first Crusades, that the main part of a Spanish chronicle of the beginning of the fourteenth century, the *Gran Conquista de Ultramar*, was taken.

While the latent authors of the peninsula were too much engaged in the solution of the problems of national existence to devise many inventions of their own, yet it is clear that the desire for fancy's play was out among them in full force, and was ready to test its vitality on any material, whether of native or foreign creation. We cannot, therefore, accuse the Spaniards of any lack of national pride, because they welcomed to their castles and their market-places the singers and the legends of France. What they received they adapted to themselves. They were in no hurry, but took their time with true Spanish dignity. And when they had completed the working-over process to their satisfaction, they produced again the old stories of feudalism and the deeds of chivalry, thoroughly permeated with their national spirit, and stamped with their national ideals. They returned to France what they had borrowed from her, refined, purified, and ennobled.

In the romances of chivalry there is something besides a definite plot to distinguish them from the prose versions of the Carolingian and Arthurian poems, and this additional something is not at all connected with style or literary polish, inasmuch as the French *Tristan* of the thirteenth century is decidedly superior, in those qualities, to the later *Amadis of Gaul*. The romances of chivalry cannot boast of much art, either in their plan or composition, and they were not written with æsthetic aims in view. On the contrary, they seem to have a distinct didactic bent, like so many novels of the eighteenth and nineteenth centuries. In the midst of their tales of knight-errantry and magic incantations they never lose sight of this ulterior purpose, nor fail to draw the intended moral.

Their French models had aspired to but a portion of this teaching. The poems of Chrétien and the prose romances of the Round Table wished, indeed, to place before their readers the social ideal of their time. But this ideal was especially chivalrous and gallant. It enjoined the defense of the weak and the rescue of the oppressed, but it did not require in the defender absolute purity of mind or body. The real heroes of mediæval society were Lancelot and Tristan. Its heroines were Guinevere and Iseult. But in Spain of the fifteenth century an advance on such views could naturally be expected. The times had grown better and the race was a more devout one. It was also more loyal than were the French of the reign of Philip Augustus. Therefore the romances of chivalry, which became the favorite literature of the Spanish people, and which represent, consequently, its feelings and aspirations, put before their readers a higher standard of chivalry and honor than did their epic progenitors.

In the hero, Amadis of Gaul, they endeavored to present a pattern of a true and perfect knight, whose fidelity to his lawful mistress should equal his prowess in the defense of the feeble, and whose loyalty to his sovereign should correspond to the greatness of his self-sacrifice for the good of others. He was to be the living pattern for the nobility of Spain. ˙In him were to be reconciled the virtues of the man and the duties of the subject, and his career, both in love and in war, was to encourage higher notions of social intercourse, and a deeper sense of devotion to the welfare of the state, among the doughty chieftains of the Moorish border and the restless vassals of Castile and Aragon. Half a century after the appearance of *Amadis of Gaul* there expired on the plains of Lombardy, dying in defense of his country and his king, a perfect knight of actual life, who probably had never read of the perfect knight of fiction, but who, though a foreigner, realized in his character that ideal more fully, perhaps, than any noble of Spain, the Chevalier Bayard, " sans peur et sans reproche."

It is not to be supposed from this digressive eulogy that all the heroes and heroines of the romances of chivalry were on the high level of Amadis and Oriana. Some approached them in chivalry and virtue, and others fell away, far away, from the standard set by the leaders. Amadis himself has a foil in his half brother, Galaor, who equals the knights-errant of the Breton legends in the lack of fidelity to one love, and in his chivalrous readiness to succor the defense-less wherever they are found. Indeed, it would seem that in many of the minor characters of the romances there had been no improvement over the French mediæval conception of honor and duty, and that these actors had been retained in order to place in greater relief, by the contrast they afforded, the virtues of the men and women who were espe-cially dear to the Spanish heart. And to realize the progress which had been made in social and political morals from the twelfth to the fifteenth centuries, there is no better way than to compare the character and purposes of the chief heroes in the romances of chivalry with their subor-dinates, who represent the survival of the traditions of the Round Table. In the latter, for instance, Lancelot was faithful to his love. Yet with him it was a guilty love, and brought, together with this fidelity, perjury toward his sove-reign, whom he dishonored. Tristan loved by the force of a magic potion, and often lamented the supernatural power which the draught exercised so tyranically over him.

On the other hand, it is not true that faithful lovers in the highest sense of the word, were wanting in mediæval French literature. While they may be but few in the tales of Arthur's court, they are comparatively numerous in one of the supposed sources of our romances of chivalry, the *romans d'aventure.* One of these, the *Roman de la Violette* (belonging to the third decade of the thirteenth century), which is repeated in part by Shakspere's *Cymbeline,* keeps its hero Girard always faithful to his mistress, in spite of the many temptations which assail him during a long series of exploits and adventures, and of wrongs set to rights. So in *Amadas et Idoine* of about the same period—a poem which has often been appealed to as furnishing the prototype of *Amadis of Gaul,* owing to the resemblance between the heroes' names—the lover is repelled at first by his lady's severity, but afterward wins her pity through his unwearying constancy, and finally, when he finds that she is to be given to a rival in marriage, loses his senses in despair, and is not cured of his madness until her tender care and nursing have come to his aid. Still we must remember that these perfect characters are found in separate and isolated poems, and are not those chosen types of chivalry that are celebrated by a whole series, like the poems of the Breton cycle.

At their very best the ideal knights of the Middle Ages were loyal only to their mistress. In their conception of duty their sovereign held but a subordinate place. But Amadis of Gaul is ever loyal to both lady and monarch, whether in favor or disgrace, whether honored or slandered. He is always true to his highest conceptions of virtue, and therefore is the personification of knightly chivalry, fidelity, and honor.

It would be too much to claim that this ideal of a true and perfect knight was developed nowhere but in Spain, especially when we see that its best representative was the champion of France. Yet it seems safe to assert that in the peninsula the notions of chivalry and knightly honor were more generally felt than elsewhere, and had penetrated deeper into the various classes of society. At least it is in Spain alone that literature made itself the standard-bearer of such conceptions, and the romances of chivalry are the only works of the time in which literature remained aristocratic. Outside of her borders feudalism and the social structure of the Middle Ages had given way before the consolidation of royal power, and the growing strength of the merchant class. Literature in the other parts of Europe had followed in the track of this revolution, and had adapted itself to the taste of the new masters of the state. In Italy there had never been a nobility which had possessed sufficient power to direct prose and poetry. Magistrates and bankers had supported impecunious authors from the very beginnings of Italian literature. In France the power of the noble houses had been broken by the vicissitudes of the Hundred Years' War and the increase of an urban population, which looked to one sovereign, the king, for protection against his vassals. Thus there arose a Louis XI. and a literature addressed to tradesmen. Charles of Orleans and his school of poets were an anachronism in the fifteenth century, and their rhymes were unknown to the general public. So in Germany and England the new social conditions were reflected in a new and plebeian style of writing.

But in Spain and Portugal the situation was entirely different. The presence of the Moors, demanding ever-recurring crusades in behalf of the Christian faith, and the independence of the provinces, which had been preserved by the absorption of the population in the work of territorial redemption, had perpetuated the surroundings of feudal times, and prolonged for generations the spirit and institutions of the Middle Ages. Thus each petty noble had remained practically his own master. Far from repressing or checking the exercise of individual force and initiative, the monarchs of the different states of the peninsula spurred on each warlike adventurer to repeated incursions into the lands held by the infidels, and confirmed him in the possession of whatever domain he might wrest from them to the profit of the general cause of Christianity. Along the frontier many noble houses were thus established, which owed but slight allegiance to any over-lord. The principle of individualism, though in a righteous cause, was developed to the highest extent and held in the greatest honor, and a career of knight-errantry was regarded by the whole people as affording a most material bulwark to the safety of the ancestral religion ; while the daring expeditions of the independent Christian knights against the common enemy fostered the popular admiration for any personal deed at arms.

When the Moslems would afford but little glory, the restless nobles must perforce direct their energy toward feuds and joustings within Spanish territory, and the northern kingdoms were fairly overrun with knights seeking adventures. A short chronicle of the fifteenth century has handed down to us a record of one of the favorite expedients to acquire a reputation for prowess on the field of battle. It tells how, in 1434, a knight-errant seized on a bridge near the city of Leon, and held it against all comers. And this *passo honroso* is but an instance—perhaps the most noteworthy, to be sure—of many others of the same kind. Personal prowess was the pass-word to glory in the land, and the Crusader was the highest type of those elements which had combined for the defense of the nation. And when the long-postponed expulsion of the Moslem invaders was felt to be at hand, and all Spain could confidently look forward to the complete supremacy of the native dynasties, the enthusiasm and pride of the Spanish people found expression in the glorification of the chief agent in the attainment of these cherished results, and consecrated, in the most popular branch of its literature, the personification of those qualities in the chivalry and loyalty of that perfect knight, Amadis of Gaul.

It is impossible to know definitely when the idea of this first romance of chivalry began to take shape among the legends of the nation. And it is no less difficult to decide the exact, or approximate, date when the story of Amadis and Oriana made its first appearance before the world. The main plot of the romance surely existed, in some embryonic form or other, as early as the last part of the thirteenth century, and was cultivated by the poets of the court of Portugal. For the *villancico*, which is found in the eleventh chapter of the second book of the Spanish *Amadis de Gaula*, and is there said to have been written by Amadis for the young princess, Leonoreta, is an adaptation of a poem recently discovered in a Portuguese manuscript. The author of the poem was a Portuguese poet, João Lobeira, who is known to have been famous as early as 1258, and was still alive in 1285. His name had given rise to a curious confusion in literary history, which was corrected by the publication of this manuscript and its contents. A chronicle of the fifteenth century had claimed that the first author, or rather the author of the first edition, of *Amadis de Gaula*, was Vasco de Lobeira, a Portuguese gentleman of the later fourteenth century. But this assertion was rather of an enigma to scholars. For it is distinctly stated in the fortieth chapter of the first book of *Amadis*, that the outcome of the love of Briolanja for the faithful hero had been changed to suit the views of Don Alphonso, Infant of Portugal. This prince was born in 1263 and died in 1312, and consequently the story must have undergone, if we are to judge from the separate versions of the Briolanja episode, at least two editions before Vasco de Lobeira was old enough to have taken a hand in its formation. Another proof of the priority of the romance to this Lobeira's time is furnished by the chronicler, Pedro Lopez de Ayala. In a didactic poem, called the *Rimado de Palacio*, this author complains of wasted hours passed in listening to such lies as *Lancelot, Amadis*, and other follies. Ayala lived from 1332 to 1407, and the lost time he laments must have been spent in his youth.

Another reference belonging to the fourteenth century throws more light on the size, at that time, of *Amadis de Gaula*. Pedro Ferrus, a Spanish poet, contemporary with Ayala, addressed to the latter some verses in which there are allusions to events that occurred before 1379. Among these verses is a strophe devoted to our romance, which expressly states that it was then composed of three books. Other poems found in this same collection (the Cancionero de Baena) bear witness to the adventures and renown of Amadis and Oriana. So from all the testimony available, and from the fact that a Lobeira was the author of the *villancico* which was the original of the poem in *Amadis* addressed to the Princess Leonoreta, it would seem that the chronicler of the fifteenth century had blundered in his statement of the maker of the romance, and that, instead of Vasco de Lobeira, the current tradition of his age assigned the merit of its composition to the thirteenth century poet, João Lobeira.

If this view of the question is correct, and if our romance of chivalry looks back to João Lobeira for a sponsor, the appearance of a French story on Portuguese soil and its complete naturalization in the Spanish peninsula is not hard to understand. For Lobeira was a member of a poetical circle whose fame, with the fame of its patron, has come down to modern times in undiminished glory. King Diniz (or Denis), who ascended the throne of Portugal in 1279 and reigned until the year 1325, is known as the great administrator and civilizer of his country. He fostered literature and learning by the establishment of the great University of Portugal, and by throwing open the privileges of his court to native and foreign poets and writers. The king himself was not the meanest minstrel of them all. Under his father, Alphonso, the influence of troubadour poetry, and the *romances* and *lais* of northern France, had already created a race of poets, who cultivated not only the love songs of their models, but also used the art thus learned in elaborating the traditions and legends of the Portuguese people itself. Diniz continued and expanded the good work thus begun. He himself was taught by a Provençal poet, Aimeric, from Cahors. His own songs, preserved in a Vatican manuscript, amounting in number to 138, are swayed by the two influences of troubadour versification and national tradition. And the poets who were attracted to his court and lived on his bounty cultivated all the themes of love and adventure which were at that time being celebrated throughout the states of western Europe. They knew of Charlemagne, of Roland and his ivory horn, of Tristan, of Lancelot of the Lake, of Merlin, and of the love and trials of Flore and Blanchefleur. The prose romances of the Breton cycle went into a Spanish translation about the middle of Diniz's reign and must have soon been carried to the various literary groups of the peninsula. The various *romans d'aventure*, one of which we suppose *Amadis* at its origin to have been, had also reached the poets of the Southwest in a form more or less complete.

It seems probable that these various contributions of foreign poetical and prose tradition aroused among the ingenious writers of Portugal and Spain a spirit of emulation, and that, unwilling to copy them directly, the most enterprising talents of this new literary set conceived the notion of combining them to the glory of their own inventive spirit. In other words, it is plausible to suppose that the Portuguese authors of the time of Alphonso and Diniz took some *roman d'aventure*, which had grown out of some chivalrous *romance*, like *Rainaud*, and which had perhaps already admitted many episodes taken from the poems of the Breton cycle, turned it into prose (if indeed it had not reached them in a form of mingled prose and verse, like *Aucassin et Nicolette*), added to it scenes from the careers of Lancelot and Tristan, or similar inventions of their own, inserted into the midst of the prose narrative lyric poems, like the " Leonoreta sin roseta " of *Amadis* (a process which had been already employed in France in *Guillaume de Dole*, and elsewhere), and finally offered to their patrons the story, thus revised and expanded, as a novelty in fiction.

Such a theory of the origin of the romance of chivalry is based, of course, entirely upon supposition. The entire absence of any facts in the case forbids any solution of the question which might be supported by proofs. But eclectic literature, if we may call it by that name, was not unknown to the Middle Ages. *Huon de Bordeaux* is a mixture of three different sources of tradition, *Ille et Galeron* of two. *The Holy Grail* itself consists of two elements, as strongly opposed to each other as were the Druidical rites to the usages of Christianity, while *Perceforest*, as we have seen, was a rough attempt at mingling stories, which in their origin and development were entirely alien to one another. So *Amadis of Gaul* may be a union of various literary traditions and may be, in a limited degree, considered as the residuary legatee of mediæval fiction. Whether it received its greatest development at the hands of João Lobeira or not, it evidently was no more sacred to professional revisers than were the other literary compositions of the time; and it must have been worked over and adapted to the tastes of successive generations, as was the case with the poems and prose versions of the Carolingian cycle.

Thus it continually renewed its popularity among the common people of both Portugal and Spain, while, to judge

by Ayala's lament, it seems to have had its attractions for
the nobility as well. In this way Vasco de Lobeira and
nameless hack-writers may have had a hand in the many
editions it received, and may have brought it down to the
time when a more ambitious author sought, in a fresh revision, an opportunity to display his own gifts of story-
telling, and a chance to gain without much expenditure of
energy a lasting renown. For *Amadis de Gaula* was already
the most popular book, in the widest sense of the word, in
the peninsula, and had thoroughly incorporated into itself
the national spirit and character. Consequently it needed
only a literary finish, and perhaps certain refinements of
expression and better connection between its episodes, to
make it most welcome to the educated and polished circles
of society, and thus raise it from the somewhat vulgar
modesty of a chapbook to the calmer dignity of literature.

The ambitious writer who gave to *Amadis de Gaula* its
final shape was Garci-Ordoñez de Montalvo. He was governor of the city of Medina del Campo, in Old Castile, and
of course a soldier in the armies of that province. But this
is all that is known of him. From hints dropped by himself
in his writings he may have been a middle-aged man before
Granada was taken, in 1492. It is the generally received
opinion that he completed his manuscript not far from the
year 1470, and that his own statement of what he had done,
and the reasons for it, is fairly reliable. This statement is
found in a preface which alludes to the conquest of Granada,
and which is probably not much later than that great event.
There Montalvo affirms he was incited to his undertaking
by the example of the ancient historians, who had chronicled the great wars of their races, and by the exploits of
such heroes of the Middle Ages as Godfrey of Bouillon. So
he would aspire to write history also, but not of the greater
men and deeds. Only the things of less importance, based
on fancy rather than fact, he deemed his pen to be equal to,

and these things he thought capable of handing his name down to posterity.   He had therefore taken up the story of Amadis of Gaul, and corrected the three books extant before his day, freeing them of their faults of language and style.   To the three he added a fourth, drawn partly from them and partly from his own invention, and the four, thus constituted from his original text, he now supplemented by a fifth, which was to be a sequel to them.   And all this effort was made, not for his own glory only, but also to encourage in the youth of Spain the knowledge of knightly arms, and to keep alive in the world the memories of chivalry.

The exact year of the publication of Montalvo's *magnum opus* is not known.   Its author evidently considered the state of the public mind after the Moorish conquest as favorable to its reception, and very likely wrote his preface with publication in view at that time.   But there is no evidence now at hand which points to an edition before 1510, at the very earliest.   So the actual marketing of *Amadis de Gaula*, as a piece of literature, is enveloped in the same obscurity as its rise among the fictions of the people.   And it is interesting to note that, when it did appear, this most characteristic offspring of the Middle Ages was made acceptable to the literary classes by the merits of its style and composition, conceptions which came into the modern world through the revival of the literature of antiquity, as Montalvo himself implies.

To give an idea of the contents of *Amadis de Gaula* will require a long and perhaps tiresome analysis, and may only be excused on the plea of regrettable necessity.   For the first four books of Montalvo, which include all the elements of the original story and to which we shall limit our outline, comprise by themselves some four hundred pages of closely printed text, containing not less than eleven hundred words to a page.   This would make a novel somewhat longer, by one hundred or more pages, than Thackeray's *Virginians,* but in amount of interest several score of times shorter than that volume. The size is a good indicator of the credulity and the leisure of the social circles of the sixteenth century.

Not many years after the Passion of our Lord, Garinter, king of Little Britain, straying from the chase, came upon a knight engaged in mortal combat with two of his rebellious subjects. The victory finally remained to the knight, who killed his opponents, and slew also a lion, which soon after appeared on the scene in hot pursuit of a stag. The knight in question proved to be Perion, king of Gaula (evidently Wales). Welcomed to Garinter's court, this lord lost no time in winning the love of Elisena, the royal princess, though in the affair he disregards the warning of a dream. Hardly has he obtained her full affection when he is constrained to return to his kingdom. As a pledge of his fidelity he leaves with Elisena his sword and his signet ring. On the birth of a son, the princess, hearing no tidings of her lover and fearing the shame of discovery, caused her maid to place the child in a chest, into which she put also the sword and ring, and a tablet on which was written his name, Amadis. She then lowered the chest into the stream which flowed by the castle, it was borne to the sea and picked up by a Scottish knight, Gandales, who was returning home from abroad. The vessel reached Scotland in safety, the boy was adopted into his rescuer's family, and brought up with the son of the house, Gandalin, under the name of the Child of the Sea.

Meanwhile Perion, at his court in Wales, has summoned a council of wise men to interpret his evil dream, but succeeds only in drawing out a prophecy from an unknown maiden. This prophecy she has no sooner given in Wales, than she hastens to Scotland to utter the same oracle to Gandales, whom she also tells her name, Urganda the Unknown. Time passes by. The Child of the Sea, when hardly three years old, attracts the attention of Languines, king of Scotland, and is summoned to court. But he refuses to go until Gandalin is also invited. Now, during these few years Garinter had died in Little Britain ; Elisena, assailed by Languines, had sent to Perion for aid, and the procrastinating lovers had at last been married. But from fear of Perion's anger the princess had denied the birth of any child. A daughter, Melicia, and another son, Galaor, had blessed their lawful union, but the latter had been seized one day by Gandalac, a giant of Lyonnesse, and carried away to his island, where a hermit protected the child and adopted him.

It is time to introduce a heroine equal to these days of youthful precocity. This is Oriana, daughter of Lisuarte, crown prince of England. Inasmuch as she had suffered from sea-sickness (a weakness we have never seen attributed to a modern heroine), her father had left her in Scotland on his way to Denmark, whither he was going to receive the crown, to which he was heir through his wife, Brisena. Oriana now at the Scottish court receives as page the Child of the Sea. From this relationship springs their perfect love. When the boy had reached the age of fifteen, and was already noted for his noble spirit and his deeds at arms, Perion came to Scotland, seeking aid against Abies, king of Ireland. While there the king consented to knight his son, not knowing him. Now, the Child of the Sea, having Gandalin as squire, begs leave of absence from his mistress, and sets out to win fame in her service as a knight-errant. Adventures come upon him thick and fast. Girded with his father's sword, wearing his ring, and aided by Urganda, who had brought him his lance, the Child of the Sea avenges wrongs, delivers oppressed maidens, chastises evil-doers, and frees knights from imprisonment, even to king Perion himself. And in the midst of this turmoil and strife he is ever mindful of all the usages of chivalry, from the protracted ceremonies of conferring knighthood to the despatching of his prisoners to his mistress at the court. A true lover, and a mighty champion is he, and worthy of the good old times. For at the present day of degeneration how could we expect a youth of fifteen to emerge alive and victorious from an encounter like the following?

" Then they started their horses at great speed and struck with their lances each other's shields, which were straightway broken, and their harness likewise and the lance heads were buried in each other's flesh. And then they came together with their bodies and shields and helmets, one against the other so bravely that both were thrown to the ground. But now it was favorable to the Child of the Sea, who got up with the reins in his hand, and Galpano stood up badly misused, and they laid hands to their swords and raised their shields before them and struck at each other so mightily that fear came over those who looked thereon. From their shields fell many splinters and from their harness many strips, and their helmets were battered and broken ; so that the ground on which they strove was dyed red with blood."

While her knight is doing all these deeds in her honor, Oriana is living at the English court, to which she returned at the command of her father, accompanied by Mabilia, the princess of Scotland. One day, finding in her possession the tablet which the Child of the Sea had given her at his departure, Oriana bursts into tears and presses the tablet so hard that it breaks. She looks within and finds there written : "This is Amadis Sin-tiempo, the son of a king." Much comforted at this discovery she hastens to share it with her knight, and sends the paper to Amadis. He, however, relaxes not at all his efforts to win glory, but hits and hews with mind intent on his mistress alone. Thus he goes from adventure to adventure, until finally he is recognized one day by his ring to be the son of Perion.

Here the author has reached the solution of one part of

his plot, the recognition of Amadis by his parents, and would seem to be on the highroad to the end of his story. But not so simply did the men of the Middle Ages look on their literary tasks. Some chapters back the writer had carefully laid the foundation for a new series of adventures, and Amadis, instead of hastening to Oriana and claiming her hand instanter, like the impetuous heroes of the present day, feels he has first a mission to accomplish, and starts off in search of his kidnapped brother, Galaor. With the aid of Urganda the brothers soon meet, but remain unknown to each other, and the elder consents to knight the younger. After the ceremony Galaor finds a sword hanging from a bough, Urganda's gift, which he takes, and with it soon overthrows a giant. Now the narrative divides itself between these two heroes and joins the exploits of one to those of the other with great celerity, to the no little confusion and weariness of the modern reader. Amadis, on his way to the court of England, passes by a castle where he is not only refused hospitality, but is in addition reviled from its walls by its lord, Dardan, a proceeding with gives rise, in the text, to extended reflections on pride. Some time after Amadis jousts against Dardan at the court. In the midst of the combat he raises his eyes to the seats occupied by the spectators and meets the gaze of Oriana. The thought of her presence unmans him, and he forgets for a while his prowess. But as he yields to his adversary a feeling of shame comes over him, he rallies and unhorses Dardan, who brings the contest to a tragic end by the murder of his mistress—who is jeering at his defeat—and by his own suicide. The wounds of Amadis are healed that night by an interview with Oriana at her window—though it must not be supposed that this feature of Spanish manners was observed by the Northern hero with the impetuosity of the South. On the contrary his answer to the greeting which Oriana gave him in the presence of their attendants is a good example of the repression practiced on theit feelings by the heroes of chivalry.

"When Oriana saw him she came to the window and said to him : 'My lord, may you be much welcome to this land, for we have greatly desired you and have taken great pleasure in your new successes, both in arms and in your recognition by your father and mother.' Amadis, when he heard this, was indeed overcome, but making a greater effort on himself than for any other encounter, he said : ' Lady, if my manners may not suffice to repay the favor which you show me . . . do not marvel at it, for my heart is much disturbed and overcome by sovereign love and does not allow my tongue its full liberty ; and as I think all things are subject to your gracious remembrance so I am placed in subjection by the sight of you, without there being any sentiment in me which remains free ; and if I, my lady, were so worthy or if my services merited it, I would ask of you compassion for this heart in tribulation, before that it be entirely undone with tears ; and the favor which I seek from you, my lady, I desire not for myself (for when things truly loved are attained much more does desire and care augment and increase) but because all being accomplished would bring that also to an end which never tires of thinking how to serve you.' "

Oriana seems to comprehend these circumlocutions and returns an answer in kind, to which Amadis replies in fewer words. And thus the conversation was prolonged until the morning. But Amadis is called away from these pleasing exercises of linguistic expression to look again for Galaor, whose absence from court he begins to regret. This hero, however, has taken care of himself very well in his wanderings, has fought many fierce fights, and gained as many notable victories. But, unlike Amadis, there is no purpose in his exploits, no end beyond them to be attained. He has no guiding star, no revered and faithful mistress. His honor is consequently no different from the conventional honor of knighthood, as exhibited in the Arthurian romances, and the current of his affections changes with the gratitude of each maiden whom he befriends. His part, though a gallant knight, is to act as a foil to the steadfastness and fidelity of Amadis' character. But their adventures are practically the same, as are those of various other knights of royal birth, who gradually come on the stage and occupy it with their achievements.

By increasing in this way the number of characters the author, whether Montalvo, or some reviser who preceded him, injures very much the unity of action in the novel, though he evidently supposes he is thereby increasing interest among his readers. To arrive at this last result he has recourse to another notion which had done such good service in the romances of the Round Table. This device is the use of magic and incantations, an agent which he employs sparingly at first, but later on, as the novelty of his inventions fades away, introduces into nearly every episode. So we see Amadis, in this second search for his brother, as he rides out guided by a treacherous dwarf, meeting with the enchanter, Arcalaus, whom he beats in a fair fight ; but he is afterward decoyed into a room, where he is overcome by the magician's arts and sinks into a deep sleep, which gives Arcalaus a chance to present himself at the court in the hero's armor and to sadden all the courtiers there, who believe then that Amadis is dead. Oriana is driven to despair. Meanwhile the perfect knight has been revived by the words of a book which a girl reads before him, and has left the castle.

New adventures await him without. A funeral train meets him, where, borne on a litter, is the image of a king cut in marble. Afterward he comes upon Galaor, fails to recognize him, and begins to assail him in consequence of statements advanced by the artful niece of Arcalaus. A knight soon arrives, however, who stops the combat, and makes the brothers known to each other. Now they start together for the court, but Galaor turns aside to avenge the murder of a knight, and does not join Amadis again until each has undergone many perils and dangers. Finally they reach London and our hero comes again before his mistress.

"When Amadis saw himself in the presence of his lady, his heart leaped from one side to the other, guiding his eyes so that they might see the thing in the world which he loved most; and he approached her in great humility and she greeted him; and putting out her hands from under the lace of her mantle she took his own, and pressed them as a semblance of embracing him and said to him : ' My friend, what pain and grief that traitor made me pass through who brought me the news of your death ! and believe me that woman was never in so great peril as I. Certainly, friend and lord, the danger was wholly reasonable, for never did any one have so great a loss as I in losing you; for as I am loved more than all others, so my good fortune demanded that it should be by him who avails more than all! ' When Amadis heard himself praised by his lady he cast down his eyes to the ground, for he did not dare even to look at her, and she appeared so beautiful to him that his senses being troubled his words died away in his mouth ; so that he did not answer. Oriana, who kept her eyes fixed on him, noticed it straightway and said : 'Ah ! my friend, and lord ! how could I not love you more than any other thing ; for all who know you love you and value you ! and I, being the one whom you love and value, much more than for all others is it right for me to hold you dear ! ' Amadis, who had now calmed somewhat his trouble, said to her : 'Lady, I entreat you to grieve for the dolorous death which every day I suffer for your sake ; for that other death which it was said I had died, if it came to me, would be held as a great rest and consolation ; and if this sad heart of mine were not sustained by the great desire which it has to serve you, and which with great force forcibly resists the many bitter tears which spring from it, I would already be undone and consumed by them, nor is this because it fails to recognize that its mortal desires are satisfied in great part by the fact that your remembrance deigns to be merely mindful of them ; but as for the greatness of its necessity it requires greater favor than that which it merits in being sustained and made good, and if this favor does not come quickly it will very soon go down to its cruel end.' "

By the account of such interviews as these did Montalvo (whom we may safely assume improved very much on his original in such passages) endeavor to furnish to the nobility of Spain, not only the sentiments but the words and phrases for their attitude toward women, and their courtship of them. And had our author been able to renew his youth with each succeeding generation he would have found himself more than rewarded for his labored sentences, and his high conception of the spirit of man toward woman, by seeing his periods taken as a model for the conversation of lovers in subsequent fiction, and even in the daily walks of life. The Hôtel de Rambouillet of the seventeenth century went back to *Amadis de Gaula* for much of its theory of social relations between the sexes, and handed down to our own day that reverence in manner and felicity in expressing his desire to serve the fair ones, which we attribute to the " gentleman of the old school." The change of circum-stances has affected a phraseology fitted to the fifteenth century, but the courtly conversation which Montalvo desired to enjoin especially on his contemporaries has been, ever since his day, the ideal of gallantry and social refinement.

With this meeting of Amadis and Oriana another solution of the plot is reached. Galaor has been found by his brother, and the troth of the lovers has been formally plighted in the presence of witnesses. So we may look for the speedy ending of the tale. Indeed, it is highly probable that the action of our supposed *roman d'aventure* terminated at this place. But not yet was the popular curiosity satisfied. The three books of *Amadis*, cited by Ferrus, had extended the love story of the *romance* to new marvels and adventures, and in order to bring these out it was necessary for the unknown author to hit on some expedient to prolong his narrative. This expedient he found in deferring the marriage of the lovers, by raising up obstacles which should postpone the ceremony. Accordingly, Arcalaus, whose malignity was still on the alert, is made to hatch up a conspiracy against Lisuarte, king of England, by the terms of which he is to be abducted from London, and Oriana is to be given in marriage to Barsinan, lord of Sansueña, who would thereby succeed to the kingdom. All of which, the author explains, has a moral end in view, namely, the chastening of Lisuarte's pride. At first the traitors are successful, as they always are in ideal novels. Amadis and the nobles about the king are lured away on a supposed errand of mercy. Then Lisuarte is tricked into making an oath. Like Herod of old, he is obliged to give up Oriana in order to keep it, and finally is himself made a prisoner. The sadness and desolation which now brood over the once bright and joyous halls move the author to an elaborate dissertation on the vanity and perishableness of human greatness, after which homily he proceeds to gather his exiles together again. Amadis is the chief agent in this undertaking. He delivers in succession himself, Oriana, Lisuarte, and the queen, and sets the kingdom once more on its foundations.

Now we might expect that true love could be at last requited. But no! Amadis is soon forced to leave London, in order to perform a vow he had made during one of his adventures regarding an oppressed princess. On his way he is reminded of a broken sword which is necessary to the success of the enterprise, and sends his dwarf back to Oriana for the pieces he has left behind. The dwarf, ignorant of the love between his master and Oriana, tells the latter about the expedition, and assures her that Amadis is the accepted knight of this foreign princess, Briolanja. Oriana, who had just given Amadis a ring as a pledge of her affection, now falls into extreme jealousy and despair, in the midst of which the narrator leaves her.

The remainder of this first book of the novel is concerned with the career of Florestan, another son of Perion, born of a love intrigue in Germany, and who now meets Galaor, and fights with him until their common parentage is made known. Together they go in search of Amadis, and find him in the kingdom of Sobradisa, where the pious gratitude of the rescued princess, Briolanja, forms a fitting conclusion to this series of adventures.

In imitation of the example set by the governor of Medina del Campo, let us also pause a moment in our course and draw a few morals from the analysis already given. The first book of *Amadis* offers, for our first moral, conclusive proof of the statement which was made about the nature of the romances of chivalry. They are stories of erotic adventure, like the Greek novels. They are, however, unlike the latter—saving the *Nimrod* fragment—aristocratic in tone, and have not only a personage of royal blood for a hero and a princess for a heroine, but also keep the adventures strictly within the limits of court life. The hero is a knight who places patriotism and loyalty before the satisfaction of his love, and whose love is respectful and unswerving. His love for his mistress is the mainspring of the story, for it was to prove himself worthy of her that he became a knight-errant. She is ever revered by him. In her presence he is always humble and a supplicant. She confers the favors which he begs. Yet in his desire to win her he never hesitates to obey the commands of his feudal sovereign. While in these particulars, which concern the spirit and sentiment of the work, as well as its unity of action, there is only a slight departure from the style of previous mediæval fiction, in the material used, and in the setting of the story, there is an imitation of the Arthurian romances, which amounts almost to a copy of them. The latter have loaned their topography. Brittany and England, with Wales—soon to be confounded with France from the likeness of its name, Gaula—are the scene of most of the exploits. Scotland and Germany, to be sure, appear for variety's sake. The knights, like those of the Round Table, pass their time in avenging wrongs, mainly the wrongs of women. Allusions to King Arthur are frequent, and Tristan also claims an occasional reference. Urganda, the benevolent spirit, is another Lady of the Lake, though in the later books she fades into a vulgar enchantress. To this fairy a giant carries Galaor, as Lancelot was carried to Vivien.

In minor details also there are many points of resemblance which have been already noted : the illegal parentage of the hero, rings as pledges and as means of recognition, dwarfs as attendants, both friendly and hostile, faithful squires and ladies in waiting, hermits who utter oracles, conquered knights and rescued maidens who bring news of the hero to court, and even down to the passive part which Lisuarte, the king, another Arthur, plays in the events which concern his throne. So strong is the influence of these prototypes on *Amadis* that up to this point no mention of Spain has been made, and no trace of Spanish customs, excepting the nightly interviews at the lady's window, has been found. On the contrary, the Spanish writer deliberately magnifies foreign courts and rulers, and enters into an especial eulogy on London, " which at that time was raised like an eagle above the mass of Christendom." There is, to be sure, other material entering into the composition of this first book of *Amadis* which might be attributed, though not positively, to the influence of the national heroic epic of France. We find occasionally in *Amadis* the account of combats, which single champions chosen for the purpose maintain in front of their respective armies, like the celebrated fight of Roland and Oliver, and the details of many other duels of the Carolingian chivalry. In the brutality of these encounters, where horses are maimed and the arms and legs of the warriors are hewn away by piecemeal, there is a close resemblance to similar descriptions in the national epic. Also the enmity of the relatives of Arcalaus and Dardan toward the race of Amadis and Lisuarte reminds one strongly of the feud which the family of the arch-traitor Ganelon carried on with Roland and the other paladins of Charlemagne. The enchantments, too, in this first book are few and simple, like those in *Maugis d'Aigremont.* One scene of magic, which the authors of *Amadis* could well have borrowed from this poem, is where Urganda casts a spell on a girl, who immediately seeks to throw herself into the water, under the impression that she is surrounded by burning torches. So Arcalaus, the plan of whose castle is like the one where the Knight of the Lion found the captive maidens weaving, uses the cloud of Maugis in *Renaud de Montauban* as one of his stratagems, while sleep is another of his devices to get the better of his foes.

The introduction of moral reflections and pious exhortations into the recital of such adventures is new, and may be safely set down to the credit of Spanish zeal. Also the great devotion with which the knights observe the ceremonies of the Church, both in the usages of chivalry and in the private practice of their faith, probably comes from the long crusade of these southern Christians against the infidels, though it may have had its beginnings in the spasmodic piety of the knights who went in quest of the Holy Grail. Another novelty of *Amadis* has already been pointed out, and is the intention to place models of refined love-making and courtly conversation before the young nobles of Spain. The prominence which this feature assumes in the romance is so great, that we are justified in concluding that it was one of the leading motives in Montalvo's revision of the story as he found it among the people. Plebeian writers would have hardly attempted a vein so obviously intended for an aristocratic public. And this is as good as saying that Montalvo looked on his services in the making over of the romance as the part of an instructor, to give dignity to what had before been purely amusing, and to raise the homely chapbook to the rank of polite literature.

There is another element which appears but rarely in *Amadis de Gaula*, and yet forms the principal part of the novels of the present day. This is the realistic view of life. Naturally, in an ideal novel, there would be little room for matter-of-fact statements. The world of nature which envelops humanity is barely mentioned, in the vaguest way, by the writers of the romances of chivalry. In this respect we know they differed little from the general attitude of mediæval literature toward natural scenery, which even in the spring poems of those remote ages wore a most conventional aspect. But we might be led by the old surroundings of our romance to expect, once in a while at least, some incidents of a different tone from the prevailing one of chivalry. It had lived among the people for so many generations, and had been so long an amusement of their leisure hours, that it could scarcely have failed to gather up some instances of popular wit and satire. Yet if this were the case before Montalvo began his refining process, he was extremely successful in obliterating nearly every trace of it. His description of combats are realistic and detailed, but aside from them there are very few passages which offer evidence of an objective point of view. We have alluded to Oriana's seasickness which determined her stay in Scot-

land. One or two other citations of the same nature can
be made. Amadis once identifies a Dane by his speech,
Oriana having used Danish somewhat in his early acquaintance with her. Also when our hero hurries along on his
war-horse, distracted by the thought that he has been
robbed of his mistress, he meets with a commonplace mis-
hap : "And Amadis, who did not notice where he was
going, missed, in his great sorrow and care, the ford of a
brook, and when he thought he could leap over the brook,
his horse, which was tired out, could not do it, but fell back
into the mud."

There is one instance of a coarse joke in this first book
of *Amadis*, a joke, to be sure, which the stern Dante had
deigned to make in his *Inferno*. It is where the dwarf who
has been maltreated by Arcalaus complains of the latter's
brutality, and says to Amadis : " 'I cannot bear to stand
on the leg by which he hung me up, and my nostrils are so
filled with the fumes of the brimstone he placed under me
that since then I have done nothing but sneeze, and even a
worse thing than that.' Great was the laughter of Amadis
and Bramdoibas, and also of the ladies and maidens, at what
he said." But where these few examples are all which can be
gleaned from a volume of some three hundred ordinary
pages we are not warranted in asserting that practical every-
day affairs entered into this rehabilitated chapbook of old
Spain. Nor does the author attempt any portraitures of
persons, on which the French novelists of the seventeenth
century, who drew so much of their inspiration from *Amadis
of Gaul*, prided themselves. He does, indeed, consent to
make an attempt at a description of the two brothers, but
remains lastingly satisfied with this effort : "The brothers
looked so much alike that it was hard to tell them apart,
excepting that Don Galaor was somewhat fairer, and that
Amadis had curly auburn hair and somewhat more color in
the face, and was larger of limb."

We have lingered over the first book of *Amadis* because in it the spirit of the romances of chivalry is made manifest, as well as their characteristic features of style and composition. With the beginning of the second book comes in a long digression from the career of the Western heroes, and we are told how the prince Apolidon of Constantinople, and heir to its throne, had handed over his inheritance to his younger brother, and had sailed away with his wife and books to Firm Island, of indefinite location. He speedily killed the giant who was then ruling over the island, and succeeded to the lordship. For many years he governed wisely his conquest and, on being compelled to receive again his ancestral kingdom, he erected on Firm Island, at the request of his wife, Grimanesa, an enchanted palace. By the nature of the spell which he threw over this building, none but true lovers might ever penetrate into its recesses. Its outer portal was guarded by images which repelled all those who did not surpass Apolidon in valor, or Grimanesa in beauty. When the lovers who could entirely break this spell should come, the island was to pass into their possession. Great is the satisfaction of the novelist as he details the splendor of this creation, for which, to be sure, he had plenty of models in many of the more notable epic poems of France.

To this island comes Amadis, with his brothers, on their return to London from Briolanja's kingdom. All the knights endeavor to break the masculine part of the spell, but our hero alone succeeds, and becomes lord of the estate. In the midst of his triumph, however, arrives a messenger, bringing a letter from Oriana, in which she gives vent to her jealousy over his supposed intrigue with Briolanja, and banishes him, on account of his faithlessness, from her presence forever. The effect of such a dismissal on a true and perfect knight is seen beforehand. After a fruitful dream, Amadis makes his will, founds a monastery, dis-

tributes his personal effects, abdicates his throne, and goes
away alone. He soon finds the hermit who is ever at hand
to comfort distracted lovers, and turns hermit himself,
under the descriptive name of Beltenebros. But the con-
soling hermit is a shrewd old fellow who soon sees through
our hero, and reproaches him for the occasion of this sudden attack of piety, which he rightly attributes, not to
religion, but to unsuccessful love. Amadis' career as an-
chorite is not long. The messenger returns to Oriana with
the true version of the affair which had caused her anger.
A little later her compassion is aroused by the arrival of
Amadis' armor. For a while she believes him to be dead,
but her confidant suspects that in the guise of Beltenebros,
whose praises are now sung at the court, the real knight is
concealed, and Oriana dispatches another letter to him,
begging him to return. The arrival of his pardon brings
Amadis' hermit life to an abrupt ending, and determines his
immediate departure for London.

This episode of Amadis' exile from despairing love is one
of the most successful parts of the romance, and a decided
improvement on the old-fashioned way in the Arthurian
legends, where Tristan, Iwain, and similarly rejected suitors
spend the time of their disgrace in violent acts of insanity.
The notion of the Spanish author is more natural, more
refined, and particularly more romantic, in the modern
sense of the word. For these reasons " le Beau ténébreux, "
as the French translated *Beltenebros*, became the type and
standard for all unfortunate suitors. Melancholy, calm, and
conscious of its own dignity, it replaced in the higher
circles of society the traditional ravings and the abuse of
the wooed one. It would not, however, be fair to assign to
the romances of chivalry the exclusive right to this conception, for in the pastoral novels of the sixteenth century the
same inevitable cause, of true love, brings about the same situation on the part of the lover. But the romances of chiv-

alry possess, at all events, the advantage of priority in date over their later rivals, and if they did not bequeath to the pastoral tales their idea of amorous melancholy and erotic despair, they did at least furnish romantic literature, in the days of the Renaissance, with a model for blighted beings, and created a sympathetic spirit which lasted the youth of France for no less than three centuries.

While Amadis is returning to the court, Oriana withdraws to the castle of Miraflores, to repent at leisure of her cruelty toward him. His absence had also given the enemies of Lisuarte a chance to rally. A knight had penetrated even to the king's palace, bearing defiance from Arcalaus and the giants. Amadis, having obtained new armor, fights his way through these adversaries to his mistress ; and at this point the author introduces a trial of true love, such as the East offered so plentifully to the West in the Middle Ages. An old man arrives at the court, bringing with him a sword, in a green scabbard of transparent bone. Through this scabbard was seen the blade of the sword, half bright, like other blades, half red, like fire. In the jasper casket, which contained the sword and sheath, was also a wreath of flowers, of which one half was dry and withered, the other half freshly blooming. The sword could be drawn forth only by the most faithful lover, the flowers revived only by the most constant mistress. It is not necessary to add that Amadis and Oriana, in disguise, succeeded in the test, where all others failed.

But the challenge of the giants leads to a general war. Amadis, under the name of Beltenebros, decides a pitched battle in Lisuarte's favor against the hostile king of Ireland. The Irish king and Galaor were wounded in this fight, which the author describes at length, and were carried away by maidens in a boat to a castle by the sea, where Urganda healed them. This fairy, who is now rapidly evolving into an enchantress, soon after approaches the court in a galley surrounded by flames, hung with garlands, and heralded by the sweetest music. When the boat stops she lands with her maidens, seeks out Oriana, casts a spell over the princess' attendants, and gives voice to a prophecy. Now there would seem to be no hindrance to the legal union of the lovers. An obstacle, however, is soon found in the awakening jealousy of the king on account of Amadis' fame, and in the growth of this jealousy, until Amadis is forced by it in true loyalty to submit to his sovereign and to retire with his friends to Firm Island. After their departure Lisuarte's evil mood leads him to play the tyrant.

With this new episode, which contains the best psychological work of the romance, in the description of the king's jealousy and alarm, and its effect on his character and subsequent acts, the second book of *Amadis de Gaula* comes to an end. It is, as it stands in Montalvo's revision, much less interesting than the first book. It would seem as if Montalvo had felt, in rewriting it, less trammeled by the authority of tradition, and had gone on to develop in the romance his own views of what the story should be. In the first book the variety of incidents, and the rapidity with which they succeed one another, would indicate quite conclusively a close adherence to the original material. But in the second the episodes are less in number, are more spun out, and yet, in compensation, they are more ornate and inspiring from a literary point of view. The element of humor in them is largely increased, conversations are multiplied, and by their dialogue form more life is given to the narrative, while the more extended space occupied by descriptions of magic may be supposed to have aroused greater interest in the childish minds of the fifteenth century. The invention of Firm Island, its buildings, and their enchantments, was very likely in the traditional three books, but beyond a doubt the older description offered to our ambitious reviser an excellent chance to show the power of his pen. The tests of chastity on Firm Island resemble like tests in previous literature, and remind one of the device related in the Greek novel of Achilles Tatius. But the trials of the sword and flowers at court are less elaborately described, and may have been inserted by Montalvo himself, either through an effort of his own brain, or by appropriating stories which were circulating among the people. So that the general effect of the second book on the reader leads to the opinion that Montalvo has quite freed himself from the restraints placed upon him by the old chapbook, and is now molding the story to suit his own views of style and plan.

Yet we must not overlook the fact that this part of the revised *Amadis* is closely related to certain kinds of mediæval literature, even though it breaks somewhat with the legends of the Breton cycle. Bridge fights are numerous. Giants and giantesses gain a more definite character, and this increased definiteness makes it plain that they are not the ogres and cannibals of folk-tales, but are the enemies of the faith of the Carolingian poems, pagans, and even devils. Later, in the third book, we shall see Amadis sparing the life of the giant Madraque in return for the latter's conversion to Christianity, just as the paladins of Charlemagne were wont to do with Fierabras and his ilk. In the same way, Sir Bruneo's horse, like the famous Bayard in *Renaud de Montauban*, aids his owner by attacking the enemy's charger while Bruneo is assailing its rider. If Montalvo had wished to introduce new material into the novel, the heroic epic of the Middle Ages, now renewing its popularity in a prose form, was able to furnish him with an abundant supply ready to hand.

The impression, then, which one receives from the second book of *Amadis de Gaula* is that the last reviser of the story, and the only one known to fame, took what liberty he pleased with the romance, as handed down to him by his predecessors, and diluted the traditional events in his own flow of descriptions and conversations. Such a treatment of the subject-matter was only the more accentuated in the books following. In the third book, for instance, conversation pure and simple occupies a still larger space than in the second, and the style seems to be entirely free of any limitations which the sentences of the original might have imposed upon it. From all that may be gathered from the incidents and surroundings related in this book, we cannot assert with any confidence at all that the plot of the original *Amadis* has contributed any situations to its action. Indeed the general tone of the third book would point to the Turkish conquest of Constantinople as the source of its exploits, and would therefore place its composition in the time of Montalvo himself. And there is no doubt but that he furnished a good share of the events, if not indeed all of them. The birth of Esplandian for instance is related early in the book, and, according to Montalvo himself, this child was begotten in order to give an excuse for a sequel to which Montalvo should have the sole right of proprietorship. Curiously enough we find here the first mention of Spain, whose king is seen at last, fighting in England with his knights.

The part of Amadis throughout almost the whole of this book is the rôle of a disguised personage, a notion afterwards fostered by the pastoral novels, and becoming, from this time down to the eighteenth century, such a favorite device in fiction. From his success in undergoing the test of chastity already narrated, Amadis assumed the name of the Knight of the Green Sword, and under that title spread abroad his fame from London to Constantinople. Lisuarte was still hostile to him. Yet in his absence Oriana gave birth to a son, whose body was found to be marked with Latin and Greek characters. Like his father and many other heroes of the past, this child was also exposed to his fate and was carried off by a lioness. But a hermit interferes, rescues the infant, and forces the beast to suckle it. Besides, the hermit knows Latin, and interprets the letters of that language which were stamped on the child's body. They spell out the name Esplandian, with which the boy is then christened. Meanwhile Lisuarte triumphs, though in an unjust cause, over the friends of Amadis. His success, however, is of short duration, for the giants, who have always feared our hero, now seize their opportunity and invade England. But Amadis and Perion come to the king's aid, in disguise, and beat back the invaders in a pitched battle, which is well described by our author. The new allies are tricked in their turn and captured by Arcalaus, but soon make good their escape. Now Amadis, still in disgrace with Lisuarte, turns his back on England and travels toward the East. He visits Germany and Bohemia—where he kills in defense of that country the champion of the Roman emperor—and Roumania, all the while bewailing his exile from his mistress, but prudently putting his time to good use by acquiring the different languages of the lands through which he passes. Finally sailing along the islands of Greece, with the wise physician, Helisabad, he is wrecked on Devil's Island, and there performs the great feat of slaying the monster which inhabits it. Thence he proceeds to Constantinople, whither his fame as Knight of the Green Sword had already preceded him. The thought of Oriana makes him supremely miserable, but does not prevent him from winning the admiration of all Byzantium by his manners and his courtly conversation. At last, after six years of unwearying melancholy, he sets out for London, as escort of the Roumanian princess Grasinda, whom he had aided when he was in her country.

During the separation of the lovers Esplandian has increased in stature, has attracted Lisuarte's attention, as the king was one day hunting in the forests, and has been taken

to the court at London, together with his lioness and hermit.
Urganda has written a letter to Lisuarte recommending
Esplandian, and Oriana has recognized her son, and confessed her fault to the hermit. But new troubles arise.
Lisuarte is ignorant of the boy's parentage, and when the
Roman emperor, El Patin, asks for Oriana in marriage, the
king gives his consent, though in so doing he runs counter
to the advice of all his counselors. But the Knight of the
Green Sword arrives in the nick of time, summons the
boastful Romans to a mortal combat, overthrows them, yet
spares their lives at the intercession of the child Esplandian,
who has dared to venture within the lists. Lisuarte, however, still insists on the marriage, and the reluctant Oriana
is given up to the Romans, and is forced to embark for
Rome with them. Amadis thinks the time for a decisive
deed has now come. He hurries to Firm Island, assembles
there his troops, and in a studied oration—in which Montalvo clearly seeks to rival the speeches delivered by the historians of antiquity—he exhorts his followers to pursue the
Romans and destroy their fleet. The approval of the idea
by Amadis' army gives the author a chance to describe a
naval engagement, in which the Romans are worsted, and
Oriana is taken to Firm Island by her own true knight.

There are certain features in this third book of *Amadis*
which, though they do not probably have their origin in
the popular story, were, without much doubt, derived from
mediæval literature, and certainly suggested the inventions
of subsequent fiction. For whatever was received into
Amadis de Gaula was clothed with undisputed authority by
the public, and was looked upon with an almost religious
veneration by later novelists of the ideal-romantic school.
We have spoken of the transfer of the action to Constantinople and the East (a shifting of scenery which was never
afterward neglected in heroic fiction), and of the disguise
under which Amadis performed so many of his exploits—a

notion that the Breton poems had often used, and which the novels of the French school carried to an extreme in the seventeenth century. Of course the latter were also subject to the influence of the pastoral stories, which were full of such episodes as the one of Beltenebros. As for the birthmarks of Esplandian, they may look back to the birthmarks of the *romans d'aventure*, though the idea of anything so definite as letters of the alphabet may have been original with Montalvo. But they and the rearing of the young prince (which reminds us of the infancy of Romulus and Remus) became standard devices with later authors. One surprising feature in the book is the animus showed everywhere against Rome. This enmity can in no way be traced to mediæval sources, in thought or in literature, for all the people of the Middle Ages revered the name of Rome ; and the Latin races in particular looked on themselves as the rightful inheritors of her scepter. There seems to be, then, no other explanation for this hostility to the imperial city in *Amadis* than that which is offered by the fact that Italy, which represented more exactly the territory of ancient Rome, had never been a fruitful soil for the institutions of feudalism, and that her plebeian wars had excited only the aversion of Western chivalry.

In this book the Spanish idea of loyalty to the monarch, which is not found, to such a degree at least, anywhere in mediæval literature, is carried out to its logical extreme. Amadis, though wronged by Lisuarte and treated by him with the greatest ingratitude, never lifts his hand against the king, nor tolerates the slightest hint of resistance to him. He comes to the assistance of Oriana, whose troubles are all brought upon her by the tyrannical spirit of her father, only when she has ceased to be his subject by having been delivered over to the ruler of the Romans. In this part of the novel, too, the didactic bent increases in prominence, and moral reflections on the result of evil-doing, or exhortations to the practice of Christian virtues, most plentifully abound.

If the third book contains little of the original plot of *Amadis de Gaula*, the fourth and last is perhaps entirely a new creation of Montalvo: This fact seems patent when we find everywhere the adaptations of old exploits and a constant repetition of the regular commonplaces. Yet though the substance of this part is but a working-over of the traditional elements, the construction of the fourth book is superior to the design of its predecessors, and reveals a higher art of composition. The improvement is particularly apparent in the definiteness of the parts which the different characters are now called upon to act. The narrative describes again, and at length, the buildings on Firm Island, while the life there, at Amadis' court, is placed before us in greater detail than had before been attempted. Conversations between knights and ladies, harangues of the leaders to the assembled councils, and frequent letters to and from allies, fill up many chapters. For the fourth book is the longest of them all, containing 130 pages out of the 400 which make up the romance. The events described include the attack of Lisuarte, aided by the Romans, on Firm Island, and a battle lasting two days, after which Amadis recalls his troops to spare the king a defeat. This act prepared the way for the peace which is brought about by Esplandian's hermit, who comes to Firm Island and discloses the parentage of the child. But a new trouble arises for Lisuarte. During his absence Arcalaus, who has bided his time for revenge, has gathered his relatives and friends. He attacks the king on his return home and defeats him. Amadis speedily arrives, however, and in turn conquers the common enemy. At last, after all these achievements, the author can find no occasion for further deferring the lawful union of the lovers. He gathers together at Firm Island their friends and relatives, and there is celebrated the marriage, which was destined to put an end to the last enchant-ment of Apolidon's palace. Now our hero can enjoy his well-earned repose. But not the author, for he has still another book to write, in order to relate the deeds of Es-plandian, whom Amadis had despatched to Constantinople to redeem a promise, confiding to him the ring which the imperial princess had formerly given to the Knight of the Green Sword. Amadis himself remains at Firm Island, while his allies withdraw to their homes, after undergoing a final harangue from their leader, the finishing touch of *Amadis de Gaula.*

It would be a matter of considerable literary importance, and also extremely gratifying to our curiosity, could we trace, step by step, the growth of this union of a love tale and warlike adventures into the first of modern novels. But conjecture is our only resource. From all the pages upon which Montalvo has based his fame with posterity, we may indeed draw our own conclusions regarding the story which was the starting-point. A comparison of the leading features of *Amadis* with various French poems of the Middle Ages might show that the original plot of the romance of chivalry consisted of an early affection between hero and heroine, of a few adventures undergone by the hero to win his spurs, of the awakening of the heroine's jealousy through some unusual exploit performed by her knight to the profit of another woman, her consequent coldness and his madness or self-exile, and of their reconciliation when she became aware of her mistake, and when he had rendered her or her parents some service of which they stood in great need, such as a deliverance from their enemies. To expand this simple story to its present dimensions required long effort on the part of writers, and a popular interest in it lasting through many generations.

Yet all these advantages would not have availed to raise *Amadis of Gaul* above the level of many other mediæval romances of the kind, had not the art of style and composition, which was revealed to the modern world by the discovery of the literature of antiquity, come to its aid and given to it a standing in cultivated society. For it is the expansion of the primitive bare narrative of mere events, erotic or warlike, by the introduction of descriptions, conversations, moral injunctions, and chivalrous instructions, which has made of the *roman d'aventure* and the chapbook of the Spanish populace the pioneer novel of our latter-day civilization.

CHAPTER VI.

MONTALVO was not content with spinning out his rendering of the old romance to the extent of nine hundred or more octavo pages. He must needs add a sequel entirely of his own make, which is good for four hundred pages more, which sequel called for other sequels by other ambitious scribes, until folio on folio was piled up in the ducal libraries of Spain and France, whose combined leaves would discourage enumeration. And besides Amadis and his race, which had some legendary reason for existence, in the celebrity of its founder, there was a rival family made up out of whole cloth, the Palmerins of several generations, and many individual heroes whose dynasties were not perpetuated in literature. A decade of years would not be too great a length of time in which to become acquainted with the biographies of all of them, nor the concentrated patience of seven generations excessive for the task. A few analyses of the best are warranted to prove this point most satisfactorily.

We left Montalvo as he was about to launch his own independent romance of chivalry. His notion of giving an heir to Amadis, who should equal or improve on the deeds of his father, was not a new one in mediæval literature. One of the cycles of French epic poems, the one which celebrates the fame of William of Orange and his house (the ancestors of the family living at Orange, on the Rhone, in the ninth and tenth centuries, are here meant) had been based on the same idea of hereditary valor and merit. To connect his sequel with his revision, Montalvo turns to good account one of the principal agents in the action of the latter, Urganda.   This lady, now in the last stage of evolution from a fairy of the Celts to an enchantress of the East, comes to Firm Island in a dragon ship which belches forth fire and smoke of midnight blackness, takes on board Esplandian, dressed in full armor and wearing the ring of the Byzantine princess, and carries him away to meet adventures.

These take place mainly in the Orient, and Montalvo, in keeping with the good old custom of the writers of fiction, claims that he merely translated them from a Greek novel of the wise Helisabad, the friend of Amadis in the East.   He thereby accounts for the title of his book, *Las Sergas de Esplandian*—the word *sergas* as he uses it meaning "deeds." The transference of the action to Constantinople and its dependencies may have been made because Montalvo assumed, and very rightly, that Amadis had worn all novelty out of the West.   At the same time, the Turkish onslaught on the Eastern Empire and its capital gave a slight historical basis for his story, and no doubt added to its interest among the conquerors of Granada.   For the crusading spirit of the book appears in the arrival of Urganda's ship at Enchantress Hill, and the commission which Esplandian there receives to fight the enemies of the faith.   Accordingly he first travels beyond the limits of Byzantine rule to Persia, where he is known as the Black Knight, from the color of his armor.   On the way, however, he has lost his faithful squire Sargil, as Amadis had before him lost Gandalin.   But still he fights, a stranger, and passes through the usual run of experiences, in which more enchantments are used than heretofore.   The overthrowing of giants goes on prosperously, and the freeing of captives knows no cessation. Among the male prisoners set at liberty by this valiant warrior are the old king Lisuarte, who has got himself into a new entanglement, and the wise Helisabad.   The enemies of Esplandian are represented as relatives of Arcalaus, and among his friends are found various hermits who attend on his repose. Sons of Galaor and of other heroes of renown in *Amadis de Gaula* also occupy the scene, while Urganda stands ever ready with magic and armor to help on the rightful cause.

A further connection with the first four books of *Amadis* is established by embarking the young knight, his grandfather, and the sage on Urganda's ship of the Great Serpent, which then moves away of its own accord and lands them all at Amadis' court on Firm Island. Esplandian later on fights with his father, not knowing him. While these family affairs are being regulated, the maiden Carmela, who has gone to Constantinople on a love errand, and a political one as well, delivers to the princess on the part of Esplandian her ring, and also induces the emperor to send an army against Persia. To Esplandian, who is now fighting at Forbidden Mountain in the Turkish peninsula, Amadis sends a strong force of English—he having succeeded to the crown on the abdication of Lisuarte, who had retired to a monastery—an example to Charles V. Leonorina the princess sends back a harsh message to Esplandian, but finally relents, and he obtains his first interview with her by being carried into her chamber hidden in a chest. For some time now the author descants on the mutual affection and emotion of the lovers, but soon returns to the wars. The great historical catastrophe is drawing near. All the pagans are assembled under the lead of the Sultan Armato to besiege Constantinople. All the western Christians are summoned to its defense. To the magic of Urganda is opposed the art of Melia on the infidel side. A new invention is the appearance among the assailants of Calafia, the Amazon queen of the island of California (most marvelously described), who devastates the ranks of the faithful by means of her fifty griffins. Assault and repulse follow sorties and pitched battles, but a large part of the war is carried on by means of single combats, in which individual knights win resounding fame.   At last the western allies, having rendezvoused at Firm Island, proceed to the Greek capital.   There Amadis and Esplandian overcome in a two-fold duel Calafia and the Sultan Radiaro, while the Christian army defeats the pagan in a general engagement.   But in the struggle both Perion and Lisuarte fall.

As a reward for his assistance the Greek emperor marries his daughter to Esplandian.   Through this ceremony the Greek characters on the knight's breast become legible, and spell Leonorina.   The emperor then kindly abdicates in favor of his son-in-law, the captive sultan is exchanged for Urganda, who had fallen into the hands of the enemy, the serpent ship disappears, and its mistress, who foresees that without her intervention the Christian heroes must pay the common debt of nature, enchants them all, knights and ladies, in Firm Island.   Into the earth they descend, never to come forth again until at some future day, like the blameless king, Arthur, they shall be brought to life by the sword of Lisuarte, son of Esplandian.

We have already called attention to the principal features of *Las Sergas de Esplandian,* and the short analysis given of that book only emphasizes what has been said regarding its inferiority to the preceding parts of *Amadis.*   One original idea, for the romances of chivalry at least, is the love by hearsay, which grew up between the hero and the Byzantine princess, but the larger part of new material is due to the desire to avoid repetition of the events related in the former books of the series.   Montalvo succeeds in this endeavor, yet in so doing becomes both extravagant and unreal.   For his imagination had not sufficient force to compensate for the exhaustion of the traditional episodes from which he at first drew, and this defect renders his descriptions of the exploits in the fifth book wearisome, and the reasons for the meetings of the knights with one another too artificial to be probable. The constant introduction of the old hero, Amadis, interferes with the unity of action desirable, and worst of all the love story is labored and stale. The style has also deteriorated, for which we may perhaps hold Montalvo's advancing years responsible. It is self-constrained, thin in quality, conscious of effort; even the moralizings do not possess the simple and honest piety of the teachings of *Amadis*. We cannot then blame the good curate of *Don Quixote* for his judgment on *Las Sergas*, since in fact the excellences of the "father" are not indeed handed down to the "son." Such pronounced differences in fancy and composition would lead us to suppose a considerable gap between the date of the fourth book and the time of the fifth, and would go to show that Montalvo had waited too long in carrying out his long-cherished plan of furnishing a sequel to the original romance.

But the dryness and tediousness of *Las Sergas* were not noticed in the novelty and freshness of the whole work, which Montalvo gave in one volume to the public, and the great favor with which the old traditions of the people were received by the higher classes of society showed that the age of Ferdinand and Isabella overlooked or forgave all deficiencies in a piece of literature which reflected so well the spirit of the times.

So enduring was the popularity of Montalvo's story that ambitious writers of the following generation thought they might gain renown by attaching themselves to its fortunes. A sixth book of *Amadis* appeared early in the sixteenth century, and under the title of *Don Florisando* related the career of Florestan, the half-brother of Amadis and Galaor. Lisuarte the Younger had his turn (for which Montalvo had prepared the way) in the seventh and eighth books, called after him *Lisuarte de Grecia*. With him was associated Perion, Esplandian's younger brother, while the object of their united love is the princess Onoloria, of Trebizond, a place that enjoyed considerable fame in the latter part of the Middle Ages. Combats, imprisonments, magic, and rescues are narrated in close imitation of the original *Amadis*. One apparent novelty, however, is Lisuarte's escape from prison, disguised in female attire. It is he who also finds the enchanted sword and frees the sleepers on Firm Island ; but their deliverance of Constantinople is retarded by the disappearance of Lisuarte, who retires to exile after the arrival of a harsh message from Onoloria.   In this story Spain appeared as a country for the first time, but even then only in passing.

So sequel follows sequel, with little variation of exploits or method. The son of Lisuarte and Onoloria, Amadis of Greece, comes to the aid of his father in the ninth book, and when he, in turn, is enchanted in a tower, he is delivered by his son, Florisel of Niquea, the hero of the tenth book. A new idea, too, is the introduction of the Russians here, who are, to be sure, placed in no highly complimentary situations. But a more important step is the admission, in this book, of fictitious material, foreign to the substance out of which were formed the romances of chivalry.

This departure from tradition is in the shape of a pastoral episode. Darinel, a shepherd, has fallen in love with Sylvia, a supposed shepherdess, but who, in reality, is the daughter of Lisuarte and Onoloria in disguise. The suit of Darinel she rejects with aristocratic disdain, and prince Florisel, who has assumed the shepherd's dress in order to assail her affections with a greater chance of success, fares no better. But her fate comes at last, and the   haughty maiden yields to the renown of Anastarax, Florisel's brother, who had been locked up in the enchantment of a flaming tower.   When the magic arts which overcame him had been broken, the true birth of Sylvia was made known to a curious world. The import of this story in *Florisel de*

Niquea does not seem to have been appreciated by writers on literary history. The verdict which the curate pronounces upon it, in his review of Don Quixote's library, has been accepted as final by all later authorities, and is surely correct from the æsthetic standpoint. But from the standpoint of the historical development of fiction, this account of Sylvia's caprice is deserving of a somewhat better fate than cremation in the honest parson's bonfire. For it shows very conclusively, that already by the beginning of the fourth decade of the sixteenth century pastoral stories had become popular in Spain, and the notion of princely characters in pastoral disguise had been definitely established in fiction. Otherwise we may be very sure that the author of this tenth book, a certain Feliciano da Silva, would not have allowed himself to bring into his narrative an element which, in its essence, was so utterly at variance with his main subject. This episode is a reliable witness to the prevalence of pastoral tales in Spain, and is itself earlier in date than any other version of them. Such evidence will be important when we come to consider the historical growth of the pastoral novel in the Spanish peninsula.

The insertion of this pastoral episode also proves another point, more germane to our present subject, which is that the romances of chivalry had worn out their own commonplaces, and were being forced to draw on other sources of story-telling to retain their hold on the reading public. Such a necessity foreboded their decline, and accordingly we are not surprised to find, after two more books on the exploits of Florisel's brothers and the beauty of his daughter, Diana, that the long series of the sequels to *Amadis* comes to an end. In two generations the great admiration for the days of chivalry had produced no less than twelve large volumes, filled with events bearing so great a resemblance to one another as to have proved—from all that our modern tastes can determine—decidedly monotonous even to the most credulous audience.   But the spirit which animated the fountain head of them all, the ideal of knighthood and of loyalty to the monarch and to the True Faith, sustained these long compilations in popular favor down to the rule of Philip II.   By the middle of the sixteenth century further expansions of the theme ceased on Spanish soil.   But it awoke elsewhere to new life and underwent additional development, which extended its increased fame to the limits of European civilization.   This second life of the Amadis family resulted from transplanting it to France.

When Francis I., after the battle of Pavia, in 1525, found himself an unwilling guest at the court of Spain, he whiled away the tedious hours of his captivity by allowing himself to be diverted with the narratives of Spanish fiction. In this way the various books of *Amadis de Gaula* were brought to his royal attention, as the story which at that time was engrossing, above all others, the minds of his hosts. Whether it was the notions of loyalty and honor extolled by the novel which won the king's favor, or, as seems more probable, the story appealed to him as essentially French in origin and thus properly belonging to French literature, the fortunes of Amadis and his descendants became so firmly impressed on the mind of the monarch, that soon after his return to France he commissioned one of his courtiers, Nicolas de Herberay des Essarts, to reproduce them in a translation.   Des Essarts soon set himself at his task, and between the years 1540 and 1548 he did into French and published the five books written by Montalvo, together with *Lisuarte de Grecia* and *Amadis de Grecia*—omitting *Don Florisando*—in all eight books of the Spanish original.

Des Essarts does not worry over the exact meaning of the original text, but adapts it in a free and easy manner to the taste of its new readers, and brings it into sympathy with the customs of the time and surroundings, as his friends had advised him to do.   Consequently the tone of the whole history is changed, under his desire to be in keeping with the wishes of his public. The deeply devout attitude of *Amadis de Gaula*, its religious and didactic tendency, is greatly weakened in *Amadis de Gaule*, while the erotic element, of the Galaor stripe, is fortified in proportion. By these changes it became more acceptable to the less severe temper of the French, and won abroad a popularity which equaled its old renown at home. Des Essarts himself testifies to the success of *Amadis* in its new environment, won "in spite of *Orlando Furioso*," so like it in matter but unlike in spirit. The favor obtained by Des Essarts' version tempted other writers of France to try their fortunes in the same undertaking. Further translations from the Spanish followed these first eight books, and when the original source had run dry, additional sequels, due to French invention, were placed on the market. The true and perfect knight of mediæval chivalry renewed his youth in the full light of the Renaissance. His fame filled volume after volume, until by 1625 no less than twenty-five books testified to the fervor of his welcome to the land which was supposed to have given him birth, and where at all events the material for his biography had been slowly collected before it was set in order by the romancers of the South. The influence of this new series of *Amadis* on the French heroic-gallant novel of the seventeenth century need not be recalled again.

Elsewhere in western Europe the Spanish romance of chivalry aroused a fair degree of enthusiasm. It was least esteemed in Italy and shared the fate of the other legends of the Middle Ages in that land, which was always so averse to the romantic and mystical. Bernardo Tasso, the father of the great poet, took *Amadis de Gaula*, in 1544, for the basis of a prose imitation, which in 1560 he worked over into a heroic poem, *Amadigi di Francia*, understanding by *Gaula*, not Wales, but France. Besides this attempt at an

Italian adaptation of the story, there appeared in Italy a long translation in many books of the original text. Yet Amadis never penetrated into Italian life and sympathy as did Renaud of Montauban or Roland and Charlemagne. The Italian people were too matter-of-fact, too logical, above all too democratic to care for a type which was the ideal of of feudalism.

In England the comparative interest felt in *Amadis* was not great, not perhaps for the same reasons which obtained in Italy, but because this repetition and expansion of the legends of the British came into competition with the direct tradition of Arthur's reign, and the renown of the Round Table. A translation from Des Essarts soon made its way across the Channel, and the *Arcadia* of Sir Philip Sidney reflects the Spanish romances of chivalry. A translation of the French version introduced *Amadis de Gaula* into Germany also, where from various accounts left by later writers it seems to have enjoyed considerable popularity. This short survey makes it evident that it was France which gave a new lease of life to the old hero and his descendants, and carried his reputation into the countries of the North.

So much for *Amadis* and its tribe. We are done with them, but not yet with their rivals. When the barber and curate united to destroy the harmful books of Don Quixote, they did not condemn to the stake all the volumes they found in the hidalgo's library. Among those which they recommended to grace was *Tirante el Blanco,* a " treasure of enchantment and mine of pastime," and particularly good for its tone of realism. It is very likely that modern Anglo-Saxon restlessness can hardly form so unbiased an opinion as the leisurely Spanish gravity of the sixteenth century, for in our eyes the curate's praise of this book seems slightly overdone. As a matter of fact *Tirante the White* has not plot enough to aspire to the rank of a genuine novel, though by its success in keeping its hero constantly in mind, it does preserve the necessary unity of action. This feature of the story might indeed give it the name of a biographical romance, like so many poems of the Breton cycle, since the erotic element in it does not appear until the second part of the narrative is reached. But if the truth may be told regarding Cervantes' favorable opinion . of the work, it seems quite clear to us that the great novelist found in *Tirante el Blanco* a predecessor of his own *Don Quixote*, and that the former is no less a parody on the genuine romances of chivalry than the latter. *Tirante* is more respectful and not so much of a burlesque, because in the middle of the fifteenth century—the approximate date of its composition—it might not have been safe to openly ridicule so cherished a story as the one of Amadis and Oriana. Whether or not this view is tenable each reader may decide for himself. Yet there are in *Tirante* so many points of resemblance to *Amadis* that our conclusion suggests itself. Either it parodied the popular chapbook, or else it furnished the latter with several novelistic elements which later on redounded greatly to *Amadis'* profit. What these elements are will appear from the analysis.

Tirante, a Breton noble on his way to London, runs across a hermit, William of Warwick, who is reading a French treatise on military art. At the approach of Tirante the hermit lays aside his book and tells him his history, already made known to literature by the poem, *Gui de War-wick*. The knight soon proceeds to London, where he mingles in court life, joins in celebrating St. John's Day, and performs many exploits at the ceremonies which attend the marriage of the English king with the princess of France. Though in the jousts Tirante receives enough wounds to kill a dozen men, he recovers from them all, while his adversaries have the additional sorrow of being hooted at for their lack of valor by the street urchins of the capital. Many descriptions interrupt the progress of events and give the author, a

Valencian noble, by name Martorell, a chance to display his facility. Thus, a funeral of one of Tirante's opponents is related in detail, combats with German knights are pictured at length, and a somewhat over-gallant explanation of the founding of the Order of the Garter is humorously given. But after the knight had practiced all the rules of chivalry which the hermit had revealed to him, and had reported his proficiency to his instructor, he turned his face toward the East, where he distinguished himself both as a warrior and a courtier. He delivers Rhodes from the assailing Genoese, and fills the office of lord high general adviser and arranger of battles and weddings. Turks, Moors, Byzantines, and Franks of all shades move to and fro on the scene. Even Arthur is summoned forth to aid the story, and mediæval traditions are freely drawn upon, among them the plot of *Éracle*, Gautier of Arras' *roman d'aventure*, whose fame seems to have been a lasting one.

Finally Constantinople is reached by the hero, and the love story begins. The imperial princess, Carmesina, coquets with Tirante, who replies in kind, while his jolly companions besiege the hearts of the ladies in waiting. Many tricks are played on unsuspecting courtiers, and the whole narrative descends to the very verge of the burlesque. A prime mover in the action, and the wit of the story, is the maid of the princess, Placerdemivida (Pleasure of My Life), whose practical jokes and free observations belong rather to the naturalist school in fiction. The frequent attempts of Tirante to gain Carmesina's favors are interspersed with scenes of jealousy, which are occasioned by the stratagems of a widow who is seeking to win the hero's affections, while all the time discourses on knighthood and honor are liberally thrown in. At last Tirante is tricked by the widow into believing that his mistress is unfaithful to him, and he leaves the court on an expedition against the Turks, without saying farewell to Carmesina.

But a storm drives his solitary ship on the African coast, where he is found by the King of Tremecen and welcomed to the royal household. He soon has an opportunity to show his gratitude by defending the king against his enemies, and then by converting both king and queen to Christianity. Placerdemivida, who had been carried to Africa with Tirante, there rises in the world, and becomes at length the ruler of a respectable kingdom. So when Constantinople is again in straits the two friends are able to bring a large army to its relief. Tirante is then pardoned by the princess, the Turks are of course defeated by him, and the marriage between hero and heroine finds no further obstacle. But suddenly, on the eve of the ceremony, Tirante succumbs to an attack of pleurisy, the emperor dies of grief on hearing the news, and the princess' life is cut short by despair.

After reading this curious tale we are compelled to believe that Martorell, its author, was not only a clever man but a bold one. The animus of the whole narrative is satire. Side by side with high-sounding theories of knightly honor are sketched the actual doings of the knights. They go out to fight the wicked, but indulge in love-making of the carnal sort much more than in single combats with their fellow-sinners. After Tirante's sojourn in London, where he did indeed joust most valiantly, he appears rather as a general commanding great armies, than as a knight-errant courting fame through the might of his own right arm alone. The other characters of the book are even inferior in tone to the hero. They possess naturally some good traits, but the qualities which they mainly display are of the commonplace, every-day order. Placerdemivida, who is next to Tirante in importance, is a genuine go-between, and plays a part which the Spanish drama developed later to so great an extent. The author must have been conscious of the low range of his conceptions, since at the end he kills off his respectable personages and leaves the future of the empire in charge of the unfaithful empress and her lover of low degree ; strokes of irony keenly perceptible to a public which had been nourished on the high ideals of *Amadis of Gaul.*

As to the exploits in the narrative, after the absurd exaggerations of Tirante's prowess and vitality at London, there are very few which do not belong to the world of fact.   Enchantments are entirely absent, excepting an absurd scene in which Arthur figures, and the deliverance of a maiden from a snake's form by means of a kiss—a favorite episode of the Arthurian legends.   Hardly a single giant appears on the scene.   No distressed girls or private individuals are avenged.   No castles are besieged or taken.   But when it comes to the plain details of battles, accidents, jokes, or love-making, *Tirante el Blanco* has no superiors in its century.   Its whole spirit is *bourgeois,* like the stories of Boccaccio or the inventions of Ariosto, and its ridicule of the aristocratic traditions, propagated by the romances of chivalry, is as unmistakable as the bent of *Don Quixote.* Skepticism is its very essence.   Why it did not destroy the faith of the people in their notions of knights-errant and chivalrous usages, can be understood only in the light of the fact that even to-day the seeming sway of realism in literature has in no way diminished the popular demand for romantic fiction, in which virtue always triumphs over vice. *Amadis de Gaula* had not yet risen to the dignity of a literary composition.   *Tirante el Blanco* found it still among the common people, and Martorell's shafts of satire glanced harmlessly away from the unpretentious chapbook.   A century and a half later, after the romances of chivalry had become the craze among the nobility and the educated classes, and were declining in favor, the plebeian, Cervantes, was able, by means of his greater talent, and with the aid of more favorable surroundings, to accomplish what the Valencian knight had attempted in vain.   It is also to be questioned whether, before the introduction of printing into Spain, Martorell's parody was known to any but his immediate friends. And its publication, in 1490, came at the wrong moment to influence public opinion.

For all Spain was then at the flood-tide of patriotic and religious exaltation. The common soldier and the knight were pressing onward toward the Alhambra in the full confidence of driving the infidel invader from his last foothold on Spanish soil. The fall of Granada consecrated *Amadis de Gaula* to the reverence of the whole redeemed nation. Ridicule and irony have no place in ages of enthusiasm, and Spanish enthusiasm was to be kept at a high pitch for several generations to come. Close on the recovery of Andalusia came the news of a new continent. A decade later Italy, the seat of the national faith, was practically annexed to the crown of Aragon. Another ten years had barely passed when the ruler of Burgundy and Flanders became the king of the united country, to be called not many months later to the Empire of Germany. The dominion of the world was almost a fact, and evident to each inhabitant of the peninsula. It was by the loyalty and valor of such knights as Amadis that this prosperity had been attained, and it was a genuine knight-errant who still sustained it in his very person before his people.

Charles V. was a paladin as well as a ruler. He honored the traditions of chivalry, and by the greatness of his power, and the elegance of his bearing, kept its spirit ever present before his subjects. Wars abroad and tournaments at home, celebrated with all the ceremony of the Middle Ages, and adorned with the splendors of a colonial empire, allowed no moment for the relaxation of chivalrous ideals among the Spanish nations. We cannot, therefore, wonder that the romances which had pictured such an existence of glory and honor were cherished and increased; that not only the family of Amadis was carried out to its remote descendants, but that also other races of heroes were created in emulation. To be sure the new narratives could only be imitations of the older, inasmuch as the latter themselves were devoid of a traditional background. But because of this absence of a previous existence in fact, the fancy of the author was all the more unrestricted in the composition of his works, and was rather incited to greater efforts through the knowledge that any interest which might be aroused by them would depend on the merits of his own inventions.

The most successful of these imitations of *Amadis de Gaula* is the series of novels celebrating the deeds of the Palmerin family, particularly the book which relates the fortunes of Palmerin of England. The series was started by the appearance of a story called *Palmerin de Oliva*, which seems to have been printed at Salamanca in 1511. Its author is unknown. The story is very much like that of *Amadis*, the hero Palmerin being the ante-legitimate son of Florendos, prince of Macedonia, and Griana, daughter of the emperor of Constantinople. The infant is exposed to its fate in the good old style, and is found by a hermit on a hill covered with palms and olives, from which vegetation it took its name. When grown to manhood the foundling leaves the good hermit in search of his parents, and does many mighty deeds, after which he is knighted by his father who, of course, does not recognize his offspring. Numerous adventures follow, in which magic plays an important part. Palmerin delivers the German emperor from his rebel vassals and wins the love of the imperial princess Polinarda, whose acquaintance he had previously made in a dream. All now goes well for a time. Palmerin adds to the budget of his fame exploits in England and along the Mediterranean. He visits even Babylon, and has the satisfaction of refusing the hand of the local princess. Now he returns to Germany for rest. But Polinarda's brother Trineus, who had accompanied Palmerin as far as the Mediterranean, had been lost in that region and had been enchanted, taking on the form of a dog. It was now necessary for our knight to seek him out, and on the way he frees his parents from the stake to which they had been condemned for murder. A birthmark makes him then known to his mother, and the emperor is glad to acknowledge him as his heir. He is not long now in disenchanting Trineus, espousing Polinarda, and becoming emperor of the East.

There is hardly anything in this romance which is new or striking, unless we consider it a novelty to introduce into the legends of chivalry certain tales of Greek mythology. For Trineus was treated somewhat like Ulysses' crew. We also find in *Palmerin de Oliva* a few traces of its native soil in the Moorish names, and in the combats which might very well have taken the duels of Moors and Spaniards for models. Otherwise there is no allusion to Spain in the book. Though the story was so commonplace, it had a fair success in the land of its birth, and was even carried into foreign countries. In France it was translated in 1546 by Jean Maugin. At Venice it was reprinted in the original and in an Italian version, and in England it was done into our tongue by the indefatigable Anthony Munday.

The popularity of *Palmerin de Oliva* in Spain was sufficient to give rise to a sequel, *Primaleon*, evidently by the same author, whose hero was the son of Palmerin and Polinarda. His half-brother Polendos, whose birth was the result of a stratagem on the part of his mother, the queen of Tharsus, comes in for a good share of its attention. Polendos begins his exploits and the novel by kicking an old woman down the palace steps, a proceeding which allows her to reveal to him his ancestry. Polendos is valiant, if not mild of manner, and on learning of what stock he was he starts off to make himself worthy of it. He fights with many opponents, and finally rescues his mistress Francelina, who had been enchanted in a castle by a dwarf and a giant.

Primaleon in the meantime had formed a close friendship with Edward of England, and had shown his prowess by slaying many knights sent against him by Gridoina to avenge herself for the death of her brother, the magician, at the hands of Palmerin de Oliva. Primaleon does even better than kill the servants of the lady. He gains access to her castle and enthrones himself in her affections, thanks to her lack of a previous acquaintance with his face.

Primaleon contains few interesting events, and its ideals are far removed from those of a true and perfect knight. Yet it suited the times well enough to receive the honor of translations into French, Italian, and English, and to be followed in Spanish by *Platir*, the story of the son of Primaleon and Gridoina. This sequel is of no particular merit, nor is a sequel to it, *Flotir* (known only by an Italian translation) of much account. From such rivals as these, who degenerated so speedily, Amadis had nothing to fear. Their exploits were but repetitions of his, their notions of honor, loyalty, and knight-errantry were on a much lower plane than his, and the literary dress in which they appeared before the public was lacking in both texture and color. The time for any genuine inspiration in the romances of chivalry had evidently passed. Neither the descendants of Amadis nor the scions of this new family had attained sufficient eminence to revive the stories of feudalism ; and the propagation of both races had nearly ceased, when an offshoot of the Palmerin dynasty suddenly imparted to his family a glory and distinction second only to the fame of the original history of Amadis of Gaul.

This new hero who was to retrieve the fortunes of his house, and with them reflect the golden days of the romances of chivalry, was a son of Edward of England by Flerida, daughter of Palmerin de Oliva. From his double line of descent he received his name, Palmerin of England. The book which recounts his achievements was curiously enough

in Portuguese, like the prototype of *Amadis*, and was probably written by Francisco de Moraes, a Portuguese noble
who had been attached to the embassy at the French court,
and who wove into his narrative one of his own personal
experiences in Paris. Moraes may have composed his work
between the years 1540 and 1548, but if this is so (as there
seems little ground for doubting) the original copy was lost,
and the story has been preserved to us in a Spanish version
of the years 1547–48, which was made by Luis Hurtado, a
poet of Toledo possessed of considerable literary reputation. The novel as we now have it is in two distinct parts,
and offers a constant parallel to the story of Amadis. The
author was also well read in the deeds of the Palmerin
family, as his frequent reference to *Palmerin de Oliva* and
Primaleon clearly shows.

The romance begins with a hunt organized by the English king, Duardos (Edward). Engrossed in the pursuit of
a wild boar, the monarch reaches the castle of the giantess
Eutropa, whose brother had been slain some time before by
Palmerin de Oliva. The king is detained here for a while,
but succeeds finally in winning the friendship of Eutropa's
brother, the giant Dramuziando, a good and courteous specimen of his race. Meanwhile the queen, Flerida, who had
gone in search of her husband, has given birth in a forest
to twins. These were forthwith carried off by a wild man,
attended by two lions, and their lives saved by the wife of
the savage. Ten years have flown. One of the twins,
Florian, has been found in the woods by a knight and
carried to London, where Flerida brings him up under the
name of the Child of the Desert. The other twin, Palmerin, with his foster-brother, Selvian, is in his turn carried
to Constantinople in Polendos' ship, where he receives cre-
dentials from the Lady of the Lake, is knighted, and elects
to serve Polinarda, Primaleon's daughter, who consequently
girds him with his sword. In a tournament which soon

takes place much fame is won by a strange knight, wearing on his shield the picture of a savage man leading two lions. Not long afterward Polinarda, irritated by the freedom of Palmerin in the avowal of his affections to her, forbids him to come again into her presence, and he leaves the court in despair.

All the heroes have now become knights-errant, and seek adventures, which arrive thick and fast, portrayed with much elegance of description. The servants of the giantess Eutropa are untiring in their efforts to get revenge against the Palmerin family, by pitting the heroes against one another. In this way, Palmerin, who has at length reached England, fights his brother, not knowing him in his disguise as Knight of the Savage Man. The heroes find a defender against Eutropa's tricks in the magician Daliarte of the Dark Valley. The objective point of all the champions is still Dramuziando's castle, where Edward has been so long confined. Here the giant has forced his prisoners to defend his home, and as each new assailant arrives some captive friend overcomes him and adds him to the others. Primaleon even is defeated by the giant in person, but this misfortune paves the way to the end. For the Knight of the Savage comes up to release his relative, overthrows all the captives in turn, and is about to subdue Dramuziando, his last opponent, when Daliarte spirits him away, in order to reserve the honor of the final deliverance for Palmerin, who soon after takes the castle and frees all the knights.

Here ends the first part of the story. In its plan one may easily see how it won for itself the favor of the public. The plot is so distinct. The center of all action is the castle of Dramuziando, and by the successive arrival of all the knights before its gates the romance gains a unity to which *Amadis* itself was a stranger. Then the interest is kept up by the delay in the punishment of the wicked and the triumph of the truly good. Evil succeeds for a time, and ·

the outcome of the struggle is uncertain until the curtain falls on the last scene. In the recital of exploits there are more combats left undecided than in *Amadis*, more are stopped by friendly intervention, and more are animated by fervent apostrophes to lady-loves. In addition to this diversity of incident, *Palmerin de Inglaterra* surpasses its model in variety of description, in love for natural scenery, and in a pleasing absence of moral reflections. Yet *Palmerin* lacks the vigor and freshness of *Amadis*, its artlessness and directness. More softened and refined, the tone of the later novel is also less inspiring and elevating. Without any foundation in popular tradition it was unavoidable that *Palmerin* should repeat what had already been said. Its crises are almost parallel to those in *Amadis*, and its central figure, the giant's castle, had already been made a familiar invention by the *Orlando Furioso*.

The second part of this romance cannot claim the merits of composition possessed by the first. The plan of the narrative is less definite and artistic, and there is too much magic in the frequent use of the black cloud and the book. Instead of exhortations to respect the weaker sex there are many slurs on woman inserted in the most unexpected places, and evidently prompted by the personal animus of the author. The changed relation of lover to mistress, already hinted at in the first part, has here been carried to an extreme. The knight is still humble and obedient, but the lady has become harsh and overbearing without a plausible reason. She claims to be offended by the very thought of service done her, and the slight favors she consents to bestow are most grudgingly granted. It is quite probable that this feature was strengthened in Moraes' work by the example of the pastoral novels, since he follows the latter in the introduction of his private mishaps, and very likely may have emphasized after their manner the coldness of his heroines. This would seem to be quite clearly proven by the fact that Moraes did borrow from the pastorals certain traits of composition, as the siestas which his characters enjoyed, and carving the names of the lovers in the bark of trees. He also may have been acquainted with some of the Greek novels, which were beginning at this time to attract the notice of modern readers, for in the action of *Palmerin of England* we find Dame Fortune to be a powerful factor. The story differs also from previous romances of chivalry in the definiteness of its topography.

In the second part of *Palmerin* there are two centers of interest—two pivots for the plot. The one is the castle of Almourol, in Portugal, where dwells the beautiful Miraguarda, whose portrait on a shield hanging from the walls of the fortress is to be defended against all gainsayers, by those knights who have come under the spell of her charms. In the location of this castle appears for the first time any mention of the Spanish peninsula as a theater of events. The other center of interest is Constantinople, as usual. This capital is once more attacked by all the forces of the infidels, and is again protected by the flower of Christian chivalry. The two rallying-points—the one romantic, the other historical—are connected in turn by the deeds which the same knights perform at both. In inventing this plan Moraes can certainly not be accused of being wanting in constructive ability. The story in the second part goes on with an account of court life in London, its joustings and festivities, together with Daliarte's revelation of the birth of the brothers, a visit to the cave of the Savage, and an excursion to Dramuziando's castle. The beauty of Miraguarda of Portugal becomes noised abroad, and Florendos is the first to appear as her champion. Palmerin is reserved for greater deeds. As he leaves England he is carried away in a boat to Perilous Island, where Eutropa has prepared many enchantments to subdue him. But he dispels these by his courage and loyalty, releases the knights whom they have

held in bondage, and makes so thorough work of the giantess'
rule that he drives Eutropa to suicide. This episode contains the best features of the novel, both in conception and
composition. Palmerin, on landing at the Island, is immediately confronted with all the creations of magic. He first
comes upon a fountain guarded by two lions and two tigers,
which, for a time, fill him with terror, and for the moment
force him to retreat :

"Wherefore having gone back a short distance he began
to be ashamed, so much so that his duty stirred and incited
him, so that he turned about. And with shield on arm
and sword in hand he came up to one of the corners
of the beautiful and limpid fountain. There one of the
tigers received him most valiantly. For with one clean
leap he jumped at the shield of the knight, bending it
toward himself with so great a might that the straps broke,
to which it was bound, and left the knight without a shield.
Which made him so angry and full of wrath that he did not
fail to burden the beast in such a way as to wound him in
one of his legs, and so severely that the tiger could not
move about freely. But to his aid came the other three
animals, and so furiously that Palmerin thought this adventure one of the most fearful he had ever undergone.
However, seeing the danger which presented itself to him,
he did not wish to appear afraid : but turned on one of the
lions, which was in advance of the others, and cut off his
two paws so that he fell to the ground. Then he stooped
down to take up his shield which the tiger had left. But
the other lion came to attack him, and approached so near
that he seized him by the helmet, pulling it toward himself
with so much force that he tore it from him so roughly that
the knight fell forward on his hands. And thus, as he was
leaning forward, the tiger seized him, and hugged him so
tightly in his paws that, without the strength of his mail, he
would have torn the good knight to pieces, but he, seeing

himself reduced to such straits, gave him a thrust through the heart. Whereat the tiger fell prostrate. And seeing this, the lion which had torn off the helmet did not fail to approach the prince, who quickly put forward his shield, upon which the lion placed his two paws, and Palmerin gave him a sword-thrust below, so powerful that his bowels gushed out and he fell dead at his feet. But still he had not made the place so safe that one would dare to drink at the fountain. For it was still guarded by the tiger whose paw he had almost cut off at the beginning. . ." And so on until the last animal is dispatched and a new trial of shadowy horsemen meets our hero.

The delight of the author in such descriptions leads him to the constant invention of new ones. Particularly does he favor bridge fights, with which he blocks up all the highways of western Europe. After the exploits above narrated he leads Palmerin, with Daliarte as a guide, to the castle of Almourol on the banks of the Tagus, a stream which Moraes eulogizes with patriotic fervor. There Palmerin finds Florendos acting as Miraguarda's champion, defeats him in a joust before her eyes, and calls down her anger on her luckless knight. Heartbroken at his lady's disdain, Florendos wanders off and becomes the companion of a sorrowing shepherd—the hero of the pastoral stories which were now coming into prominence. Soon afterward Dramuziando reaches Almourol and offers to defend Miraguarda's shield. Against him all the lesser lights of the romance ride in vain, until the adventures at this place are brought to an unwelcome end by the theft of the shield by the pagan Albayzar of Babylon, who had been urged on by his mistress to this unchivalrous action. Albayzar, however, is not allowed to rest with his booty, but is forced to sustain many combats, while during his absence from Babylon his lady, Targiana, is hotly wooed by the prince Florian, who has reached that place after many warlike and amorous exploits. For Florian is the Galaor of *Palmerin de Inglaterra*, just as his brother is its Amadis.

With the filching of Miraguarda's shield the scene of action shifts gradually to the East, and after a time settles down at Constantinople. There Albayzar appears with the shield of Targiana also, which he places by the side of Miraguarda's and challenges to a trial at arms all unbelievers in the superior loveliness of his mistress. A condition of the combat is that his opponents should bear on their shields the portraits of the ladies whom they champion. As each is vanquished by Albayzar his shield, with its portrait, goes to join the trophies won for Targiana. So the miscreant overcomes the devout and accumulates his gallery of European beauties, until one fine day there enters the lists a knight clad in black armor pictured with flames, and carrying a shield having flames on a black field. But because the shield has upon its surface no portrait Albayzar refuses to joust with its owner. Whereupon the black knight makes reply :

"'Sir knight, you ask much of him who has little power. For if the shield which I present is not accompanied by that wnich you demand and which I would fain desire, it is for nothing else than to make it resemble the life of him who carries it ; thereby informing you that I have seen a time when I could have shown upon it a likeness, as the condition of your jousting wishes ; which would have given you food for thought and to me a heart to but little stand in fear of you. But at present I can show you only this somber color in which you see me clothed, while begging you to pardon me. For it is the larger part of that which fortune has left me.' 'Sir knight,' answered Albayzar, 'I would indeed that the face with which you threaten me were in your hands. For then I would make you know that I carry another which all the faces in the world do envy. However, seeing that the emperor of this state long ago stayed his progress to look upon you, let us do our knightly duty. For the honorableness of your words and the chagrin which you feel have abundantly satisfied me.'"

Thus with fine speeches and hard blows the exploits of Almourol are renewed at the capital of the East. As all the knights had first found their way to the banks of the Tagus, so now they approach, from all directions, the shores of the Bosphorus. Joust succeeds joust, and festivities close the daily tournaments. But Moraes is not content with portraying combats alone. The more subtle inventions of *Amadis* tempt him to friendly rivalry, while one episode on which he evidently spent much effort, and by which he set great store, is a duplicate to the trial of chastity in *Amadis*. He tells how once on a time a noble of Thrace had killed his daughter's lover and had sent her his heart in a cup. The heartbroken girl fills the cup with her tears and then leaps from the castle window to her death. The King of Thrace, who is also a magician, gets possession of the cup, congeals in it the tears, and offers his enchanted daughter, Lionarda, to the knight who can melt them. The successful man must be both brave and faithful in love. In the trial at Constantinople all fail, and Florendos is even set on fire by the cup. But Palmerin breaks the spell at last, frees the princess, and, being provided with an eligible partner himself, turns this additional blessing over to Florian.

The story now returns to the usual theme of knight-errantry. Duels and wars multiply. Particular attention is paid to a campaign in Navarre, where Florendos and Albayzar unite against its nobles, who for some reason which does not come to the surface are decidedly in ill repute with our author. Miraguarda's shield is won back by Florendos after many adventures, and Albayzar marries Targiana, whom Florian had deserted. Finally a series of weddings invite the presence of all the Christian knights to Constantinople, while the Turks, stirred up by Albayzar, attack the city. Bloody battles follow in which fortune favors now the one and now the other side. Many heroes are slain, the ladies of the court are removed by Daliarte to Perilous Island, and the city is razed to the ground. After several reverses the despair of the faithful and the valor of Dramuziando, their ally, accomplish the total rout of the pagans. Constantinople is rebuilt, but Perilous Island remains enchanted and invisible.

The merits of *Palmerin de Inglaterra* are sufficient to make it worth our while to read it at the present stage of novelistic decadence, though we may not share, after all, the eulogistic enthusiasm of the curate in *Don Quixote*. Its movement is lively, its solution is kept well in abeyance, its episodes are well arranged, and many of its scenes are excellently developed. And there is one feature in it which deserves especial mention. It is the greater regard for the setting of the story. Indeed, in the definiteness of its scenes of action Moraes' romance may be said to prepare the way for the actual portrayal of real events. And the story leaves us with the feeling that the exploits in *Palmerin* might possibly be facts, whereas we know that all the happenings in the shady topography of *Amadis* are impossible. From the moment natural scenery is sketched, and geography plays a part in the story, we can fancy that characters of flesh and blood may perform the tasks assigned to the creations of the fancy. So that immediately in the footsteps of *Palmerin* might come a novel which would relate the deeds of men, celebrated in the world's past, and would conform to historical data. Thus the historical novel would be born, and the traditional magic of the Middle Ages, which intervenes in the romances of chivalry, like a *deus ex machina*, or the Tyche of the Greeks, would give way to a more natural agent in the solution of crises, to wit, the blunders or the foresight of the actors themselves. *Palmerin*, to be sure, comes nearer the truth, regarding the infidel attacks on Constantinople, than does any of its successors, but in the rôles of its kings and generals it is as far from real life as the most extravagant among the romances. A little more courage on the part of its author and he would have had the credit of creating a new type of novel. But he stopped short on the way, and when the romance of chivalry passed from his fatherland into France, it fell into the hands of a finical few who delighted in retaining its obscurity and its unreality. In becoming in a foreign land the property of the educated classes exclusively, the modern novel of erotic adventure was deprived of its foundation of realism, or at least of the belief in its reality, on which it rested while among the Spanish people, and thus lost the advantage which it would have gained from the intellectual progress of its own proper constituency. In the hands of the *précieuses* of the seventeenth century it grew stale and insipid like themselves, and when they had converted it into the heroic-gallant novel of their coterie, the vigor and freshness of its original current was found to be absorbed in the sands of the literary desert which bounded the Sea of Tendre.

Of course *Palmerin* is not all merit. Its faults are numerous and evident. There are too many heroes in it, the outcome of the larger number of its adventures is known in advance, and its enchantments are feeble imitations of what had gone before. Having no traditional basis it appealed only to a limited set of readers, and very probably never penetrated to the common people who had cherished the deeds of Amadis so long and so faithfully. It therefore had no influence, or but little, in reviving the declining interest in the romances of chivalry, and it seems to have had no effect at all on the French fiction begotten by *Amadis.* Yet there is one favorite theme of the seventeenth century novel, which Moraes, judging by his *Palmerin,* could have fathered quite as well as Montalvo—the liking for that species of discourse which goes under the name of courtly conversations. We have seen how deferential were the knights in *Palmerin* to one another, but we should read the account of the meeting of the prince with his mistress Polinarda. When this is compared with the interviews of Amadis and Oriana it is clear that, in the half century or more between the two novels, the knights have become more loquacious and better exercised in subtle discourse :

"'My lady, if the happiness of my fortunes has kept this reward for me to put an end to my labors, I shall have no occasion to complain, being very well assured that your presence is able to make me forget all the vexations which I have suffered up to this time. For which I remain under obligations to Love, toward whom I have always been faithful and obedient, so that by his favor I have been led to this place, where I receive unspeakable contentment as a reward for my labors, which I find of little importance compared with the good that presents itself before my eyes, so great an honor that I esteem myself under perpetual obligations ; yet I would much wish that this great obedience should not put undue restraints upon me. Assuring you, my lady, that Fortune has always availed me at the time when I wished the more to hold your greatness in high repute and to esteem it, which will not be satisfied in seeing me deprived of liberty'"—and so on indefinitely. We can hardly wonder that the princess manifested considerable impatience at this verbosity, and had to be exhausted by a second installment of relative clauses before she would condescend to grant the boon so oratorically desired, namely, to graciously allow her faithful servant to salute her imperial hand. Yet harangues like these and love-making by rhetoric were the delight of polite society long after the romances of chivalry had passed away. Reduplications of words and periods between the leading characters, and particularly between the hero and heroine, are one of their most abiding legacies to romantic fiction.

There is not much to be said regarding the further history

of the Palmerin family. Sequels to *Palmerin de Inglaterra* were published in Spain, but met with little favor. In France the romance soon appeared (1552–53) in a translation by Jacques Vincent, dedicated to Diana of Poitiers. In 1555 an Italian translation was published, and in 1567 Moraes himself gave it once more a Portuguese dress. Munday, as usual, did it into English from the French of Vincent. On French soil also Chapuis, a professional translator, gave it a sequel called *Darinel*, after a son of Primaleon. But in spite of this attempt to acclimate the series in a northern atmosphere, no new life entered into the Palmerin family as it had into the race of Amadis. Nor at home did the heroes of this house ever enjoy the popularity of their older models, at least so far as the test of few or many editions may prove. The heyday of the romance of chivalry in the peninsula was during the reign of Charles V., the last of the knights-errant. With the rule of the gloomy and retiring Philip II. a change came over the popular fiction of Spain, very like that alteration in the tone of French literature under Louis XI. The aristocratic story of courtly life passed away with the decay of the nobility. The popular adoration for the feudal chieftains, who had led the long onset of the nation against the Moors, was undermined by the rise of the *bourgeois* class, which had come into greater prominence from the discovery of America and the conquests of the Empire. The first half of the sixteenth century was for Spain its crowning period of power and glory, and the romance of chivalry, which eulogized those qualities that were the mainsprings of national expansion, retained its hold on the imagination of the people long after the state of society which produced it had passed away, and long after the exhaustion of its own original and traditional material. But after the sixth decade of the century, when the tide of temporal prosperity was fast ebbing, and the armies of the nation were retreating from their outposts in every land, when the poverty, which had succeeded the sudden wealth caused by the inflow of the precious metals from the colonies of the West, no longer secretly lurked in the cabins of the farm-hands, but was invading in full light of day the old castles of Castile, at this time of dishonor and want, Spain had no heart to blind herself with fresh visions of fanciful glory. The hard reality of national decay was bearing down with its full weight on the imaginations of the people, and the new and disagreeable conditions of private and public existence demanded new representatives in fiction.

Yet we must not conclude that the romance of chivalry willingly relaxed the powerful grasp it had so long maintained on the minds of the nation. Though its two great families had ceased to awaken popular interest in their descendants of later generations, it was possible that other heroes, whose exploits should not come into competition with those of Amadis and Palmerin, might be welcome on their own account. So the novel of erotic adventure was continued for another score of years, and as many as forty more specimens of it sought a permanent place in the affections of the readers of fiction. Most of these works, however, failed completely in their desires. So to enumerate them here would be of little profit, and to analyze them less. Still, there is one among them which stands out from its fellows, as being not only the best of them all, or rather the least poor, but also as having obtained the honor of a somewhat extended criticism by the curate of *Don Quixote.* This romance is *Don Belianis de Grecia*, written in 1547 by Jeronimo Fernandez, a native of Madrid, and expanded later on, so that by 1587 it was composed of four parts, and contained some eight hundred octavo pages.

It tells how Belianis, son of Beliano, emperor of Greece, and of the Spanish princess, Clarinda, distinguished himself at the early age of twelve by killing a lion and a giant.

Afterward he and his friend Arfileo, prince of Hungary, were entertained by a maiden who dwelt in a cave. But Belianis had brothers whom he must find, and so he went in search of them, attended by the maiden. On his way— strewn with many combats—the maiden tells him of the beauty of Florisbella, princess of Persia. After Belianis has been deemed worthy of the ceremony of knighthood on account of his deeds, he rescues his father from peril—not being recognized, of course—and proceeds to Persia, where he undergoes all kinds of trials in joustings, abductions, magic spells, enchanted fountains, and the like. He delivers the princess from her enemies, fights his father, again unknown to him, and accomplishes all the feats familiar to the romances of chivalry. Under the pseudonym of Knight of the Basilisk he is entertained by kings and receives flattering attention from queens and princesses; and in all his career the wise Belonia is his ever-present aid, and the epic account of the wars of the Greeks and Trojans his constant stimulus. After fighting unawares with one of his brothers, Belianis wins Florisbella's love, but is immediately obliged to leave her in order to avenge a suppliant. During his absence the emperor of Trebizond, by demanding the hand of the princess, starts a new series of obstacles to her happy union. General wars ensue, in which Babylon is the center of events, until the prowess of our knight compels the revelation of his ancestry, and all points to a speedy solution, when suddenly every one of the princesses is stolen away, and the author takes breath for a while, in promising a sequel which never appeared.

So we do not yet know how it fared with Belianis and his lady-love, and this is little loss to us, as is plain from what we do know about him. For the author had no idea of plan or composition. The episodes of the book are strung together with little sequence, and the stuff of which they are made is not at all new. The memory of the deeds of

Amadis and Palmerin was too strong with Fernandez for the success of his own story, and in imitating his predecessors he had not sufficient talent to improve on them. He is prolix also, is overfond of letters and conversations, and delights to a wearisome extent in disguised characters. That the curate should have taken the trouble to save him from the pyre of Don Quixote's library is, perhaps, to be explained by his late date, and by a popularity revealed in the successive expansions of the book. But no other proof that the romances of chivalry had run out, and that the way was fully prepared for Cervantes' satire of them, is needed, than the very existence of such a conglomeration as this last exponent of their ideas, *Don Belianis de Grecia.*

It is well understood at the present day that the change in the tendencies of Spanish literature in the last half of the sixteenth century was not due to the mere alteration of the social condition of the country. Out of the wars against the Moors of Andalusia and the South, and the stalwart piety which those wars had fostered, had arisen a practical organization of the religious sentiment of the nation, which in process of time became a powerful instrument in the hands of the central government for the discomfiture of its more independent subjects, and the establishment of its unquestioned sway among them. The hold on the popular mind of this perfected administrative machine has never been questioned It did not stop with the exercise of civil jurisdiction, or with the defense of the true faith against the inroads of heresy. It investigated private life and pried into the secrets of individual thought as well, while of course the favorite literature of both nobles and *bourgeois* came within its assumed field of activity.

As early as the fourth decade of the sixteenth century, the religious guides of Spain sought to adapt to their own ends the universal passion for the romances of chivalry. In 1543, or thereabouts, they tried the popular taste with the publication of a novel enjoining piety and devotion, but composed after the pattern of *Amadis* or *Palmerin.* This story, called *Lepolemo,* from the name of its hero, tells how the son of the emperor of Germany was stolen away to Africa while but a child, and how he was brought up among the infidels. When grown to manhood he gained great fame at the court of the sultan, under the title of the Knight of the Cross, from a cross which had been marked on his shoulders in early boyhood. He was still a Christian, and refused to turn Moslem even to win the hand of the sultan's daughter. On the contrary he returns to Africa in search of his old nurse, and experiences many adventures; is made a prisoner, frees his parents, who had been captured on their way to Jerusalem, and suffers all manner of hardships. Finally he reaches France, wrests Calais from the English, is entertained by the dauphin—whom he had liberated from a Moslem prison of the East some time before— falls in love with Andriana, the royal princess, and marries her after having been recognized by his parents.

The remarkable thing in all this narrative is not so much its devout spirit as the fact that hardly an adventure is described which is not a possible one. No tournaments are held in *Lepolemo,* the enchantments it recounts are few, its topography is real. In these particulars it bears a close resemblance to *Palmerin de Inglaterra.* Yet to the reader this zealous defender of the faith seems a conscious imitator of the old heroes of chivalry, but in a kind of pious parody. The knight's parents, for instance, are on their way to the Holy Land, not to interview Persian beauties and combat Oriental magic, but to assuage by a pilgrimage the grief they felt for the loss of their son. And instead of dwarfs and maidens and Urganda, who carry the letters and tell the news in the traditional stories, we find here chaplains and friars acting as their substitutes. But such as it was, the religious departure in *Lepolemo* aroused imitators later on, and called out the inevitable sequel to itself, which, strange to say, did not uphold the principle at the foundation of the original. For *Leandro el Bel*, published in 1562 by Pedro Luxan, returns to the style of the regular romances. Leandro, who is the son of Lepolemo, goes through the same series of adventures as Palmerin of England, unless perhaps Leandro's are more unreal. And there is no moral purpose whatever, either in the episodes of the story or in its solution with the marriage of the hero to the daughter of the Eastern emperor. So we may infer that Luxan, who also claims to be the author of the twelfth book of *Amadis*, has perhaps been guilty of a little satire in thus perverting the moral intent of his predecessor.

The Church, however, was not to be rebuffed by the ill success of this first venture in pious romancing, and in the palmy days of the Inquisition it returned to the charge more than once. But these new ventures differed decidedly from the first in the material out of which they were made. *Lepolemo* was content with giving a religious bent to genuine exploits of chivalry, and with the introduction of a few minor characters in clerical dress, but the religious romances which followed this pioneer, during the subsequent decades of the century, were more directly doctrinal. The earliest of them, and one of the best, appeared in 1554 at Antwerp, at that time under Spanish rule. It is called *La Caballeria Celestial*, and was written by a certain Hieronimo de San Pedro. ·In a letter to the reader the author states that the characters in his romance will not be Merlin, Urganda, Amadis, Tirante, Oriana, or Carmesina, but lovers of the truth and holy women. The subject of the book is taken from the Old Testament, and its contents are divided into " marvels " instead of into chapters. The narrative begins with the creation of the world and of a Round Table, occupied by both earthly and heavenly knights. Angels are naturally the members of the latter class. After the fall of one of them, Lucifer, Prince Adam is engaged in a war with the Knight of the Serpent. In this way the narrative goes on, setting before us various Scriptural events, until it reaches King Hezekiah, who finally conquers the Knight of the Serpent, and thereby ends the romance.

La Caballeria Celestial does not fall far short of an allegory, for besides the presentation of Biblical personages, and evil and good angels in the rôle of mediæval champions, it contains two actual personifications, Allegory and Moralizing, whose office it is to point out the religious doctrine which each episode is intended to convey. So we have a mixture of history and of fancy that may have been edifying to the subjects of Philip II., but which does not stir the pulse overmuch at the present day. Nor indeed is there any evidence to indicate that this romance, and others of its kind, were ever in demand in ascetic Spain of the sixteenth century. The religious novels, in spite of the temporal might back of them, rarely received the honor of a second edition, while the genuine romances of chivalry survived all imitations, and all attempts at repression on the part of the state. Edicts were promulgated forbidding their exportation to the colonies, on the ground of their being pernicious literature, and petitions were presented to the crown asking that their sale at home be prohibited. Yet notwithstanding all attacks from the clergy, and all the competition of the rising pastoral and *picaresco* novels, and more fatal than all enmity from without, notwithstanding their own internal decline, the long line of volumes which celebrated the fame of the race of Amadis and Palmerin kept their hold on the mass of the Spanish people many years after the vogue of their rivals had passed away. Cervantes' satire marks their downfall with the more intelligent classes only, and booksellers still found profit in new editions of the stories he had ridiculed, even when Don Quixote had become as familiar a knight as Amadis.

To be sure, this fact is an ever-present one in the history of fiction, that whatever is aristocratic or assumedly so, whatever is unreal, romantic, punishes vice and upholds virtue, takes the mind out of the narrow rut of daily existence, and diverts it by exciting the fancy and by picturing what might be rather than what is, that the very stories which ignore toil and drudgery, or pass lightly and hopefully over their unwelcome attributes, in a word, ideal fiction, will be read by the large majority of readers, if not by the most intelligent, and will outlast all changes in fashion, whim, or style. And thus it was with the romances of chivalry even in the Spain of Philip II.

CHAPTER VII.

THE ITALIAN PASTORAL, NARRATIVE AND DRAMATIC.

IT seems rather late in the day to be talking about pastoral literature. The march of man has left all that sort of thing so far behind. No one retires in this present epoch to remote Arcadian glens to commune with nymphs, or sport with Pan and his wanton train. Naiads, nereids, satyrs, Diana and her maidens, all have ceased to allure mortals to their rustic abodes, and when humanity seeks nature now it is for relaxation and calm repose. The forests are merely trees and underbrush, the river banks turf and flowers. To give them inhabitants is to violate the principle of modern recreation, release from thinking and from social intercourse. Yet the pastoral idea has survived in art to some extent. The school of Boucher and Watteau in painting, and tapestries adorned with woodland scenes, retain some hold still on the public taste, while sculpture continually renews itself through the ideal outlines of classic forms. But in literature there is not a trace of this old-time fashion. The return to nature of Rousseau and St. Pierre was prompted by political beliefs rather than by a disgust for the world's corruption, while *Atala*, *René*, and the effusions of the whole romantic school lent to natural scenery the subjective coloring of their own emotions. To-day the storm has passed and the outer world has reappeared calm before the gaze of mankind. It neither is required to reflect the turmoil of human passions, nor supposed to be alive with the creatures of man's idle fancies, for the present generation desires a nature absolutely peaceful, unruffled by the personification of even her own attributes.

It is therefore a practical impossibility for us, cosmopolitans and latter-day as we are, to appreciate the feelings of the more localized inhabitants of the Peloponnesus and the islands of the Mediterranean in regard to fostering nature. The ancient Romans themselves did not enter into these views even with all their striving after pastoral sentiment. Nor can we sympathize fully, in the midst of our progress in civilization, with the more recent enthusiasm with which the descendants of the Romans greeted the renewal of the pastoral idea in Italy under the Medici. Yet the cause of their ardor is clear. The overwrought minds of the promotors of the Renaissance sought relief from the failure of their ideals in a nature which appealed to them by its absence of all art and culture, just as the heroes of romanticism looked to it for a response to their wild longing to overturn the whole universe. We can understand the desires of both these generations. We can share to some extent the spirit of the latter, for we still experience the results of its struggles; but the surroundings of renascent Florence or Rome are in no direct communication with our own environment, and the period of discouragement for the future of humanity is still so remote, that the despairing records of past failures appeal to our minds only as facts in the historical expression of thought by literature. It is therefore as literary history only that this chapter and its successor can be of interest to the reader.

The development of the pastoral in Italy corresponds quite closely in time to the evolution of the romance of chivalry in Spain. Here, however, the likeness begins and ends. For the romance of chivalry is a product of the Middle Ages. It portrays the feudal ideal, and its constituent elements were expressed in the new vernaculars of Europe. But the pastoral, so far as its career in Italy is

concerned, reaches back into the life of antiquity, and its
forerunners spoke in the Latin tongue. The romance of
chivalry also, though aristocratic in tone, was popular in the
widest sense of that word. It represented the accumulation
of national traditions, which had been fostered by the people
no less than by the nobles, and it had circulated among all
classes of society long before it claimed any standing as
literature.

But the Italian pastoral went through a very different
development. It was not in the least popular, because it
was unknown to the people. It grew up among students of
antiquity, literary men by profession, who cultivated it
sporadically and as an exercise in Latinity. Consequently its
development was slow and uncertain. Occasionally such
writers as Boccaccio, who considered his mother tongue a
more natural vehicle for the expression of ideas than the
conventional Latin, turned their attention to these survivals
of Roman poetry, and gave them a modern dress and a
more national setting. In this way Italian legends entered
into the formation of the pastoral, and combined with the
material inherited from the ancients to make up a composite
literature, half learned, half popular, which obtained a wider
circle of readers than the Latin eclogues of the humanists
could expect. Yet, in spite of the infusion of this element
of folk tradition, the Italian pastoral in its literary form
remained wholly artistic both in its conception and in the
treatment it received. It was therefore highborn in sentiment, not after the manner of the romance of chivalry in
celebrating people of noble birth only, but highborn in its
appeal to refined and cultivated feelings, to a nobility of
education rather than an aristocracy of blood. For this
reason the Italian pastoral throughout its whole existence
continued to be the peculiar diversion and property of the
literary circles of Italian society.

Before the appearance of the pastoral in mediæval Italy,

rural life had been the theme of a distinct kind of lyric poetry in France and Provence. The *pastourelles*, as they were called, set their action in natural scenery, and made shepherds and shepherdesses the actors of the story. Soon, however, the shepherd was replaced by the court gallant, and the plot of the poem weakened to a mere love episode. The *pastourelles* were very much in favor with all classes of society, and quickly spread from France to her Romance neighbors of the South. In Italy they very likely gave rise to the first musical operas as early as the last half of the thirteenth century, but in no way do they appear to have affected the wholly classical material of the Italian pastoral.

Nor did the pastoral notion of the Greek novel have anything to do with this later application of the idea to fiction. Whatever was known of the Greco-Roman novelists in the Middle Ages was confined wholly to the stories of erotic adventure. *Daphnis and Chloe* attracted attention only in the later years of the Renaissance. Yet the predecessors of Longus, the elegiac poets of the Hellenistic period, were discovered early in the revival of learning by the collectors of the Italian courts, and appear to have served as models for one kind of pastoral composition, the dramatic. But with the other kind, the narrative, or more strictly speaking the narrative-lyric, Greek authors and Greek literature had nothing whatever to do. It was born into the modern world before Greek manuscripts had come out of their hiding places, or the Greek tongue had been taught to the dialecticians of Bologna. So the pedigree of the Italian narrative pastoral is direct and easily traced. It is the legitimate descendant of Latin pastoral poetry, whether mediæval or classical, and its great master in both epochs was Virgil. The *Eclogues* of this poet from the birth of Dante to the death of Sannazaro were the models for all bucolic poems among the humanists; and directly through his own works, and indirectly through the imitations of his disciples, Virgil's conception of nature became also the conception of the pastoral narratives in the vernacular.

The conditions which gave rise to the revival of the pastoral idea in mediæval Italy were not like those which fostered it in Rome of the Cæsars. In the latter it was the result of an endeavor to turn away the mind from intrigue and corruption to the contemplation of a primitive simplicity, untainted by the refinements of civilization. With Boccaccio and Sannazaro, the fathers of the modern narrative pastoral, the portrayal of rustic life was mainly an æsthetic diversion. In their hands pastoral writing was purely a branch of literature to be cultivated for its own sake, with no moral object in view. Or, if they had any subjective motive for their theories, it extended no further, and was no more serious, than to represent in disguise certain episodes of their own lives. In this notion their teacher, Virgil, had set them a well-known example. And then Boccaccio may possibly have had also an allegorical purpose in view, but Sannazaro was probably mainly influenced by literary fashion, and may not be accused of any ulterior objects.

So much for the narrative pastoral. With the dramatic, which was confined almost entirely to Italy of the sixteenth century, the conditions were the same as those which inspired the poets of decadent Greece. The revival of learning had come, the renaissance of art had followed. Style and taste had been elevated and purified, erudition had ceased to be a rarity. Yet with all this intellectual quickening, and with all the improvement in the direction of the senses, no moral foundation had been laid for the firm abiding of lofty aspirations. State and people had come far short of the standard set for them by the humanists and artists of the first period of the awakening. The rulers of the sixteenth century practiced the administrative principles illustrated by Machiavelli's *Prince*. The heads of the

Church, though promoters of learning, were opposed to all admission of scientific methods into the study of ecclesiastical doctrines, or the investigation of natural phenomena. Too lax in their daily walk and conversation to present to the world shining examples of Christian character, they relied for the advancement of religion on the temporal power, while the terrors of the Inquisition guarded the orthodoxy of the people's belief without being able to conform its heart and life to the profession of its lips.

Thus liberty, civil and religious, thus progress in the seeking after truth, psychical or physical, had been checked, oppressed, and finally rooted out in Italy of the sixteenth century. And yet there can be no doubt that it was the anticipation of this liberty, the confident expectation of this knowledge, which had inspired the minds and souls of the leaders of the Renaissance. But when, in the stead of these gains to mankind, they saw cunning become all-powerful in the political world, and bigotry gather to itself all sacred things, their disappointment was the more bitter as their hopes had been the more exalted. Discouragement is the tone of Italian literature after the popedom of Leo X. and the career of Lucretia Borgia. Satire and irony, with excessive worship of form, are its characteristics. Ariosto and Aretino are its exponents. And after the wave of incredulity had retreated, and the eyes of the soberminded were no longer dazzled by the brilliancy of its manifestations, those who had learning and science truly at heart saw that the enthusiasm for antiquity had spent itself. Freedom had not profited by it, in Italy, at least ; truth had apparently not been the gainer by all this expenditure of strength. It was then that the ideals of ancient Greece revived again. Refinement in manners and in expression was once more accepted as an evidence of moral and material retrogression, and the yearnings of those who despaired of social progress turned back to the primitive ages of mankind; to the patriarchal simplicity of rural existence. It was under the influence of such feelings that Italian pastoral drama was created, and that the Age of Gold became the theme of Tasso and Guarini.

We find, then, two distinct currents in the life of the pastoral in Italy, which run side by side without attempting to blend. The older of the two and the stronger is the stream of the narrative pastoral, appearing for the most part in a prose form, while the dramatic pastoral chose poetry for the expression of its sentiments. In order to understand the history of the narrative pastoral in Italy it will be necessary to glance back to its development in antiquity, and examine its characteristics in Virgil and Theocritus. The appearance of the pastoral in literature dates from the time of the Sicilian poet. His *Idylls*, in Greek meter, show already, in the third century before the Christian era, a perversion of the genuine original rural poetry. They are half real and half fancied. In many instances they portray the actual shepherd life of the island, but elsewhere it is the author himself who appears in pastoral dress. This transition, of course, is a natural one ; and it is interesting to note that it arose so early in the history of the literary pastoral, since it is the substitution of the authors and his friends for the shepherds and shepherdesses of the nomadic state that gave the prose pastoral its popularity and continued success in modern society.

When Virgil took for the model of his *Eclogues* the *Idylls* of Theocritus, he extended the latter's notion of self-disguise to the action of nearly every theme. He himself appears in a leading part in almost all of his pastorals, though he very skillfully keeps the setting of his little dramas entirely rural. The exposition of his *Eclogues* is generally in the form of a dialogue between shepherds, or it may develop into a poetic tournament between two shepherds, who thus while away their noontide rest surrounded

by their flocks. Virgil's landscape is the scenery of his
native place, just as the nature described by Theocritus is
Sicilian, yet neither the Roman nor the Greek hesitate to
bring in Arcadian herdsmen from that region of the Peloponnesus which was sacred to folds and the god Pan.
Virgil, however, goes further than the introduction of himself, his friends, and neighbors into his bucolic poetry. He
changes often the tenor of the conversation, so that instead
of discussing the interests and affairs of his assumed actors,
it more frequently dwells on the joys and trials of the poet
and his acquaintances. Even thinly veiled allusions to his
benefactors and to the events of the time are not absent
from his verses. And in this way allegory entered into the
composition of the pastoral.

In the Middle Ages, Virgil shared with Ovid the admiration of students and authors. He was more popular than
his rival, even though his reputation for wisdom may not
have been so great as the latter's. It was therefore to be
expected, that whatever Virgil and his earlier disciples wrote
would be imitated most faithfully by his uninventive followers of more modern times. The beginning of allegory
in his *Eclogues* set the fashion for subsequent pastoral
poetry, and by conforming so well to the didactic bent of
mediæval scholasticism, became the peculiar feature of
mediæval bucolics. The Latinists of the Christian monas-
teries preserved, to be sure, the Greek names inherited from
Theocritus through their great example, as well as many of
his typical commonplaces. But the sentiment of their
pastorals is Virgilian, and their purpose is allegorical.
More and more in the bucolics of these writers subjective
ideas are seen to displace objective, while their personal
emotions and the narrative of their own adventures become
the confessed subject of their verses. Through the extension of this process it was inevitable that the share of
nature in their works should be reduced to smaller and

smaller dimensions. Fictitious characters made the setting of the action a purely conventional one, and eliminated all freshness from the pastoral descriptions. And the kind of literature which these eclogues at first represented gradually changed into a kind which was the exact opposite of its parent.

An instance of the extreme to which the allegorical pastoral was carried is found in a certain class of mediæval poetry of a religious nature. Virgil, in his *Eclogues*, had disguised as shepherds persons of rank belonging to his acquaintance, but his characters still remained actual living beings. His later imitators among the pious schoolmen went much further than he, and in their pastorals substi-tuted for human actors outright personifications of senti-ments and emotions. In this way the primitive poem of rural life was turned into an allegory having the object of advocating the doctrines of the Church.

This phase of imitation, however, was not long-lived. The secular writers of the fourteenth century checked it in its development by a direct return to the fountain head, where they learned the real intention of the master. Per-haps the first author to disregard the allegorical fashion of his time was Dante, who at the threshold of the Renaissance went back to the original Latin of Virgil and wrote Latin eclogues patterned closely after the Virgilian manner, as witness his correspondence with Giovanni del Virgilio. In his turn Dante was imitated by Petrarch and Boccaccio in their Latin poetry. And so by the authority of these three great names was established again the Mantuan tradition of disguised characters.

The first pastoral in the vernacular of the fourteenth cen-tury was not an eclogue, and no direct connection between it and Virgil's *Bucolics* can be traced, though the latter exercised upon it an undoubted influence. It is one of Boccaccio's earlier productions, written in 1341 or 1342, some years before his Latin eclogues, or those of Petrarch. The title it received from its author is *L'Ameto*, or *La Commedia delle Ninfe Fiorentine*. Like the later pastoral novels, of which *L'Ameto* is beyond question the prototype, Boccaccio's story was made up of both prose and verse, the verse being in extent much less than the prose. Such a mixture of the two kinds of composition in the same production was not uncommon in the literature of the Middle Ages. A century and more before Boccaccio there had appeared in France one of the most charming examples of the kind, the still popular *chante-fable* of *Aucassin et Nicolette*. The plan of these literary compounds was to have the prose part tell the story and recite the adventures, and to use the poetry for the expression of feelings and ideas. In Italian such a notion had been successfully carried out by Dante in his *Vita Nuova*, though with him the songs were to be the chief element, and the prose merely a running commentary. It is quite probable that Boccaccio, with his wide range of literary knowledge, knew other examples of the sort now lost to us, and so may have modeled his *Ameto* on a story more pastoral in nature than either of those we have mentioned. But whatever may have been his direct model, or even were *Ameto* due to a conception wholly its author's own, it is plain that the *Vita Nuova* has shaped, to a great extent, the thought of *Ameto*, though in its form, and in the purpose of each of its constituent parts, it would seem nearer to the idea of *Aucassin et Nicolette*. For in the *Vita Nuova* there is traced the evolution of earthly love into heavenly. In *Ameto* the same theme is attempted, but in a manner much less refined, and in a spirit more sensuous than devout.

Ameto opens with a prose prologue, wherein the author displays much learning in mythological lore and shows his mediæval training by a closing invocation to Love and the Lady. After the prologue the story begins. With the feeling of a born artist the setting of the action is first described, a wooded hill near Florence. Next the hero is introduced in the person of Ameto, a hunter who pursues the game in the forests of that region. One day as he was resting by the stream, meditating on the rough pleasures of the chase, he heard a song such as he had "never before heard," and arousing himself and going toward the sound he saw a group of maidens " amidst the flowers and the tall grasses of the river's brink." These maidens are in fact nymphs, the lawful dwellers among classic shades. They notice the approach of the mortal hunter, they bid him welcome to their company, and the nymph Lia sings again to him the song he had just heard. It is a song in praise of love. It fills Ameto with delight. It leads him to confess his ignorance of love, and ask for instruction in the ways of such an entrancing passion. The nymphs are won over by his modest bearing and his ardent prayers. They not only furnish him the desired training, but when he returns to the hunt he finds in Lia a constant helper. He rejoices in her presence, until winter (here pictured with a rhetorical out-burst savoring strongly of Virgil) interrupts by its snows their happy meetings. The approach of spring brings them together again. Now midsummer is at hand and with it the festival of Venus, to which Ameto is led by Lia and her companions. After the celebration of the feast the nymphs and our hero withdraw to a meadow, where they sit down in the shade of the trees close by a cool fountain. Lia, whom Boccaccio describes here at length, speaks of the gods and of human frailties. But her discourse is interrupted by the arrival of two other nymphs, whose beauty and charms are likewise minutely delineated. Suddenly the sound of a shep-herd's pipe breaks in on this quiet party, and turning they see near at hand Teogapen, accompanied by his fleecy flock. At the request of the nymphs the newcomer extols in song the might of love. No sooner is his melody at an end than two other most beautiful nymphs arrive. The assembled company demand further entertainment, and to amuse them Teogapen induces two friends of his (one of them an Arcadian) to engage in a singing contest. This musical duel, which passes off like those in Virgil—whom Boccaccio here imitates—results in the crowning of the victor by the nymphs. At last two more nymphs appear, the final couple, and Ameto, after feasting his eyes anew on the loveliness of these last recruits, breaks out into a hymn to the gods, whom he praises for his rescue from the existence of a rude hunter and for his initiation into the realms of love.

This invocation by the hero brings the first and purely pastoral part of the narrative to an end. Nothing had as yet been introduced into the story but what was entirely in keeping with the rural life of primitive man, as it appeared to the eyes of antiquity, and there is no jarring difference in the tone of *Ameto* thus far from the more spiritual tenor of the *Vita Nuova*. Though his pastoral reveals a freshness which those of the Latins did not possess (for Boccaccio can hardly be supposed to have had any direct acquaintance with Greek pastoral poets), yet in substance and in accidental allusions it shows no practical divergence from the ideas of the classical bucolics. The artistic paganism of the palmy period of Roman culture is successfully imitated here by the citizen of mediæval Florence, and his knowledge of ancient literature had been so thoroughly assimilated to his thought, that the material which he drew so freely from his elders seems to be spontaneously his own. The only reservations which may be made in regard to the genuine classicism of *Ameto* are, on the one side, the sensuously detailed descriptions of the nymphs, which would not be allowed by the severe taste of the Augustan age, and on the other, the occasional hints that something higher, in sentiment or purpose, was to come than had yet been vouchsafed.

But suddenly into the purity of the pastoral tale breaks the realistic coarseness of the mediæval story-writer. So entirely does the spirit of the narrative change that its first part would appear to be a prolonged introduction to the main body. For at the proposal of Lia, each one of the new arrivals among the nymphs agrees to tell the story of her earthly love, and to close the story with a hymn to the deity she especially honors. Ameto is made president of this symposium, and the stories begin. The nymphs are seven in number, and the stories are seven. As each tells her tale, Ameto falls in love with her, but recovers in sufficient time to become enamored of her successor. Unfortunately the stories are not in line with the avowed moral intention of the author. They greatly resemble the less elevating of the adventures told in the *Decameron*, and the mechanism or framework by which the stories are introduced in *Ameto* is practically the structure which Boccaccio used later in the *Decameron*. Their main topic is the theme of unhappy marriages, which most of the nymphs seemed to have contracted with little divine foresight, while the delight of these supernatural beings in relating the more repulsive features of their hymeneal state is only equaled by the joy with which they picture their final happiness in non-matrimonial alliances. The contrast of these exploits with the comparative cleanliness of the beginning of the pastoral is not agreeable to the modern reader, nor complimentary to the taste of the author.

The accessories, however, to the material of these stories, the digressions and incidental descriptions, are not to be neglected in a study of the pastoral novel, for they indicate clearly the sources of Boccaccio's inspiration, and illustrate the character of his erudition. The dedication of each of the tales to some goddess of the old religion gives frequent occasion for allegorical amplification, and in the literary allusions which follow, Virgil's *Æneid* plays a prominent part. Many of the descriptions are elegant in diction and classical in tone. Among them are the picture of Pomona's garden, the details of Venus' loveliness and—somewhat different but none the less striking—the account of the loathing excited in a young bride by her repulsive old husband. One of the nymphs, Fiammetta, relates the tradition of the founding of Naples in connection with the history of her love affairs. Lia, also, prefaces the account of her acquaintance with Ameto by the legend of the building of Florence. And her hymn to Cybele, which closes the series of stories, is remarkable for the manner in which certain doctrines of Christianity, as those of the Conception, the Trinity, and Transubstantiation, are interwoven with the commonplaces of heathen mythology. Indeed the hymn may be considered as typical of that uncertainty of outline and feature which characterizes the whole of *Ameto*, and contrasts it with the definiteness of the *Decameron*. Up to the very end of the pastoral we are vaguely suspicious that there is a solid basis of fact at the bottom of all this fiction, and are quite ready to believe that the author is amusing himself at our expense, by placing his own personal experience just outside the boundaries of our recognition.

But Boccaccio had an object in the confounding of paganism and Christianity in this hymn to Cybele. It is a shrewd artifice on his part to bring back his story from the contemplation of earthly passions to a higher plane of thought, to the idea with which he began his work. So in harmony with this idea he now at last throws aside his sensual scenes, and presents the attributes of the celestial Venus before the eyes of the enraptured hunter. As these are revealed in the heavens there sounds down into the ears of Ameto the hymn of divine and eternal love. Yet his eyes are still too gross to gaze upon the ethereal radiance. He must first be purified from all terrestrial thoughts. To accomplish this cleansing Lia dips him in the fountain, and removes from him the stains of sinful desire. And now, a new being, he looks back in wonder on his former state of animal existence, "and in short from a brute beast he seems to have become a man." This change of heart he consecrates by a hymn to the Trinity. Here the moral teaching of Boccaccio ends, and the closing sentences of his story bring us out of the realm of allegory into nature's kingdom again. Evening is drawing nigh, and with its deepening shades the happy company of the groves disperse. The nymphs depart and the mortal, abandoned to himself, laments in a final poem his forced leave-taking of divine associations, and his return to an unsympathetic father's roof.

Thus the beginning and the end of *L'Ameto* were made to agree in purpose, and this purpose was to present a moral truth. So if we keep this first intention of the author in mind, the story, like the *Vita Nuova*, should be placed on the list of didactic treatises. But it was not the moral element in *Ameto* which attracted to it the attention of later writers. It was the form of mingled prose and poetry, the pastoral scenery and characters, and the biographies of individuals which gave to this production of the fourteenth century its significance in the history of literature. Boccaccio, like his masters, Virgil and Dante, has disguised events chosen from his own life or from the experience of his acquaintances. But this was not an unusual proceeding in his day nor before his time, and it seems quite evident that his contemporaries did not consider *Ameto* to be a novelty. At all events they did not imitate its plan or style. And when this first bloom of Italian literature had passed, its productions—saving the *Divine Comedy*—remained unnoticed for at least a century. The humanists of the revival of learning turned away in disdain from the vernacular of the people, and endeavored to restore in their writings and conversation the Latin of Cicero and the *Æneid*. Their attempts at sketching nature were pure imitations of the eclogues of antiquity, or of the mediæval Latinists, while the cultivation of such pastoral compositions as the example of *Ameto* would incite, was postponed for many generations. When the Italian language became again the vehicle of cultivated expression—in the last quarter of the fifteenth century—it found the conditions of literary activity entirely different from the surroundings of the age of Petrarch.

These differences were peculiarly in favor of those sentiments which promote the growth of the pastoral. In the time of Boccaccio, when the discovery of manuscripts was adding every day to the world's stock of knowledge, and was increasing the zeal for learning, the educated classes of society were enthusiastic over human progress, and thoroughly confident in a Utopian future for the world. In *Ameto* there is not the slightest trace of discouragement. It pictures, in its way, the birth of a soul, as Hawthorne has done in his *Marble Faun*. But by the end of the fifteenth century, in the Florence of Lorenzo di Medici, where the most brilliant results of the long period of intellectual quickening had been brought together, hope had failed, and the minds of men were shaded with sadness. For the Renaissance had revealed its treasures and could no longer attract its devotees by the allurements of fresh discoveries. The mental stimulus of a century and a half had not been accompanied by a corresponding moral awakening, and thus in the time of its exhaustion learning possessed no enduring foundation on which to build its own structure of independent scientific investigation. Literature deprived of knowledge, its ally, frittered itself away in debasing pursuits. Art and form became its end; thought and truth departed from it, and hence it is that *Orlando Furioso* is the fitting representative of its age.

Under such conditions the more meditative souls slipped away from the doubt and discouragement which faced them, and sought refuge in that haven always open to decaying civilizations, the original state of man, the primitive simplicity, and the rustic happiness of the Age of Gold. The pastoral life of this ideal existence was revived in Florence and in Rome after the example of both Greek and Roman traditions, and the restful consolation which it could offer to the weary and despairing found expression in the Italian poets from Poliziano on. Now, this sentiment of despair is the more especial theme of the Italian dramatic pastoral, while the narrative kind follows rather in the footsteps of Boccaccio. Yet it was inevitable that the atmosphere of its surroundings, and the prevailing fashion in literature, should affect the narrative pastoral as well, and in the *Arcadia*, the best specimen of the school, this contemporary longing for a pure life on earth and the return of the Age of Gold is disclosed by many a passage, and affects, however unconsciously, the tone of the whole work.

We must, then, study Sannazaro's story, both in its relation to *Ameto*, of which it is the undoubted successor, and in the light of its attitude toward its own times, which it was bound to represent, like any successful literary composition. The *Arcadia* was published in its complete form in 1504, more than 160 years after *Ameto*. It contained twelve prose narratives and as many eclogues or songs. Between these detached pieces an artificial connection was preserved by the presence of the narrator himself, who speaks in the first person, and who claims that the different episodes of his story are events in his own personal experience. This union of prose with verse is, perhaps, more artistically accomplished by Sannazaro than by Boccaccio, but the likeness of the two pastorals in their general plan, and the fact that many ideas of the *Arcadia* seem to have been suggested by corresponding ones in *Ameto*, point quite conclusively to a certain correspondence between the two, and thereby offer a reasonable explanation for Sannazaro's divergence from the spirit of the dramatic pastoral of his time. The title of the *Arcadia* may have been suggested by its author's general acquaintance with ancient pastoral literature, or by his familiarity with Virgil, who speaks of that favorite province in his tenth *Eclogue.* In keeping with its rural setting, the actors of the *Arcadia* are shepherds. But their disguise is very slight, and is so easily penetrated that Sannazaro himself becomes aware of the fact, and in the seventh *prosa* steps forward in his own name to relate events pertaining to his own career. Others of the shepherds are to be recognized as friends of the author.

The *Arcadia* begins like *Ameto*, with a short prologue, where the superiority of nature over art, both in content and form, is confidently asserted. Next the scene of the action is given, a valley among the mountains of Arcadia, delightful for its deep shade and cooling streams, where the shepherds are wont to resort to rest from labor and to carry on their rustic amusements. There Ergasto, melancholy on account of unrequited love, is cheered by his friend, Selvaggio. All this is but the setting to the picture. In the divisions of the story following this introduction, the prose parts serve at first as commentary to the poetical, while the subject hinges wholly on the recreation and games of the shepherds. A festival is held in honor of the goddess Pales, the deity of the flocks, on whose temple are painted scenes from rural life, which reminds one of the pictures in the Greek novels of antiquity. Considerable space is also given to the account of various superstitions dear to the shepherds, among them the belief in the evil eye, which is still so strong with the people of Italy. The power of incantations is also shown ; and lovers obtain relief, as they do in the pastorals of all ages, by cutting the names of their loved ones in the bark of trees. A direct imitation of the *Æneid* is the reverence which these Arcadian herdsmen pay to their dead, and the manner in which they recall to grateful memory their departed friend, Androgeo, by singing songs at his tomb.   Then in the sixth eclogue comes the praise of the days of old, together with the lamentations of an aged shepherd over the evil present, and forebodings of a still darker future.   On the other hand, in the portraits of his heroines Sannazaro follows closely after his fellow-countryman, and the description of the object of his affections, the nymph Amaranta, abounds in those sensuous details which flowed so freely from Boccaccio's pen.

With the biography of the author in the seventh *prosa* these parts of the *Arcadia*, which had been hitherto fairly equal to the songs in length, begin to expand proportionately to the eclogues proper.   Sannazaro here appears in the character of an unhappy lover, the melancholy Sincero, and to comfort him for his bereavement his companion, Charino, relates to him an unlucky love affair of his own with a nymph.   This consolation closes with the praise of rustic life, and various rules for bird-catching—that favorite subject of boudoir painting in more modern times.   Now the assembled shepherds pass again to the discussion of magic arts and eulogies of Pan and his woodland temple. Laws are laid down for the guidance of him who pursues a shepherd's vocation (Sannazaro copies freely after Virgil in these rules), and incantations for the cure of love are enumerated.   Afterward the fifth book of the *Æneid* is again put to use in the description of athletic sports, which take place before the tomb of Massilia—who is supposed to be the mother of Sannazaro—and in the eleventh eclogue the author, under the name of Ergasto, sings his lamentations over her death.   In this lament is found the only digression, and a slight one at that, from the skillfully maintained paganism of the *Arcadia :*

> " But thou, beautiful above all and soul immortal,
>   Who from the heavens perhaps dost hear me . . . "

It was now high time for the return of Ergasto to his native town and to active life once more. For this purpose a nymph became his guide, and led him, in a dream, through many subterranean marvels under the sea from the Arcadian groves to Naples. As he is approaching his home he hears two shepherds bewailing in verse the death of his mistress, Phyllis, and overcome by this new grief he bursts into a farewell to his rustic pipe, and brings his wanderings to an end.

The composite character of the *Arcadia* did much to help on its success. Besides its reflection of *Ameto*, evident to Sannazaro's contemporaries, the devotees of the vernacular literature were won over by its many paraphrases of Petrarch, while the admirers of antiquity were flattered by the allusions to the fabled Golden Age and frequent imitations of Virgil. Even the journey of Ergasto underground was taken from the experience of Aristæus in the fourth *Georgic*. The humanists of the age also were not left without some representation in the pastoral, for the lamentation on the death of Phyllis is an open adaptation from a Latin eclogue of Pontano, Sannazaro's steadfast friend. To make his work the more successful, Sannazaro deliberately excited the curiosity of his public by confessing to certain disguises among his actors, thereby arousing social interest in determining their identity. Novels with keys began with the *Arcadia*, and like their model they never failed to meet with at least a temporary popularity.

But when we come to look at the plan of the *Arcadia* we are obliged to admit that it merits less the name of novel than even *Ameto*. Unlike Boccaccio's story it has no general theme, and it is entirely devoid of any unity of action. A most artificial tie binds its separate parts together so slightly that it might well be looked upon as a simple collection of prose and verse. It would also seem as though the original intention of its author was to make the poetical eclogues the chief part of his story and to subordinate the prose narratives to a purely introductory function. As he progressed with his task, however, this intention,· if such existed, was lost sight of, and the eclogues became musical variations on a theme which the preceding prose parts had separately developed. There is certainly no plot running through this changing scene, and we are therefore obliged to consider the *Arcadia* as a mere literary amusement of its author.

Sannazaro did not aspire at all after originality in thought or material, and was not content with the imitation of ideas alone. Many of his sentences are skillful paraphrases of the periods of his predecessors, and where one writer failed to fill out the exact notion which he wished to convey, his words were supplemented with a clause borrowed from another ; so that in the *Arcadia* we are constantly meeting with compounds of authors, and the deficiencies of Virgil are supplied by Petrarch, and *vice versa*. From the frequent occurrence of such additions, we may very properly consider the *Arcadia* to be the triumph of eclecticism in literature. The talent of Sannazaro seems, indeed, to lie in his appropriation of clauses of greater writers, and in his deftness in joining together his loans. But he certainly showed, in addition to this talent, a remarkable faculty for word coloring, and a keen sense of musical rhythm, and it was the combination of his eclecticism in expression with the harmonious flow of his period which won for his pastoral its great and enduring popularity. Nor must we forget that the *Arcadia* thoroughly suited the taste of the literary public to which it was addressed. It appeared at a time when people were tired of new conceptions, and preferred repetition in thought to the exposition of new ideas. Art for art's sake was the watchword of Italian literature in the closing decades of the Renaissance, and the *Arcadia* is one of the best exponents of that law.

To the success of his pastoral Sannazaro contributed not a little by the variety and excellence of his verse. In the eclogues of the *Arcadia* he employed nearly all of the strophes known to Italian lyric poetry, while *Ameto* had been content with the use of the modest *terza rima*. The novelty of his rhymes appealed to the finical spirit of his contemporaries, and their brilliancy cast all previous Italian verse endings completely into the shade. In the descriptions of the *Arcadia* there is also an advance both in color and in rhythm over the most elaborate periods of Boccaccio. Sannazaro's word pictures of games, festivals, the life and habits of his Arcadian herdsmen, composite as they were, and the result of a recast of what former authors had expressed, became the standard for the imitation of his successors, and entered into the later pastoral novel as truly classical scenes. And with the *Arcadia* begins that public lament of unsuccessful love, that solicitation of consolation, while all the train of sorrowings by day, of watchings by night, of relieving the pent-up passion by carving the names of the loved ones on trees, will follow closely in the footsteps of the passions depicted by this Italian master. So his half-actual, half-mythological surroundings will live on in fiction with a vitality which the changes of time and race and civilization will not be able to entirely destroy.

It is a curious fact, however, that these novelistic contributions from the *Arcadia* have had a greater influence on literature outside of Italy than they had within their native land. The imitations of the *Arcadia* by Italian authors are numerous enough, to be sure, but are so inferior to their original that they added nothing new to the pastoral idea, and consequently demand no especial notice here. Their most palpable bearing on literary life is in the pastoral pseudonyms which they gave to the members of the various Italian academies, and in the fashion of poetical improvisation cultivated by these assemblies of *dilettanti.*

But in foreign lands the fancies and spirit of Sannazaro received a much greater development than at home. The *Arcadia* was not long in attracting the attention of students and tourists of France and Spain. In the latter country it played an important part in the development of a new school of lyric poetry, and affected strongly the tone and structure of the pastoral novel. In France the verse of the Pleiad reflected the elegance of Sannazaro's lines, and the wonderful novel of the great D'Urfé re-echoed many of the sentiments and ideas of its Italian forerunner. In England Spenser both admired and followed it, while Sir Philip Sidney borrowed from it its name at least. Still, after all the reckoning is made, the singular fact remains that no foreign author directly imitated the plan or composition of the *Arcadia*, as was done by so many Italians. And within Italy itself the narrative pastoral, in prose and verse, produced, curiously enough, but two works of any significance, *Ameto* and the *Arcadia*.

The other branch of the Italian pastoral, the dramatic, is represented by a larger number of masterpieces than the narrative, but, on the other hand, has exercised less influence than its rival on the development of the modern novel. The pioneer writer of the pastoral drama was Boccaccio, the originator of the narrative, and his *Ninfale Fiesolano* is the first example of the kind in the modern vernaculars. In form this work belongs to the department of narrative poetry, being composed of nearly five hundred strophes in *ottava rima*. But in thought it is a genuine tragedy.

The story of the *Ninfale Fiesolano* is a combination of the tradition of Fiesole's origin with an account of rural love. Nature furnishes the scenery. The time is prehistoric, or perhaps mythological, for the heroine of the tale is Mensola, one of Diana's nymphs. One day as the goddess' train was sweeping by him, this nymph was seen in her beauty by the shepherd Affrico, who lost no time in becoming infatuated with her and in laying siege to her heart. The nymph rejects him with disdain ; yet the more ardent for his rebuff he plans a stratagem to win her. In spite of his father's warnings, Affrico dresses himself in a maiden's dress and mingles with the nymphs attendant on the deity. The disguise succeeds in its object. Mensola is deceived, and finds out her mistake only when it is too late.

Though in the midst of her error and its consequences, the fear of her mistress restrains her from another interview with her lover. At the trysting-place, where they were again to meet, Affrico awaits in vain the return of his beloved. Days pass by, but still he lingers. Doubt changes to certainty and sadness to despair. At length on the banks of the stream, which was ever afterward called by his name, he succumbs to his sorrow, takes his own life, and dyes with his blood the clear waters. A burial is given to his body by his heartbroken father. In the meantime Mensola had been assailed by a fate hardly less unrelenting. Sheltered from Diana's wrath for a while by a friendly nymph, she is finally surprised by the virgin goddess in the act of bathing her child. Fleeing in terror, she endeavors to escape through the waves, but is herself changed into billows by the act of the outraged divinity. From her the other stream in turn received its name. The child, however, was saved, was brought up by its grandfather, and became in manhood the founder of Fiesole.

The purpose of the *Ninfale Fiesolano* is plainly an adaptation of such stories as are found in abundance in Ovid's *Metamorphoses*, and for this reason it closely resembles the Greek erotic tales, from which the Roman poet borrowed so freely, and which we have seen were one of the sources of the Greco-Roman novel. The plot of Boccaccio's poem contains also all the distinguishing features of the later pastoral drama: the meeting of the lovers, their courtship and their punishment, which is often self-inflicted. It presents, besides, the notion of disguise in sex, which afterward obtained so great success in the pastoral novel. But the intention of Boccaccio's poem is not so clear as its literary import. What he wished it to be we do not know. Surely there is nothing allegorical about it, as was the case with *Ameto.* He seems to have made use of the two streams near Fiesole to tell a story in the style of antiquity, and very likely considered his composition in no other light than as a work of art. At all events this pastoral of his attracted no more notice from his contemporaries than his narrative in prose had done, and its influence on subsequent literature was even less than the influence of *Ameto,* if we may form an opinion from the evidence at hand. The rise of humanism submerged this poem with the rest of Italian compositions, and when the dramatic pastoral reappeared a century and more later on, it built itself up on as original foundations as though the *Ninfale Fiesolano* had never existed.

It was in 1472, at the brilliant court of the Medici, on the banks of the Arno, that the versatile Poliziano conceived the idea of inventing a new species of poetry for the pleasure of his generous patrons. It was to be a mixture of antecedent literature and, like so many inventions of the Renaissance, consisted in grafting a shoot taken from antiquity on a tree of modern stock. For during the Middle Ages there had grown up among the peoples of western Europe a kind of drama in the vernacular, which had its origins in the liturgy of the Church. The form the plays of this popular theater assumed in Italy went under the name of *Sacra Rappresentazione.* Poliziano, with the cleverness characteristic of the man, here saw ready to hand, and familiar to his public, a convenient framework for a new dramatic departure. Looking about for a subject for this setting, he hit upon the myth of Orpheus and Eurydice, typical of the spirit that redeems the body from death and darkness by the breathings of its divine harmony. The theme was consonant with the traditions of his liturgical model. He adapted it to that model, and thus produced the beautiful pastoral drama of *Orfeo*.

Naturally, Poliziano was obliged to change his story to suit his purpose, yet he varied but little from the beautiful legend of the ancients. The shepherd Aristæus is first presented to the spectators in the character of a longing swain. For he has learned by hearsay that the nymph Eurydice is endowed with charms lovelier by far than those of Diana herself. So he is incited to seek after such a wonder. . On his approach Eurydice flees in terror, but as she escapes a serpent bites her in the foot, she falls, and soon expires. Her husband, Orpheus, comes up when too late to save her life, and follows her in sadness of heart to the lower world. The songs of the skilled musician prevail even against the hardheartedness of Pluto. The god of shadows gives over Eurydice to her suppliant spouse under conditions not fulfilled by Orpheus, for he looks back on his wife before their feet are clear of the infernal regions, and she vanishes forever from his sight. Now in his grief the singer forswears henceforth all womankind, and for this oath is torn to pieces by the maddened Bacchantes of Thrace.

Orfeo was not only a drama having a pastoral leaning, but, as may be surmised from the calling of its hero, it was a drama set to music, and may thus be counted among the best specimens of early Italian opera. As a matter of fact, when the theater of the ancients was imitated by the Italian writers of the first quarter of the sixteenth century, this play of Poliziano was divided, to conform to their supposed ideas, into acts and scenes, and through the excellence of its verse in octaves and *terza rima* it was regarded for many decades as the finest musical drama that had yet been represented. But *Orfeo* did not take a high stand among pastoral plays pure and simple. The purpose of Poliziano in composing it was quite foreign to the spirit of such works as the *Ninfale Fiesolano*, and we place it here among the examples of dramatic pastoral mainly because of the pastoral dress of its characters. However, it begot successors which approached nearer to the kind of literature in question. In these imitations the action is more developed, while new features are added which emphasize both the unrequited love of shepherds for nymphs, and the unfortunate passions of the nymphs as well. The hatred of nymphs for satyrs becomes conventional in them. A favorite form of plot is to make a satyr love a nymph, who in turn loves a shepherd who loves another nymph, who loves another shepherd, and so on into an infinity of parallel loves which never meet, until a tremendous mental upheaval brings all back to the realms of finite life and forces a solution. These ingenious devices were afterward incorporated into the pastoral novel.

Many of the musical dramas which the success of *Orfeo* called out in Italy were first given at the court of Ferrara, where the house of Este extended a never-failing patronage to whatever was eminent in art or in letters. It was for the head of that house that Ariosto wrote *Orlando Furioso*, and under the generous protection of his descendants Torquato Tasso lived and labored half a century later. During all these years the elaboration of the incipient opera went on with increasing enthusiasm as the last product of the Italian Renaissance. Tasso, surrounded as he was by the cultivators of the musical art, and seeing daily before his eyes evidences of its adaptability to dramatic purposes, could not have failed to be incited to try his hand at so popular a theme, and perhaps from the performances of these followers of *Orfeo* he conceived the idea of *Aminta*. Tasso's libretto, however, is a genuine pastoral drama, although it is divided into the standard five acts of the classical theater, and makes use of the traditional chorus. Its setting is rural, and its actors are herdsmen and woodland deities. The time is in harmony with the surroundings, carrying the hearer back to the uncertain epoch of mythological tales.

Aminta opens with a prologue, which dedicates the play to the god of love. Then Cupid, who has escaped from his mother, Venus, appears in the disguise of a shepherd. From his lines we learn that he is about to direct his arrows against Sylvia, a nymph of Diana's train, who is treating with scorn the suit of the shepherd Amyntas. Now the story proper begins with a dialogue on love between Sylvia and her friend Daphne. This is followed by an eclogue, in which the singer Thyrsis endeavors to console Amyntas for Sylvia's disdain. But the sorrowful shepherd refuses to be comforted. On the contrary he excites his own desires with the remembrance of Sylvia's charms, and relates the stratagem he had used to approach her—which is the story of the bee, borrowed by Tasso from Achilles Tatius. Up to this point all has been in keeping with the assumed rusticity of the times. But suddenly the author breaks in upon this simplicity by contemporaneous allusions. In bitter terms he condemns the vices which town life is supposed to breed, and discloses the true sentiment of his work in a beautiful chorus on the innocence and happiness of the Age of Gold.

The second act transports us back again into the fabled past. A satyr appears, who plots before our eyes the abduction of Sylvia. Then Amyntas' friends arrive and propose to betray Sylvia to him, while she is bathing in the fountain—a situation already exploited in the *Ninfale Fiesolano*. But Amyntas, who is filled with the true idea of love, refuses to do violence to the mistress of his heart, and the chorus seconds him, in a song on the power of the tender passion. The action is ripening rapidly into a tragedy. Thyrsis and the chorus hold the stage. The former tells his sympathetic listeners how the satyr had caught Sylvia and how Amyntas had bravely rescued her from him. Yet this act of devotion has not won her affection.   The ungrateful nymph flies from her generous deliverer, and in despair Amyntas attempts his own life. But a new situation is developed which seems to be another loan from the Greek novels. Sylvia is supposed to have fallen a prey to wolves, and portions of her dress are offered on the stage as evidences of her death. At this, Amyntas, who has been restrained from suicide, disappears, and the nymph returns to the scene to explain the error into which the shepherds had fallen regarding her. While they are talking a messenger arrives, who tells them that Amyntas has evaded his friends and has thrown himself from a high cliff—like so many heroes of the Greek elegiac poetry. Then pity softens the hard heart of the terrified nymph. She hastens to find the corpse of her lover, and to give it a fitting burial, but on reaching the foot of the cliff she sees that breath is still in the body. Overhanging bushes have broken the force of the fall, and, in the arms of his beloved, Amyntas comes to life again.

Aminta was played before the nobilty of Ferrara exactly one hundred years after the production of *Orfeo* in Florence. During that long period of time no other pastoral drama of note had been written in Italy, though the stage had been flooded with many second-rate productions. These inferior plays, however, had done their work in keeping alive the taste for rural scenes ; and in the process of their development they had become by degrees more like their original model, the *Ninfale Fiesolano.* So we are obliged to account for the unbounded enthusiasm which greeted Tasso's dramatic poem on the ground of the excellence of its style and composition, rather than on the supposition that its sentiments were in any way a novelty. To be sure the author mars constantly the peace of his rustic surroundings by the bitterness and cynicism of his references to the court which sheltered him, and to the vices of his contemporaries. Yet this manner of procedure was well calculated to excite the curiosity of his frivolous public. For by openly violating the assumed time of *Aminta's* plot he showed to the gossips that its whole setting was but superficial, and thus led them to the necessary conclusion that his shepherds and nymphs might be persons of their own acquaintance in disguise. The story would then have a key and be assured of success from the start.

It is in the perfection of his verse and in the adaptation of his material that Tasso has retained the admiration of posterity. He borrows freely from the ancients, though less literally than did Sannazaro. In the prologue to *Aminta* he follows Theocritus. In the main body of the poem Virgil is often in his thoughts, and is openly imitated in the lines where Tasso praises his patron in the manner of the Roman poet's first *Eclogue*. Ovid also, and the minor lyric and pastoral writers of Greece, come in for their share of influence, as well as the Greek novelist whom we have already mentioned, and even the Italian Ariosto. The characters of the play are the traditional ones, and the hero is still the despairing lover, who pours out his sorrows in song, and cuts the name of his mistress on the bark of friendly sighing trees. Still the accessories of pastoral existence are almost wholly absent in *Aminta*. The grazing flocks are far away from the scene of action, and instead of the cooling shades of noon, which bend to hear the tender lament of the unfortunate lover, we are startled in the gloomy forest by the mad rush of feverish passions, the barbarous wooing of the satyr, or the exalted melancholy of the rejected shepherd. Sylvia's harshness toward her suitors was not new to ancient or mediæval literature, but was the disdain of the nymphs of Greece. The revival of the tradition of antiquity had affected the demeanor of many heroines before Tasso's time, yet it was a novelty in fiction that this trait of the maiden should be made so prominent in the development of the plot.   The predecessors of Tasso in pastoral drama had either caused the nymph to be in love from the beginning, or at least to yield after prolonged entreaty.   In the *Arcadia* the lover did not give up hope so long as his mistress lived.   In *Aminta*, however, the conception derived from the ancients of a mortal who is proof against Venus' power, is repeated in its entirety.   The stress which Tasso laid on this characteristic is unmistakable, and it is undoubtedly to his delineation rather than to the portraits of the other repellent maidens of Renaissance fiction that the French novelists of the seventeenth century owe the frigidity of their glacial heroines.

Through the *Astrée* and, in real life, through the blue-stockings of the Hôtel de Rambouillet, Tasso's attitude of the mistress to the lover was handed down to the present day.   Amyntas is the lovelorn hero of many a society novel during the last three centuries, always despairing, always looking on suicide with a longing eye ; and the romantic movement in literature, which proved so fatal to the reign of Sylvia, multiplied his race to such an alarming extent that the reverberation of the sighs and groans which the shores of the Ægean re-echoed to the banks of the Arno has not yet died away over the waters of Lake Leman or the islands of Windermere.

One more example of the Italian dramatic pastoral remains to be noticed before this chapter can be brought to an end.   It is Guarini's *Pastor Fido*, which in no sense is so important a work in the history of literature as *Aminta*.   In fact it was inspired by the latter play, and the object of its composition—later by a decade than its model—was to rival Tasso on his own chosen ground.   Consequently in the *Pastor Fido* we meet with the same general trend of events as in the earlier poem, and with imitation in verse we find a considerable imitation in expressions and sentiments.   In his choice of the place of action for his story, Guarini returns to the opinion of Sannazaro and revives the scenery of Arcadia of the Peloponnesus. His prologue, a eulogy of his patrons, he puts in the mouth of the river god, Alpheus. His plot he borrows, with change of names, from that supply of erotic tales which Pausanias never tired of telling, and so adapts to the taste of his Italian audience the old Greek story of Coresus and Callirrhoe.

The priest of Diana, Amyntas by name, loves the nymph Lucrina. But his love is scorned, and in answer to the prayers of her servant the goddess sends a pestilence to ravage the country. The inhabitants demand from an oracle the means of staying the plague, and are told that to accomplish it Lucrina must first be sacrificed. Accordingly she is brought as a victim to Diana's altar, where Amyntas officiates as priest. But her lover, true to his passion for her, kills himself rather than shed her blood, and she, repenting too late of her hardheartedness toward him, pierces her own bosom with the very dagger which had taken the life of her suitor. The blood shed at her shrine once more arouses Diana's wrath, and the oracle, again consulted, demands an annual human sacrifice of a virgin. This grievous burden may be removed only when two heavenly races have become united, and a faithful shepherd atones for the faithless nymph. To bring about this result the wise men of the land betroth Sylvio, a descendant of Hercules, to Amaryllis, of the race of Pan, but each unwillingly. For the shepherd, who is the counterpart of Tasso's Sylvia, scorns all love as unworthy of a man's attention, and Amaryllis is already in love with Myrtillo, and is beloved by him in return.

So much for the principal plot of the *Pastor Fido.* At this point, however, the first story is complicated by the introduction of another, which the author interweaves with his main narrative. Corisca, wooed by a satyr whom she abhors, and whom she finally lures to his death, is enamored of Myrtillo, and consequently is filled with hatred toward Amaryllis. She tries to compass that maiden's destruction by raising against her the charge of faithlessness. Amaryllis does indeed fall into the snare, and is condemned to execution. Already at the altar, Myrtillo hears of her peril and hastens to offer himself as her substitute. Montano, who is both the priest of Diana and the father of Sylvio, is on the point of accepting Myrtillo's sacrifice, in spite of many inward misgivings, when an unknown shepherd appears on the scene to delay the ceremony. This stranger tells how he had found Myrtillo, when but an infant, on the banks of a stream which had overflowed its bed. With the child were tokens of his ancestry and rank, and these the shepherd brings with him. By means of them Montano recognizes in Myrtillo the lost brother of Sylvio, and his own son. So the justice of the oracle is proven. Myrtillo is united to the vindicated Amaryllis, Sylvio allows himself to be touched at last by the devotion of Dorinda—who through love of him had disguised herself in a wolf's skin, and had been wounded by him on a hunt—while Corisca is disposed of by a simple disappearance.

The chief feature which distinguishes Guarini's drama from the plays of his predecessors is the intricacy of its plot. The wheel within a wheel was something new to pastoral fiction. The action also of the *Pastor Fido*, in spite of many allusions to the fickleness of woman, and particularly of the city-bred, is also to be preferred to the action of *Aminta*, which is not so faithful to the assumption of a pastoral existence. In these respects Guarini's play is more dramatic than the simple and emotional poem of Tasso. But in other things the *Pastor Fido* reveals an author of inferior talent. A good share of its episodes are not original, but are openly imitated from the scenes of *Aminta*. In its choruses, especially the one on the delights of kissing, and another extolling the Age of Gold, the sentiments of Tasso are merely repeated without variation. Guarini's originality mainly consists in the minor ornaments of his style, such as proverbs, conceits, refrains, and the celebrated echo verse, a forerunner of which may be found in *Orfeo.* In his descriptions of shepherd's games and the sports of the nymphs, he approaches again the genuine pastoral idea which Tasso had abandoned somewhat; and yet, when all has been said regarding his poem, and when its merits and defects have been balanced from the pastoral point of view, we must admit that the success of the *Pastor Fido* was due to its voluptuous imagery, its sensuous coloring, and the softness of its rhythm, rather than to the excellences of its plot or action. In his exposition of Arcadian surroundings Guarini violated the very principles of simplicity and directness, on which the idea of pastoral composition was founded. Those qualities which have given him his place in literature were fatal to the conception of the very kind of writing which he cultivated, and were so many elements of decay in the life of the school. In fact, after Guarini, the pastoral drama, which had held so high a place in the Italy of the Renaissance, produced no work of prominence. Pastoral composition was continued, to be sure, and even swamped by its popularity the legitimate drama. The disguise of shepherds and shepherdesses invaded, as we have seen, all the literary life of the people, and became a leading trait of their operas and academies. But real development of the pastoral in Italy stopped short with the *Pastor Fido*, and its further progress must be traced on foreign soil, in the dramas of the early seventeenth century in France and in the episodes of the renowned *Astrée*, to which Guarini's poem contributed its quota of inspiration.

Yet it would hardly be fair to Italian pastorals as a whole, taking together the narrative and the dramatic, to say that they remained without direct imitations of a novelistic character. For in France particularly, they did not fail to incite to literary compositions, made up in great part of prose, to be sure, yet containing numerous poems also. Such productions, which took their form from *Ameto* or the *Arcadia*, but admitted in addition the notions of *Aminta* or the *Pastor Fido*, fell little short of being genuine novels with a plot and a solution. It is true that these attempts at romancing do not seem to have ever been popular with the reading public, and nowadays they are recalled only as literary curiosities. The best example of them, beyond all doubt, is *Les Bergeries de Juliette*, by Ollenix du Montsacré, a pseudonym for the French dramatist, Nicolas de Montreux, who is the author also of the sixteenth book of the French *Amadis*. The work is divided into five volumes, which were published at intervals from 1585 to 1598. The first two volumes of the five appear to have met with considerable favor, and attained the honor of several editions, but the remaining three evidently fell flat from the very outset. The author indicates the plan of his novel in the sub-title of the first volume, so to cite his words is to give the best idea of the contents of the pastoral: "In which through the loves of shepherds and shepherdesses one sees the different effects of love, with five jocose stories told in five days by five shepherdesses, and several echos, enigmas, sonnets, elegies, and stanzas. Together with a pastoral in French verse, in imitation of the Italians."

This new combination of various devices to attract all sorts of clients includes the realistic matter of the *Decameron*, with its framework, and the ideal divagations of the pastoral muse. But the setting is wholly rural. The action takes place in Arcadia, where dwelt the herdsman Phyllis, his sister Juliette, and eight other shepherds. In this primitive society of ten love ran rampant. Each loved someone who did not love him, but who loved someone else, and so on until the circuit was complete. The usual assemblies, were held, with which we are now familiar, the audience was entertained at them with stories and songs, while the flows of soul were broken in upon by the evil-minded satyrs, who rushed from their hiding-places in the groves to steal away the kindly nymphs. But in *Les Bergeries de Juliette* the satyrs are not so successful as in the Italian pastorals, and the shepherds, who are enamored of their fair entertainers, drive the unwelcome suitors back to their dens. The stories told in these reunions are not of the most elevating character, nor the most refined in sentiment, but they know no geographical limits, reaching from Spain to Poland, and are re-enforced at times with the performance of magic arts, a trait Nicolas may have borrowed from Spanish fiction. The only character of prominence, Juliette, is a duplicate of the heroines of Tasso and Guarini. Her cooling attitude toward the ardent supplications of her admirers never fails to have an effect opposite to the natural process, raising the temperature of their affections rather than lowering it.

There is, however, nothing in this work to call for particular comment. The author himself was aware of some of his shortcomings, and declares in the last volume he published that he will write sequels which shall excel in piety what he had written, though not in poetry or invention. But this promise was not fulfilled. No further addition to *Les Bergeries de Juliette* was made, and the absence of a solution to the plot of the story makes what we have before us resemble rather a succession of scenes than an unfinished novel. Nicolas did not have sufficient talent to mold his material toward the end he desired. His models did not help him at all, inasmuch as those among them which were partly in prose did not aim at the same end he did. They were content in being purely artistic episodes, without demanding the least connection or progressive development. The pastoral novels of the seventeenth century were not to look for a model to these Italian predecessors. When, ten years after Nicolas de Montreux had ceased to publish, Honoré D'Urfé tried his hand at pastoral fiction, it was not the dramas and eclogues of Italy which inspired his pen. For the construction of the *Astrée* he chose rather the example of a genuine novel in prose and verse, regular in plan, and consonant in tone, which half a century before his day had received its completed form from the more exacting romancers of the Spanish peninsula.

CHAPTER VIII.

SPAIN of the sixteenth century gave birth to the pastoral novel, as Spain of the fifteenth had done to the romance of chivalry. So much is conceded on all sides. But whether Spain originated the pastoral novel or imitated it, with some improvements in the way of construction, from her Latin neighbor to the eastward, is still a mooted question in literary history. At first sight the arguments seem to be all in her favor. She invented beyond dispute the novel of chivalry half a century before the pastoral novel appeared, and just as unmistakably did she fashion the *picaresco* novel, the pastoral's contemporary. Possessing the genius for creating this style of fiction, and, indeed, endowed with it peculiarly, when compared to the incomplete talents of the other lands of modern Europe, all the weight of analogy would incline the balance to the side of Spain in the matter of the pastoral novel also. Still we must remember that in the case of the romance of chivalry there was abundant testimony to the previous life and popularity, with the Portuguese and the Spaniards, of the embryonic *Amadis of Gaul.* And so far as the *picaresco* novel is concerned, while it lacks any known antecedents in the peninsula—or elsewhere for that matter —its whole spirit and scene is thoroughly and entirely Spanish.

With the pastoral novel, however, the evidence is not so clear. Italy had far outshone, with Boccaccio, Poliziano, and Sannazaro, all other countries in the cultivation of this branch of fiction, and the glory of *Ameto* and the *Arcadia* had eclipsed all faint gleams of the pastoral idea which had appeared here and there in the literature of the remaining Latin peoples. So when Montemayor gave out his *Diana*, toward the middle of the sixteenth century, it was assumed at once that such a brilliant production, appearing without any notable predecessors in its own vernacular, must necessarily have been prompted by the great *Arcadia* and patterned after it. But the setting of *Diana* is Spanish, its tone and customs are Spanish, and there is nothing in its contents which would testify to a loan from foreign sources. The great contrast between the two works of the Italian writer and the Portuguese would suggest another explanation for the *Diana's* existence ; and when it is studied by itself, without any mental reservations, it appears entirely indigenous to the Iberian peninsula. If then it can be shown that antecedent to the *Diana* there was in its home any local cultivation of the pastoral either in poetry or prose, however humble and infrequent, the likelihood would be that the *Diana* is the outgrowth, in the main, of these obscure beginnings. And, to go one step further, if it appears that this literary fancy had enjoyed any considerable popularity, and its current could be followed for any length of time down the stream of national production until it was strong enough to sustain the burden of a great work, then it would be admissible to claim that the existence of the *Diana* could be explained sufficiently from the circumstances surrounding it in its own fatherland.

While occasional specimens of pastoral composition are to be found in Castilian and Portuguese poetry back to the Middle Ages, no connected line of works is seen until Ferdinand and Isabella had strengthened their throne by the expulsion of the Moors and the discovery of America. The romance of chivalry had already lived its life among the people, and under the revision of Montalvo had just risen to favor with the nobility. Peace had been secured from domestic foes, and the mind of the nation, wearied with the long discords and fond of the herdsman's life, was ready to turn aside from the martial strains of ballad poetry to the quiet pipings of the shepherd's muse. The period of military glory had not passed by any means, for the Empire was about to begin, but still the time had come when other literary themes could be introduced in the place hitherto held exclusively by the warlike. And it would seem as though the reign of Charles V. witnessed the evolution of the pastoral novel, very much as the religious wars of the preceding centuries had fostered the development of the romance of chivalry.

For ideas foreign to the territory of Spain and Portugal were always welcome there, and often received the rights of citizenship on the banks of the Douro and Tagus. So the likeness in the formation of the pastoral novel and the romance of chivalry does not stop with the adaptation of their respective contents to a new locality and an alien race. Both nations of the peninsula worked together in the production of the pastoral, as they had done in the evolution of the romance, and each of them must be credited with the honor arising from its labors, share and share alike. Or rather, as the Spaniard has won the greater praise in the romance of chivalry, so the Portuguese must be accorded the chief glory in the shaping of the pastoral. *Amadis of Gaul,* whatever its antecedents, came into literature in the Spanish tongue and fathered by a Spanish noble. But the author of *Diana,* though using in his work the more widespread idiom of the peninsula, was by birth a Portuguese, and his most important forerunners could lay claim to the same ancestry. However, there is no call for any exact differentiation between the two nations at the time of the Renaissance, since in all literary matters, and in their sensitiveness to outside influences of style and thought, they acted as one people, and their authors wrote indifferently in either tongue.

But in following out the path of the pastoral in Spain and Portugal our task is not by any means so simple as it was in exploring the ways of the romance of chivalry. The material for the pastoral came from more than one source, and though these sources can be roughly located, as springing from Roman literature, from Italian, and from the indigenous poetry of the peninsula, yet to define more exactly the contributions of each to the resulting product is a most difficult matter, and one to which the present knowledge of the subject is certainly inadequate. The bucolic poetry of the fourteenth and fifteenth centuries, both in Latin and in the vernacular, still awaits the investigation of modern scholars. Consequently it is too early to pretend to write the final history of the evolution of the modern pastoral novel, and the pages which follow are to be taken as indications, plausible but not assured, of the way in which that evolution may have taken place.

The first definite appearance of pastoral poetry in the literature of the peninsula was at the court of the Portuguese king, Diniz. There *pastourelles*, in the manner of France and Provence, were cultivated by the native poets, and very likely may have become thoroughly acclimated. In Spain proper, however, there is very little evidence of the presence of bucolic verse. The influence of Provençal lyric during the fourteenth and fifteenth centuries, and particularly in the provinces of Aragon, Catalonia, and Valencia, led to the imitation of the rural poetry of Provence, as the writings of the Marquis of Santillana clearly prove. But whether this foreign fashion awoke any native sentiment among the more popular poets, or whether the Provençal strophic form was imitated because it afforded a more polished framework for indigenous material, we have at present no means of ascertaining. It is known, however, that the economic conditions of the country would of themselves naturally conduce to the popularity of pastoral subjects, and did, in fact, guide the steps of the rising drama, whatever may have been its effects on lyric verse.

For Spain was always a land of flocks and herds, and remained an agricultural community long after the cities in the other parts of western Europe had inclined the industrial balance of their nations in favor of the artisans. The larger towns in Spain were under the control of the Moors until a comparatively late date, so the population of the North was divided between warriors and shepherds, for its two largest classes. When the drama arose under the auspices of the Church, and developed out of the sacred liturgy its mysteries and miracles, the people of Spain strongly favored the cultivation of a kind of religious play which appears hardly at all in the mediæval drama of the other Romance nations. And it was under the influence of the national industry that the Christmas *auto* came into being. The visit of the shepherds of Judea to the manger at Bethlehem was an especially pleasing subject for the husbandmen of the Spanish tablelands, and as a result the *auto* multiplied itself in Spanish literature. Scarcely a poet wrote, during the Renaissance, who did not attempt to win the applause of the multitude by the production of these cherished scenes. And when the strictly liturgical character of the play yielded to the encroachments of the secular theater, the pastoral disguise of the original actors coincided no less with the taste and demands of the same public they had interested in their first surroundings. Besides, there is not much doubt that the example of the Latin eclogue confirmed, among the educated classes, this natural inclination of the people.

In this way the ground was unusually well prepared for the reception of the pastoral narrative, while its growth was further favored by the previous expansion of the secular pastoral drama, or eclogue. As early as the year 1472, when Montalvo was giving to *Amadis* its final revision, the seeds of its later rival were already bearing fruit in a series of strophes in dialogue form, which are known to literary history as *Las Coplas de Mingo Revulgo.* Their subject was anything but pastoral, a genuine satire on the evils of the times, when the country was being wasted by the civil strife which the feeble king, Henry IV., allowed to go on unchecked. But the actors who carry on the dialogue are two shepherds, one of whom, Mingo Revulgo himself, personifies the common people. The piece is, therefore, an eclogue in appearance, probably suggested by the Christmas *autos.* At all events, it became a great favorite with the Spaniards, and its success lasted well into the following century.

Some twenty-five years later than the anonymous *Mingo Revulgo,* a Spanish poet, known to fame, who had been a student at the great University of Salamanca, and who became afterward the celebrated chapel-master of Pope Leo X., Juan de la Encina by name, produced an entire set of dramatic eclogues. They were of both types, sacred, after the style of the Chrismas *autos,* and profane, in the manner of the Italian school. Among the latter there is one which seems unmistakably patterned on a French *pastourelle.* It contains the traditional village scenes, allegorical allusions and descriptions, all of which are portrayed in the acting and conversation of shepherds, both in leading and subordinate parts. More significant is a dramatic pastoral of Encina's, after the Italian style, and no doubt inspired by a Latin or Italian original, though it was written in 1497, before pastoral dramas had advanced very far in Italy. The story is simple, and tells how the shepherd, Fileno, confides to two friends his love for Zafira and her rejection of his suit. It concludes with the suicide of the melancholy hero.

Encina was fond also of translating Virgil's *Bucolics,* and the use of classical names for his actors, even in pastoral inventions of his own, points quite clearly to the source of his conception.   With his successors foreign influence prevails in a steadily increasing degree. The second and third decades of the sixteenth century saw the literary career of the great poet Garcilaso de la Vega, an acknowledged admirer and disciple of the ancients and one of the most ardent supporters of the revival of learning.   It was Garcilaso who called the attention of his countrymen to the excellence in form of Italian poetical work, and started the new school of lyric poetry in Spain.   His own individual writing was not extensive, though excellent in quality and important in its bearing.   About one-half of it was made up of three eclogues, rather lyric than dramatic in nature, the content of which discloses on the part of Garcilaso a great admiration for Virgil, Horace, and the Italian Sannazaro.   But the most interesting feature about them is that the three poems are clearly based on facts of personal experience, and present so many episodes taken from the life of the poet. Their setting is Spanish, the names of their characters are anagrams or suggestions of living Spaniards, and one of the princely families of Spain is directly eulogized in them.

Whatever then may have been the influence of the pastorals of Latin antiquity or of the style of the *Arcadia*, it is beyond dispute that the chief element here is local and Spanish, and that the purpose is to place the writer and his friends before our eyes in pastoral disguise. We find, therefore, in these lyrical narratives of Garcilaso that fusion of indigenous and extraneous material—the former furnishing the story and the latter the ornamentation, the substance original, the form borrowed—which would appear to be the embryo of the pastoral novel in Spain. If this conjecture be true, the poems of Garcilaso take on an importance in literary history which has not heretofore been assigned to them.

The story which the first poem tells runs after this manner : On the banks of the Tagus a shepherd, Salicio (anagram of Garcilaso), is seen complaining to his friend, Nemoroso (who is probably the poet Boscan), of the coldness of his mistress. And such was the grief excited by the recollection of these woes that at the end Salicio expires from unrequited love, and leaves Nemoroso behind to close the eclogue with a lamentation over the loss of his own beloved, Elisa. The second poem is much longer and more detailed. It opens with a description of the surroundings of the action, which takes place near a fountain beneath the trees—the conventional scenery. Next is introduced the hero, Albanio, a truly melancholy shepherd, who proceeds first to recall his woes in verse and afterward to forget them in the oblivion of sleep. But soon the song of the shepherd Salicio awakens him to his grief again, and in the midst of a fresh outburst of lamentations he tells the story of his sorrows to the newcomer : One day when Albanio was resting from the fatigues of the hunt, in company with a nymph of Diana's train, he was besought by her to disclose the face of his heart's love. He pretends to comply with her request, and bids her look for the features of his mistress in the waters of the neighboring fountain. Unsuspecting, she follows his directions, and the calm surface returns to her the reflection of her own countenance. She understands at once the mystery, and in shame and confusion flees away. This is Albanio's story. Salicio, in pity, now tries to comfort the deserted lover, and the two finally leave the scene.

No sooner are they out of hearing than the nymph who has occasioned all this suffering, Camilla by name, arrives at the fountain. She has no confidant, and must fain soliloquize. So in her monologue she declares that she truly loves Albanio, but yet desires to keep the vows she had made when she entered the service of Diana. At last she also falls asleep in the midst of her perplexity, and is discovered in that condition by Albanio on his return. His joy at seeing her again is cut short, however, by the approach of Salicio and Nemoroso. In his vexation he falls on these unwelcome friends most valiantly. The strife arouses Camilla, who disappears. Now the poet, using Nemoroso as his spokesman, runs off into a long eulogy of a country-seat by the river Tormes, and the family of Alva— a digression which became the fashion in the later pastoral novels. So the device, which Garcilaso employs here, of an urn adorned with the portraits of the famous men of the time, and bearing inscriptions recounting their mighty deeds, was also much used in subsequent pastoral literature. The eulogy ends the second eclogue. The third eclogue is unimportant. It describes a vale of the Tagus, and celebrates a nymph who dwelt there. A poetical tournament between two shepherds concludes the series.

Whether the notions which Garcilaso has expressed in these three poems were original with him, or whether they were borrowed from native or foreign predecessors, the fact remains that a generation previous to the appearance of *Diana*, the most popular poet of his age had outlined in Spain all the essential features of the pastoral novel. There are hints in his eclogues of the dramatic pastoral, such as Boccaccio cultivated, and they contain conceptions which very likely were prompted by the love legends of antiquity. And in his own participation in disguise in the action of his story, Garcilaso may have been guided by the example of Sannazaro in the *Arcadia*. Yet, when all concessions have been made to the foreign influence in his work, we must still admit that the Spanish poet showed a great advance over his supposed models in other literatures. In the matter of scenery he was not affected by them at all, but chose deliberately, in the very face of the Arcadian fashion of his day, the banks and valleys of Spanish rivers. As regards the time of his action, he coincides somewhat with the ideas of

Sannazaro, making it half-mythological by the presence of nymphs, and half-actual by the anagrams of his actors. His eulogy, however, of living men inclined the balance of sentiment to the side of modern feeling, while by citing the names of their patrons he revealed so plainly the identity of his fictitious shepherds, that the slight dose of mythology in the story must have seemed to his contemporaries an inartistic anachronism. Other elements of the traditional pastoral he seems to have disregarded entirely, notwithstanding the opposite trend of the Italian writers, and by dwelling, without digressive episodes, so strongly as he does on true emotion, he carried the probability of his plot to the verge of the narration of true events. In other words, time and place were almost entirely modernized in the eclogues of our poet, and required no further handling to be prepared for the appearance of the pastoral novel. The idea of selecting episodes from the life of the author and his acquaintances was not new, of course, but Garcilaso, by localizing it in well-known Spanish scenery, must have contributed very much to its popularity and future adaptability. After his eclogues a developed plot and a prose form alone were needed in order to produce a genuine pastoral romance.

Garcilaso's influence was not confined to subsequent Spanish literature only. The educated classes of Portugal, who were familiar with the language of their neighbors equally with their own vernacular, came under the charm of his verse, and acknowledged his authority as leader of the new Renaissance school of poetry. And besides this reception by the literary class, his eclogues, though lyric in their essence, almost elegies indeed, were considered as fair game by the wandering troops of actors which were beginning to overrun the peninsula, and through them found access to the popular theater. Thus their dramatic side was emphasized. In this way they were kept before the minds of the public, and by their popularity they were made the starting-point for a whole series of pastoral plays, which in their turn prolonged and extended Garcilaso's conception of pastoral composition. How many obscure and nameless poets became his imitators is not recorded, but among the authors whose merits have handed down their writings to posterity, there may be found some who seem to have received from him their inspiration for pastoral literature.

Among such admirers of Garcilaso we may probably count his relative, Francesco de Sà de Miranda, a native of Portugal. It is possible, to be sure, that this brilliant writer obtained many of his views of pastoral poetry directly from Italian sources, since he visited Italy between the years 1521 and 1526. If so, his resemblance then to Garcilaso is merely accidental. Yet the ties of blood which held the two poets together, and the popularity of the Spanish writer throughout the whole peninsula, make the theory of Miranda's relationship to him in literature, as well as in family, the more plausible one. At all events the Portuguese author employed the same method in the treatment of his subject that Garcilaso had used, and gave to the material which he selected, and to the Italian forms of versification he had borrowed, the same vividness of local coloring and the same realistic basis in nature. Many of Miranda's eclogues are arranged as dialogues, and contain nothing which need be here mentioned as in any way distinctive. But the first poetical narrative which came from his pen is interesting for many reasons. It is is told in the first person, and is called *The Story of the Mondego*, written in the winter of 1527–28.

The theme is the love affair of an orphan, Diego, who lived on the banks of the river Munda. One day, as Diego was returning from the chase, he heard near at hand the voice of a nymph who dwelt in the plain between the river and the mountain. He advanced toward the voice and descried the maiden, whose appearance and attire were most attractive. Her song was on the birth of Diana and Apollo. But as the hunter approaches she becomes aware of the gaze of mortal eyes, and in confusion vanishes, to be seen no more. Her flight, however, comes too late for the peace of Diego, for already had the arrows of love transfixed his breast. After seeking in vain for the nymph, he takes the hills and groves into his confidence, and pours into their sympathetic bosom the words of his lamentations. Though a victim to the god of love, he celebrates his power as it was revealed of old in the life of Orpheus, and when consolation delays to come he yields to his passion's consuming flame, pines away, and dies. Now his neighbors who had tried to comfort him in his grief give his lifeless body burial by the side of the stream, which they ever after call Mondego in remembrance of him. And they placed on his tombstone an epitaph, which told the passer-by of the might of love and the sorrow of nature at the death of the youthful hunter.

The general trend of this poem is clearly like the course of Boccaccio's pastorals, and it may be even considered a less tragic *Ninfale Fiesolano*. The elaborate description of the nymph's figure and dress reminds one also of the fondness of the Italian author for such delineations. So we cannot say that in its contents Miranda's eclogue marks any advance toward the later novel. But in his style and in the accessories of his story the Portuguese poet contributed no inconsiderable share to the reality of pastoral pictures. He was not content with the repetition of the conventional phrases on the beauties of nature and the charms of country scenery. He is modern and his sketches are living. His grass is thick and growing, his meadows are strewn with flowers of many hues, and in the background of his landscapes are grazing the fleeciest flocks in all Portugal. Miranda loved nature for herself, and his hero found in her a friend who could soothe his sadness. His love for her vitalized the touches with which he expressed his delight in her charms—a trait we are too often inclined to limit to the writers of the more modern romantic school—and in the *Story of the Mondego* there is that renewal of natural vigor, which is always felt when an ideal conception descends to refresh itself by contact with its real substance. Nature is now valued for the pleasure she can give to sentient man, and no longer for the literary uses to which she may be artificially adapted. After Miranda had provided a genuine rural setting for pastoral things, the task of subsequent authors would be to place within that frame the expression of personal emotions and real desires. This work the writers of Portugal successfully performed, and by their narratives of actual human experience attained the end for which the more artistic Italians had vainly striven. They founded indeed the pastoral novel.

It was a friend of Sà de Miranda who first united these two essentials of a living pastoral composition. He was also a Portuguese, but, unlike his associate, chose his mother tongue for his literary language. His name was Bernardim Ribeiro, was born about 1486, and lived until, perhaps, 1554, being thus Miranda's senior by some years, and his contemporary as well. Ribeiro, like the other literary men of his time, tried his hand at lyrics and eclogues. It cannot be claimed that he was at first influenced by his compatriot, for he had composed some poems before Miranda had proved his own talent. But it cannot be questioned that the two exercised a mutual control over each other, and quickened their mutual inspiration. Ribeiro came also under the same literary influences as the other poets of the age. The Italian pastorals no doubt furnished him with many suggestions, both for the style and the composition of his work, while the bucolics of Virgil and the poems of Garcilaso are not to be left out of account, in a study of this Portuguese author. Besides he may have come into sympathetic contact with the ideas of Provençal poetry, which were now dying away before the oncoming of the Renaissance standards of taste. Yet whatever may be his indebtedness to all these sources for inspiration or material, it is not open to much doubt that the foundation of Ribeiro's pastoral writings is the same as the one which supported the eclogues of Juan de la Encina, for in the case of both the secular *autos* of the popular theater seem to have shaped their literary career. Other influences, to be sure, came in, but mainly for the bettering of their style and the dramatic development of their episodes.

In keeping with the theory of Ribeiro's dependence on the *auto*, we find that his first eclogue is a dialogue between two shepherds on the subject of love. The one who is ignorant of that passion gives a deal of sound moral advice to the other, a lover, disconsolate because his mistress had married a richer swain. In this little scene it is possible we may have the echo of an event in the life of the author himself, for in the poem following an episode of personal experience is certainly the theme. He there tells how a shepherd, Jano, disregarded the warnings of an older comrade, and, at the age of twenty-one, left his rural peace for the turmoil of court life. Soon he falls in love with a shepherdess, Joanna by name, of noble birth, in which hopeless attachment he perseveres in spite of the knowledge that it is hopeless, and notwithstanding the lessons taught by a previous unlucky affair of the heart. But a relief is at last found for him in the sympathetic breast of another shepherd, Franco de Sandovir, the anagram for Francisco de Sà de Miranda.

Other eclogues later in date provide this story with a sequel. The third in the series relates the lamentations of the solitary Silvestre over the unhappy state of his affections, and the arrival of Amador, who has fled from his own private grief. In the fourth Jano reappears, but as an exile in foreign lands on account of his unsuccessful suit. All these four poems were written previous to 1516. The fifth, composed many years later, is in dialogue form again. Two exiles, Ribeiro and Agrestes, meet as wanderers banished from their native country, and talk over their mishaps and their chances of returning home.

The importance of these five poems consists almost wholly in the facts they relate, which are undoubtedly so many leading events in the career of their author. They show his departure from his native village, his sojourn at the court, his love for one above him in social station, his consequent exile from his fatherland, and finally his supplication to be allowed to return to his home. Put these incidents into prose, turn the poems into chapters, tell the story in the first person, and you have an autobiographical novel, in pastoral disguise. This is precisely what Ribeiro did, in after years, and the result of the transformation is the pastoral romance *Menina e Moça* (Girl and Maiden).

This unusual title is taken from the opening words of the story, which are spoken by the girl in question. A sub-title often used is *Saudades* (Regrets) *de Bernardim Ribeiro.* Perhaps the latter furnishes a better indication of the contents of the book, for after carefully reading the many short chapters of which it is composed, we are still in doubt as to the purpose of the author, and " Regrets " do not commit him to one thing or another. To increase our uncertainty in regard to his intention, Ribeiro has imitated in many of his scenes the characteristic episodes of the romances of chivalry. So the work is not strictly pastoral in spirit, though its setting is rural. Nor are all of its characters in pastoral disguise. And as a last objection there is no unity of action in its plot, for it is unmistakably divided between two distinct stories.

The first part introduces a girl sitting on the banks of a brook, and bewailing the absence of her lover. But soon the approach of a woman of noble presence puts an end to her complaints, and starts the maiden on an account of her past life. Nothing particularly fascinating is seen in her story, and our own familiarity with such longings will excuse its omission here. The only new feature in it is the idyl of a nightingale, which, while singing its sweetest song on the overhanging bough, falls lifeless into the water and is borne away by the rushing current. The notion of this delicate sketch was probably derived from Provençal poetry, where the nightingale is the singer of the shepherds' loves. After the girl has finished, her audience reciprocates, and unfolds the occasion of her own sorrows : Lamentor, a knight renowned, comes from a far foreign land to escort two ladies. On approaching a bridge he is challenged by its keeper to a combat. He accepts the defiance and overthrows his opponent, who dies from the effect of his wounds. Now Lamentor pitches his tent near the fateful bridge, and for a time repels assaults and enjoys the company of his friends. But sorrow presses close on his footsteps. His own lady-love, Belisa, dies in childbirth, and leaves her knight and sister, Aonia, behind, to bewail her loss. The latter, however, is not long in finding a partial distraction, in the proffered suit of a new arrival, the knight Narbindel.

Here the first division of *Menina e Moça* comes to an end. The pastoral element up to this point is hardly more than a pretense and an introduction. The principal theme is the episode of chivalry, and the love of Lamentor (anagram of Manoel, duke of Beja) for Belisa, the anagram of Isabella of Seville, who married Manoel in 1496, and died in childbirth two years later, approximately the time when Ribeiro appeared at the court of Portugal. So that his recollection of the sad ending of this happy marriage now serves him as a prelude to the recital of his own misfortunes. For the second part of *Menina e Moça* is the expansion of the five eclogues we have already reviewed.

Narbindel arrives at the bridge and desires to fight with its keeper, in order to prove the greater loveliness of his own lady. But the bridge stands deserted, while Lamentor, in his tent, is mourning by the side of his dead mistress. Narbindel's sympathy is aroused by this sight, he follows Belisa's body to the tomb, and in the funeral train his eyes encounter the downcast face of Aonia. He does not delay in becoming smitten with her charms, though a recent unfortunate experience with Cruelsia, who had sent him to the bridge, might have taught him better. Yet he still fears this former flame and, to give her the slip, now dismisses his squire and changes his name to Bimnarder. Near a castle where Aonia has found refuge the fickle lover lingers for a while until his horse is devoured by wolves, and a herdsman receives him into his hut. Under the calm influence of this rustic friend, Bimnarder's spirit becomes softened. He renounces the ways of knight-errantry, and turns to the pastoral pursuit of a cowherd. But through all these outward changes his heart still beats true to Aonia. Night after night he watches her window, seeking to attract her attention, and at last his perseverance is rewarded by a private interview with her, which he owes to the kind offices of the chambermaid. No happiness is durable here below, and Bimnarder's was no exception to the rule. One night he is overcome by sleep at Aonia's casement and, falling to the ground, is so injured that he can no longer keep his daily tryst. But his mistress seeks him out in his wretched hovel, and by this decided assurance of her affection renews his amatory delights. Nevertheless his destiny must be fulfilled. Lamentor gives Aonia in marriage against her will to a wealthy suitor, Fileno. Bimnarder cannot endure this grief and flees the country, and the closing chapter of the romance shows us the unhappy Aonia bewailing her forced hymen.

There can be no mistaking the thinly veiled actors in

this part of *Menina e Moça,* and the anagrams might as well have been the true names of the persons they represent.   Aonia is certainly the Joanna of the second eclogue, while Narbindel or Bimnarder varies little from Bernardim. The story here is the story of the eclogue without much variation.   The characters are not all pastoral, but include real nobles undisguised, while the hero's adoption of a rural garb is not more serious than was the hermit life of Amadis himself.   On the whole, then, there is a stronger tendency in this last half of the book toward the style of the romances of chivalry than toward the tone of the pastoral compositions, and perhaps were it not for the beginning of the story it would be an error to number *Menina e Moça* among pastorals.   But this very hesitancy between the two leading kinds of fiction in fashion at the time expresses most clearly Ribeiro's literary independence.   And he is not content with suggestions offered by moralistic literature alone, but looks in other directions for hints in perfecting his narrative.   For instance Aonia's chambermaid in the castle performs the part of the go-between, which became such a feature of later Spanish comedy, and which was already in favor among the popular dramatists; and the story of a bull-fight told by her is borrowed entirely from the great forerunner of Spanish drama, the play of *Celestina.*   In regard to the mingling of prose and poetry, which Boccaccio and Sannazaro had carried out so persistently, Ribeiro's pastoral does not call for much comment.   Possibly the substitution of prose for the original poetry of his plot had caused him to adhere more closely to one style of writing. At all events he introduces into *Menina e Moça* but two pieces of poetry, and they are both entirely foreign to the conception of the poems in *Ameto* or the *Arcadia.*   One of the two again reveals Ribeiro's fondness for Provençal literature, being an imitation of that poetical form of the troubadour song which goes by the name of *solatz.*

Of pastoral traits, besides the introduction and the disguise of Narbindel, there is little to be said. Aonia's beauty is lightly touched upon, when Narbindel surprises her as she sits weeping with "loosened hair," but this is about all which recalls the usual pastoral descriptions, and this may just as well have been a non-pastoral epithet— practically the opinion we are obliged to form concerning the whole work. For when full justice has been done to Ribeiro and to his story, the importance of it, after all, is seen to be, not in itself, but in its effect on other authors and other works. Especially strong must have been its influence on the mind of Ribeiro's friend, Montemayor, the author of *Diana*, whose experiences tallied so closely with the account of this more modest composition.

Ribeiro's eclogues were published during his lifetime, but *Menina e Moça* is posthumous, and was found among his papers after his death. Accordingly, it was not printed until 1554, but it must have been familiar in manuscript to his associates a score of years before. On its own account it received some attention among literary men, and when a second edition appeared in 1557 a sequel was appended, wholly in the style of the romances of chivalry, and patterned after the episodes of *Amadis*. Undoubtedly this sequel shows that the impression the story made on the public was one of a novel of erotic adventure, and any idea that it was an autobiography in the pastoral manner had died away. Ribeiro's merits as a pastoral writer may, therefore, be summed up in the one statement that he made the personal side so prominent as not to be mistaken by those who knew him or were aware of his history. But he failed decidedly to convey his intention to strangers, and they looked on his few pastoral traits as so many digressions from the true way of knight-errantry. Still, he pointed out to the initiates of his circle the road to success in romancing. After him a greater talent could give to the world the account of his own fortunes, and could profit by Ribeiro's failure to conceal, by a pastoral disguise, the apparent identity of his characters.

The period of the development of the pastoral novel in Spain includes, therefore, the last quarter of the fifteenth century and the first half of the sixteenth. It was thus a much more sudden growth than the romance of chivalry, which had been gathering headway for generations before it claimed a place in the literature of the nation. The reasons for this early maturity of the pastoral are evident. Its style of composition could never be popular with the masses. It appealed purely to the taste of the more refined classes, and particularly courted the sympathy of the educated. The pastoral is rarely plebeian, and the moment the pastoral idea in Spain and Portugal passed from the *autos* of the popular theater into eclogues, after the manner of Virgil and the Italians, or into narratives which represented artificially the vicissitudes of their author's experiences, that instant did its conception become too subtle for the crowd, and its further cultivation lose all interest with the populace. Consequently it became purely the property of literary men, and as such was susceptible of a more speedy development. Notions foreign at first to its spirit were incorporated into it as diverting accessories, and artistic devices from literatures of every age and race were turned once more to literary profit. So, when the pastoral novel was fully ready for the public, it offered to its readers a union of novelistic elements most diverse in origin.

Yet in all its transformations and accretions the chief characteristic of the modern prose-pastoral remained true to the conception of its great authority, Virgil. It told the personal experience of its author under the cloak of a pastoral disguise. This feature is the leading one among the authors of Spain and Portugal, as it had been pre-eminent among the literary artists of Italy. In other respects the pastorals of the peninsula are widely different from their Italian predecessors. In Ribeiro or Montemayor there is no sign at all of national decadence, or of longing for a primitive era of simplicity and innocence. The idea of the Age of Gold gained no foothold among the prosperous subjects of Charles V.; and when the hopes of the world-empire faded with his abdication, the disappointment of the people took a more severe and realistic direction than had been the case with the less seriously minded courtiers of Florence and Ferrara. The theme of the most successful examples of the Spanish pastoral was the private life of their authors, and the pastoral cloak which concealed the true history of the writer would seem to have been merely the result of the influence of a literary fashion.

It is probable also that the growth of the pastoral in the Spanish peninsula was favored by the improvement in the taste of the educated classes, and the consequent decline in their esteem of the romances of chivalry. Like the historical novels of the nineteenth century, the tales of feudal prowess and magic arts soon palled on the more refined palates of the nation, and were gradually allowed to descend to the position of chapbooks and stories for children, while the pastoral novels with their higher aspirations after literary style and plan were taken as substitutes for the romances of national tradition ; and in this substitution it is very likely that the influence of Italy, whose literature commanded during this period the admiration of all Europe, played a leading part. It was also undoubtedly a relief to escape from the didactic sentences of *Amadis* and *Palmerin* to a kind of composition which had no serious purpose and pointed no moral. In the pastorals there are no conflicts of virtue and vice, no heavy villains (unless we call the satyrs such) to bring down on their heads the condemnation of the galleries, and no suffering heroines to stir the pit to pity. They are distinctively a literature of amusement, and being amusement and depending on gossip for the interest they excited, their career was neither so broad nor so enduring as the vogue of either their ideal predecessors or their matter-of-fact followers. The Spanish pastoral did not attain its complete form until the middle of the sixteenth century, and it did not last, even in its weak dilutions, more than two generations longer. And in spite of all attempts to attract and hold the attention of the public by excellence of style or novelty of subject, it produced really but one work which is readable at the present day, or indeed which appears to have excited a more than momentary interest among its own contemporaries. And this unique success of its kind is Montemayor's *Diana*.

CHAPTER IX.

MONTEMAYOR'S DIANA, ITS SEQUELS AND SUCCESSORS.

JORGE DE MONTEMAYOR—or Montemôr, to give the Portuguese spelling—was both a compatriot and friend of Sà de Miranda and Ribeiro, who had preceded him in the trade of pastoral writing. Like them, he seems to have early deserted his fatherland for the wider field of action in Spain. He united in his person the qualities of a soldier and a musician, and in this latter capacity acquired a livelihood at the court of Castile. Montemayor was also a lyric poet, cultivating both the national and the Italian forms of verse. But, as is the case with the other literary men of his time, the events of his life are but little known. His love for nature may very well be traced to his youth spent on the banks of the Mondego, whose praises we have heard sounded by Sà de Miranda, and his notion of revealing in pastoral disguise the misfortunes of his own heart may be assigned to the influence and example of his two associates.

Still, all assumptions as to the origin of his work remain purely theoretical. The *Diana* is independent of any definite model, unless we consider *Menina e Moça* to have served it in that capacity, and the whole tone of its plan and composition is completely individual. The difficulty of discovering literary progenitors for this book is further enhanced by the uncertainty regarding the time of its appearance. Authorities vary, by a score of years almost, concerning its date, though 1558 seems the most acceptable, since a writer speaks of the *furore* created by it at the Spanish court in 1559. But whatever may have given rise to the *Diana*, it is essentially national in tone and feeling, while the loans it makes from foreign sources are thoroughly assimilated to its indigenous material. And these loans affect rather the form than the substance. *Diana* is a record of private life, an autobiography of love, and the consistency of Montemayor in upholding this conception, and in subordinating to it all ornamental digressions, lies at the foundation of his success. For by this logical development of the plot his pastoral gained a unity of action and a vigor of inspiration, which the half-mystical stories of Boccaccio and Sannazaro had not been able to attain.

The idea in *Diana* is the familiar one of unrequited love. Its contents are divided into seven books, for the most part prose and in Spanish. However, poetry is by no means lacking, of both the native and Italian varieties, and occasionally a poem in the vernacular of Portugal is found. The opening scene is laid among the valleys of Leon, where the shepherd, Sireno, is discovered lamenting the loss of his former companion and mistress, Diana, who had been married while he was away on a year's absence from the kingdom. Yet he still sings her praises and cherishes the letters he had received from her. While Sireno is sighing over the names he had cut in the bark of trees, and is gazing sadly at the fountain where he had passed so many happy hours, the voice of Silvano is heard near at hand. Silvano had been his unsuccessful rival in the past, and was now another victim of Diana's marriage. Misery ever loves company, and the gloomy swains entertain each other with both prose and poetical lamentations, until their desolate symposium is finally interrupted by another prey to amorous misfortune, in the person of the shepherdess Selvagia. This damsel proves to be a most vigorous champion of her sex, valiantly repelling the attacks on woman made by her masculine colleagues. After a while of polemics truce is established, and Selvagia consents to furnish entertainment by the recital of her own troubles.

Her story is somewhat intricate. On the banks of the Douro she had met at a festival the lonely shepherdess, Ismenia, with whom she soon became intimate. She finally discovered by Ismenia's confession that the latter was a shepherd in disguise, Alanio by name, and Selvagia accordingly proceeds to fall in love with her acquaintance on the new basis of sex. But Ismenia's confession was false. She was a woman strongly resembling Alanio, whom she loved. The genuine Alanio now takes advantage of his great likeness to Ismenia, and passes himself off for her to Selvagia, who is not aware of the substitution. The real Ismenia, finding herself deserted by her lover, seeks consolation in the company of another shepherd, Montano, but with a change of amorous fortune, for Montano in turn does not delay long in becoming enamored of Selvagia. So we have a series of cross-loves, such as the imitations of Poliziano's *Orfeo* had made popular in Italy. The tangle can be unraveled only by Selvagia's disappearance, which in due time takes place.

After listening to this story, the two melancholy shepherds and their new friend agree to watch their flocks together, and to make a daily exchange of their sentiments in conversation and song. While they are dragging out in this manner a sorrowful existence, one morning they are delighted by the arrival of three nymphs, who come up singing *villancicos*. After the singing they tell each her history, until the entertainment is broken up by the appearance of three wild men (evidently Montemayor's modernization of satyrs), who lay violent hands on the nymphs and are about to carry them away. But the ravishers are transfixed by the arrows of a shepherdess, who comes upon the stage of action in the nick of time. As reward for the service she has thus rendered them, the valiant archer, Felismena by name, insists on using the assembled company as an audience for her story, the longest in the book.

Felismena's mother, having dared to question the justice of Paris' award of the golden apple, had a dream wherein Venus appeared to her and foretold her death in childbirth, and the unfortunate career in love of the fruit of her womb. On the other hand the distressed woman was straightway assured by Minerva that the child would be both prudent and brave. Now when Felismena had reached the age of discretion she became violently smitten with a young nobleman, Don Felix. When he was sent to court by his father she followed him, entered his service disguised as a page, and served as a messenger between him and a new mistress, Celia. The latter inconsiderately falls in love with the supposed boy, and dies of grief at the rejection of her love. Thereupon Don Felix disappears, and Felismena assumes the shepherd's dress.

This story is very like the tale told by Eustathius in his *Hysmenias and Hysmene*, and from the use which Montemayor has made of one of the proper names of the Byzantine narrative in his heroine, Ismenia, it seems quite certain that he was acquainted with at least some portions of the Greek novel and has adapted them to his purpose. But he has handled this foreign material in the most artistic manner ; and by cleverly filling in the borrowed outlines with Spanish customs and Spanish characteristics, he has imparted to his revision of Eustathius such a local coloring and impression of reality that it might pass very well for the recital of an actual occurrence.

Now the rescued nymphs, whose conduct had been irreproachable during this extended discourse, wisely head off any further speeches by offering to lead the way to Diana's temple. All gladly accept their guidance and the journey is begun, thus giving the author an opportunity for a picture of nature, which he improves: " With very great contentment the beautiful nymphs were journeying along with their company through the midst of a dense wood, and when the sun was about to set they came out into a laughing valley, through which a wild torrent flowed, adorned on either side by thick willows and alders, among which were many other kinds of smaller trees that entwined themselves with the larger and interlaced the golden flowers of some with the green branches of others. The sight of them gave great pleasure. The nymphs and shepherds followed a path which led along between the stream and the beautiful grove, and they had not gone far when they reached a broad meadow, where was a most charming pool, from which the brook came and rushed down the valley with great force. In the midst of the pool was a small island, where some trees were growing, which almost veiled a shepherd's hut. Back of this was a flock of sheep grazing on the green grass. Then as that place appeared to the nymphs suitable for passing the night, which was now upon them, by means of some stones which had been placed in regular order from the meadow to the island through the middle of the pool, they all crossed over dry-shod and went straight toward the hut they had seen on the island."

In this hut they find a shepherdess asleep. When she wakes she tells them that her name is Belisa, and that she had formerly, in another condition in life, been courted by both father and son. The father made the son, of whose passion he was ignorant, the bearer of his letters to his beloved, and the singer of his songs in the nightly serenades. One night the supposed son is talking to Belisa from a tree near her window, when the father chances to come that way. He hears the vows addressed to his mistress, does not recognize their author, and in a rage shoots an arrow into the tree-top. The son falls to the ground, and the father, discovering his mistake too late, kills himself on the spot.

After telling this story, which bears all the marks of a genuine Spanish comedy—love, jealousy, night scenes, murder—Belisa concludes to join the company and go with them to the temple. As they approach the building nymphs come out to meet them, together with a wise and mature beauty, Felicia. The temple, which the author describes in detail, is adorned with the statues of the national heroes and women of high rank in the kingdom, and each statue bears its own private eulogy in rhyme. The entertainment at this place was furnished by Orpheus, who, being preserved there by enchantment, was able to extol in song the charms of the Renaissance beauties. To this *musicale* succeeded a feast of reason, in which love, as the offspring of reason, was made the subject of discussion. After this *tertulia*, Felismena recites a Valencian tale she has heard, and which forms the most interesting part of *Diana.* But unfortunately there is not much doubt nowadays that this story is an interpolation of a later editor of the book, and that it was not found in the original during Montemayor's lifetime. It is in style a Moorish romance, and its subject is the love of Jarifa and Abindarraez, the last of the Abencerrages.

This narrative, as it appears in *Diana,* is the account of an adventure which had already found its way into literature, or popular tradition, and of which various other renderings appeared about this time, notably that of Antonio de Villegas. Yet the celebrity of this episode in foreign lands, where it had many imitators, was due mainly to the version which the renown of *Diana* circulated so widely. It is most romantic in character and proceeds as follows :

In the reign of Ferdinand of Aragon, during an expedition against the Moors, the Spanish knight, Rodrigo de Narvaez, went out one night to reconnoiter the position of the enemy. On reaching the banks of a river he divided his escort of nine warriors, left five of them to guard the ford, and passed the stream with the remaining four. Soon after their companions had disappeared, the watchers by the ford heard the sound of music, and from their ambush became aware that a young Moor was passing near on horseback, singing as he went songs in praise of his lady-love. The Spaniards rush from their hiding-place and fall upon him, but he resists them most stoutly, and is on the point of routing them all when the appointed signal from a horn reaches the ears of Rodrigo, and hastens his return. On his arrival a single combat is arranged, in which the Moor, who has been exhausted by his previous efforts, is finally worsted by his fresh adversary. On the way back to his castle with his captive, Rodrigo is struck with the latter's melancholy, and after a long insistence receives the confidence of his prisoner. He was Abindarraez, the only survivor of the princely house of the Abencerrages, whose execution had shaken the walls of the last Moslem stronghold in Spain almost to the ground. Abindarraez had escaped the general massacre of his kindred by having been sent, while a mere child, to a castle on the frontier, the warden of which, an old friend of the young Moor's father, had reared him like his own son. This warden had an only child, a daughter, Jarifa by name, who supposed Abindarraez to be her own true brother, as he believed her to be his sister. The affection and trust between them was only strengthened by the later revelation of their real position, and when Jarifa's father was ordered to a new post, and the young Abencerrage returned to serve his king, the lovers kept up a frequent communication with each other. It was on one of these visits to his lady that he had fallen into the hands of the Spaniards, and his chagrin at his captivity was embittered by the thought that Jarifa would look in vain for him.

Such a story could not fail to appeal to the chivalrous spirit of Rodrigo. He grants his prisoner temporary liberty on the condition that in three days he will place himself again in his power. Abindarraez joyfully accepts the offer, hastens to the castle of his beloved, and in her presence forgets for the time all perils, past and to come. But when the three days are nearly over, and the hour approaches when he must fulfill his promise, sadness begins to oppress his noble mind. His mistress perceives it and wonders. Silence only adds to her anxiety, and so he is at last obliged to apprise her of the situation and his compact with Rodrigo. After the first outburst of grief the Moorish maiden takes counsel of her love, and determines to return to the Spanish castle with her lover, where they arrive together in season to redeem the plighted word. Their fidelity to the pledge and to each other arouses still further Rodrigo's magnanimity. He does not delay to restore to them their freedom, and couples with this gift a letter to the Moorish sovereign, in which he asks of him pardon for the Abencerrage. The king cannot fail to yield to the petition of so courteous an enemy, and nothing now stands in the way of the future happiness of the faithful lovers.

After the insertion of this truly romantic episode, the revised *Diana* returns to Montemayor's narrative, and to the temple where the company was assembled. There the arts of enchantment reign. Felicia sinks Sireno, Silvano, and Selvagia into a deep sleep by the innocent means of a draught of water. When they are brought to consciousness again, Sireno finds himself entirely cured of his love for Diana, and Silvano and Selvagia become aware that they are prepared to reciprocate each other's affection. After a while they all leave the temple and go each his own way. Felismena, as she travels on alone, hears by accident the complaint of Arsileo, who is the youth that was supposed to have fallen a victim to his father's rage while he was courting Belisa. In his lament Arsileo accuses a hostile necromancer of conjuring up two spirits in order to deceive Belisa and drive her to despair. It was exceedingly opportune that Arsileo should have detailed all these circumstances in Felismena's hearing, for she straightway interrupted his sorrow, sent him away to find Belisa, and thus made two loving hearts one. She is also instrumental in reconciling another couple of which the swain had been jealous of Arsileo. Now all the chief characters are satisfied and peaceable save Diana, who begins to bemoan her marriage and upbraids Sireno for his change of heart.

But Felismena is not yet rewarded. She wanders over Spain and Portugal, and at last reaches the vicinity of Coimbra. There on an island in the river she sees a mortal combat of three against one. She comes to the assistance of the one, beats off his foes, and finds that she has thus rescued her own knight, Don Felix. Water cures his wounds, the balm of his affection her lacerated heart, and finally united in holy bonds they commence a pilgrimage toward Diana's temple, where the author temporarily leaves them.

The intention of Montemayor, as declared in the closing pages of *Diana*, was to continue that book at some future time, and to bring the remaining features of his plot to some definite solution. Consequently, the part which he actually wrote is to be considered as a portion of the whole, and its sins against unity of action, which is not as complete in *Diana* as it was in the far less artistic *Menina e Moça*, are perhaps to be pardoned on that account. For, as the book now stands, the heroine of the beginning of the story, Diana, is supplanted by the later arrival Felismena, and the adventures of the latter are brought to a happy end, while the reconciliation of Sireno to his mistress is yet to be accomplished. Besides this unfinished ending, the author hurries the matter of his concluding chapters to such an extent that the reader becomes entangled in the different threads of his narrative. Yet his principal object is plain in spite of all digressions. He wishes to show how Diana is punished for her inconstancy, and how Sireno, who is evidently Montemayor himself, becomes indifferent to her without acquiring the consolation of a new love. There is also a didactic strain in the story, where reasonable affection, which depends on enduring charms, is typified by the image of the goddess' temple.

The general movement of *Diana* is quite attractive. At first the author is disposed to tell his tale quietly and leisurely, while by judiciously mingling poetry with his prose he relieves the modern reader, at least, from the tediousness which would be necessarily begotten by the lack of solidity in his scenes. His descriptions also are excellent, whether of nature, people, or buildings, and are pleasantly varied. In all of them a hearty regard for Spain and Portugal, and pride in the greatness of the former nation, pierces easily the assumed covering of prehistoric surroundings. In strong contrast to the Italian pastorals there are in *Diana* no traces of Arcadia, and no employment of genuine paganism. Nor on the other hand is there anything in the book which is distinctively Christian. Yet its tone throughout is personal and modern, and its episodes and allusions are peculiarly local. So strongly indeed does this flavor of actual experience pervade the material which Montemayor has gathered together from so wide a field, that all events which are not of the sixteenth century appear like anachronisms, and the introduction of any heathen deities at all seems a sin against literary taste.

It is interesting also to notice how Montemayor's loans from the romances of chivalry, especially the features of magic and enchantment, jar with the tone of his observation of real life. We feel that in *Diana* there is no need of supernatural agencies to heighten the merits of the novel in the eyes of the public. The author is so thoroughly bent on giving his own statement of his career (once even he appears in the first person) that any use of marvels for popular consumption seems entirely superfluous. For there cannot be much doubt that the delight of the Spanish courtiers of Philip II. in the story of Sireno and his mistress was due to the element of gossip which they discovered in it, quite as much as to its beautiful descriptions and its varied verse. To be sure, it was the first good specimen of Spanish prose which dealt with love as a principal theme, and thus it afforded a change of literary diet to the lords and ladies who had become weary of the extravagant prowess of Amadis and Palmerin. In fact, *Diana* contains no small dose of sentimentality, which evidently suited the palates of its day, while there is in the style of its composition a sufficient tendency toward conceits (which later became so popular under the name of Gongorism) to allow the literary set of Madrid, to which these were particularly addressed, a pleasurable feeling of superiority over their rough and unfinical contemporaries. For there are times when literary success may be achieved by an appeal to intellectual esteem, and by an open disregard of the common herd, though we cannot say that *Diana* depended for the welcome which might await it on this sentiment of caste alone, or a certain degree of initiation into literary *arcana*. Its novelty of subject, its personal bearing, and its flowing periods, all had their share in the favorable result. But the novel never was known in Spain outside a select circle, and it was not adapted to the comprehension of the vulgar. When the crowd abandoned the romances of chivalry it demanded stronger mental nourishment than was afforded by the pastoral novels.

Not only in the matter of magic did Montemayor's pastoral feel the influence of the romances of chivalry. Its whole conception of gallantry was borrowed from these aristocratic predecessors. This is shown in various ways, as in the frequent appearance of epistles in the first part of *Diana*, thus continuing the fashion set by the authors of *Amadis*, or in the courtly conversations between the lovers in the different episodes of the pastoral. Perhaps Montemayor's style marks a progress in the use of conceits over the narratives of erotic adventure, and thus may point the way to the subsequent *préciosité* of the Hôtel de Rambouillet. A good example of highflown conversations may be taken from the Felismena-Don Felix story. In this part Celia, who does not reciprocate the affection of her vehement suitor, makes answer to him in this manner:

"'Never was a thing, which I might suspect of your love, so far from the truth as to give me occasion for not believing my suspicion many times more than your excuse. And if in this I do you wrong lay it to your forgetfulness, that you could indeed deny past loves and not give occasion to be condemned for your confession. You say that I was the cause of your forgetting your first love. Console yourself with this, that another woman will not be wanting to make you forget your second. And be assured, Sir Felix, for I affirm to you that there is nothing worse for a knight than to find in any lady whatsoever an occasion for becoming lost on her account. And I shall not say more, because in evils without a remedy it is the best thing not to procure it for one's self.'" All of which is certainly frank, and framed so that Don Felix can hardly have failed to see the point.

It is hardly necessary to trace out the imprints of the previous pastoral poetry or prose of Spain and Portugal on the content of *Diana*. They are visible everywhere, and particularly in the great allegory of the novel, Diana's temple, which was erected to the glory of the great names in the nation, and to the memory of their deeds. In his poetical passages Montemayor naturally imitates the stanzas of the Italian pastorals, and the latter undoubtedly contributed also to the ease and amplitude of his style. Poetical contests are not absent from his work, nor mottoes, eulogies in verse, nor songs. The richness of his strophic forms excited the admiration of his countrymen, and of foreigners as well, while the emulation they aroused at home and abroad did much to preserve the popularity of the novel. No less interest did the Spaniards show in its disguised characters, and we read in the histories of the century, that some fifty years after the author's death his heroine, the real Diana, was visited in her old age by the court of Philip III. Such was the honor in which Montemayor was still held. Yet we must not suppose that in his disguised personages he attempts character painting at all. The actors on his stage represent but one emotion or one talent, and in no way could they pass for delineations of real human beings.

From what we already know regarding the career of successful novels in the sixteenth century, we shall not be surprised to find that the popularity of *Diana* tempted the ambition of many other writers, who fancied it was necessary to their renown to furnish that continuation to the original work which its author had himself promised, but had not lived to accomplish. Consequently in 1564, but three years after Montemayor's death, two sequels were placed on the market, one by Alonzo Perez and the other by Gaspar Gil Polo. The production of the former is roundly rated by the curate in *Don Quixote*, and put with the combustibles of the hidalgo's library ; and it certainly merited the trial of fire.

For Perez did not heed altogether the plan which his friend had in mind, and which he had expressed near the end of his *Diana*, but after obeying his wishes so far as to renew the lamentations of the heroine, and to lead the company, increased by new swains, through conversations and singing back to the temple, he branches off into inventions of his own. He introduces a character, Parfiles, who is seeking for his lost daughter, Stella, and when she is found the attention of the reader is invited to the perusal of her love affairs. Stella is of the haughty type in matters of affection, though when she is accused of undue coldness to her suitors she defends herself very much as Marcella afterward did in the pastoral episode of the first part of *Don Quixote.* After the second book of such a sequel very little of the original plot is naturally to be looked for, and when, after unfolding many times in various descriptions the abundance of his mythological erudition, Perez is reminded at the end of his eighth book to kill off Diana's husband, Delio, it is too late in the day for Sireno to profit by her long deferred widowhood. So nothing has been accomplished, and Perez concludes by promising still a third part in which he hopes to reach a solution. This promise he luckily never kept.

The other continuation, known as *Diana Enamorada,* met with Cervantes' approval, and is not so very uninteresting as a literary type, even to a reader of the present day. First and foremost it has the virtue of brevity. Like Perez, this rival brings in at the beginning a new character in the person of the shepherdess Alcida, who endeavors to console Diana for Sireno's change of heart. Their confidences are cut short by the arrival of Delio, who at first indulges in a scene of jealousy, and afterward falls violently in love with Alcida. But the latter's suitors are already too numerous and too persistent for her comfort, so she escapes from this last addition to them, and leaves the stage to one of her former adorers, Marcelio by name. He has a long tale of woe in store for us. He had been betrothed to Alcida in Africa, had sailed with her for Lisbon, but had been overtaken by a storm at sea, and had been shipwrecked and was carried off by the sailors, thus completing a series of episodes, which may very well have been suggested by the Greek novels. After Marcelio has had his say, Ismenia takes the floor and abuses her husband, Montano, in a story which could easily furnish high comedy with a good plot. After Ismenia is done the adventures of new actors fill out a couple of books. Here we have long-lost relatives and sweethearts to be recognized, disguises to be assumed and penetrated, songs to be sung, and eulogies to be pronounced. One digression is a glorification of the men of Valencia, much after the style of Montemayor's praise of Spanish grandees, and among the names cited by Polo we recognize the familiar one of the poet Ausias March. Finally, after long wandering samong subjects of his own invention, the author returns to the task he had inherited, kills off Delio, changes the spirit of Sireno by the oracles of the stars, and marries him to Diana. The fifth book is occupied with an account of the wedding festivities, told in most extravagant language, and *Diana Enamorada* comes to an end, like the original, with the promise of a sequel in which the new threads of the plot are to be untangled, and the long-deferred fate of Danteo and Duarda, which had rested so heavily on Montemayor's conscience, is to be revealed. But literary men, even in the sixteenth century, were as fickle as their heroes, and no third part was published by Polo or anyone else until 1627, when a writer in Paris, by the name of Texeda, foisted on the public a jumble of Polo and stories from other Spanish authors which can claim neither value nor consequence.

But Polo's sequel is not to be dismissed with a mere analysis only. He was a man of no inconsiderable talent, though his book may hardly pretend to the originality or the freshness of its model. He was a good versifier, and extended his poetical acquisitions to the use of French and Provençal, as well as Spanish. He has, however, too high an idea of pure rhetoric, and becomes too labored in his striving after artistic effects. More worldly minded than Montemayor, he courted the favor of polite society and incorporated into his fiction many of its games and tableaux. Besides, in his rôle of the continuator of *Diana*, he shows himself too subservient to his predecessor, exhausting his reader by his frequent references to the original pastoral. Yet Cervantes' praise proves that Polo was appreciated by his countrymen, while abroad his book had no small success and received the honor of several translations into French. It is also of such a nature that it can be read to-day, a remark that cannot be made perhaps of any other pastoral that followed in the wake of *Diana.*

For in the two generations which succeeded the publication of Montemayor's novel not a few Spaniards tried to repeat the success of their Portuguese master in the pastoral art. What reward crowned their efforts is best seen in the judgment of the curate in *Don Quixote.* Of the five pastoral novels which he enumerates, four he condemns without deeming them worthy of further remark, and the fifth, which he praises, is not much better than the rest. Its author, Montalvo, was Cervantes' friend, whence the difference, perhaps. Still his book was shorter than the others, and one needs only to read the specimens composed by his contemporaries to appreciate the part that the element of brevity plays in any literary criticism of the Spanish pastoral.

The first of these novels which have a subject independent of *Diana,* is the *Ten Books of the Fortune of Love,* published in 1573 by Antonio de lo Frasso. The contents are mainly in verse, and are a mere compilation of scenes without plot or conclusion. Letters and poetry are couched in the most flowery and bombastic style, and the inevitable palace comes in for a gorgeous description. There are traces of the Italian dramatic pastoral, as in the discovery of the torn veil of a shepherdess, which presupposes her death by wild beasts. Local pride is present in the praise of Catalonia, and in the jousts which take place at Barcelona, while even politics, of the anti-democratic kind, are not eschewed. A more tiresome and pointless volume it is hard to find, though literary history may get a crumb of interest out of it from its unconscious collection of the germs of all those defects, which have made the name of Gongora so notorious in the annals of Spanish authorship.

Montalvo's *Filida*, which appeared in 1582, is a novel of disguised characters where the disguise is very apparent. It has no plot, or at least no solutions of the many scenes in which we see Philida and fellow-shepherdesses being wooed by a larger number of shepherds, some of whom are not really in love with the maidens to whom they are paying court, but are merely taking that method to arouse the jealousy of their chosen mistresses. The usual temple of Diana is built again (here displaying all the wonders of the world), and the ladies of Spain are again gratified by seeing their names in print. The romance of chivalry comes in for a share of influence, as it had done in Lo Frasso's pastoral, and an interesting touch of realism is revealed in the passage where Montalvo feels called upon to appear in person, and defend himself against the criticism that ordinary shepherds do not pasture their flocks near the hiding-places of wolves. But even without a plot *Filida* has redeeming features in the excellence of its style. It is simple, without bombasts or conceits. There is no attempt to keep up the threadbare fiction of pagan surroundings, and the poetry of the book is good and varied. But when one has read the *Diana*, even the best of its imitations are somewhat wearing.

Cervantes himself tried his hand at the kind, a few years after *Filida*, in his pastoral *Galatea*. The prologue of this book remarks on the fashion of writing eclogues, and states the author's own inclination toward poetical composition. At the same time it very justly apologizes for the metaphysical disquisitions which are woven into the body of his narrative, yet forgets to excuse his many conceits and the euphuistic tone of his descriptions. Even later, in *Don Quixote*, when Cervantes has occasion to refer to this production of his earlier years, he still seems to be unconscious of its most striking deficiencies. The heroine of the story, Galatea, is a kind of Felicia. The court ladies esteem her for her wisdom. She is indifferent to love, and, as a sad consequence, is all the more harassed by the pursuit of indefatigable rustic swains. This is about all that can be found concerning the chief character. Cervantes' efforts are all centered on the various episodes he describes, and in which he relates events which are far more dramatic than any we have yet met with in the Spanish pastoral.

One of the episodes is the familiar tale of love between children of hostile families; and the murders which thereupon ensue—some of which are due to mistaken identity—give anything but a cheerful picture of the village life of the time. Other episodes supply us with an assortment of imperfect suicides, increase our knowledge of contemporaneous happenings by repeated allusions, and narrate to our delectation fierce combats with infidel Turks. Naturally, in the midst of these gleanings from active existence, the intended portrayal of pastoral life stands very little show. Let once the shepherds get well under way in recounting their experiences, and a series of most startling occurrences cuts short their reminiscences before any crises are reached. In the same way their assemblies are often interrupted by the approach of some powerful vocalist. Therefore unity of action cannot be looked for in such a compilation, and even the pastoral pretense often goes by the board. Still Montemayor was evidently a powerful influence in the thought of Cervantes, and imitations of *Diana* abound in *Galatea*, particularly the long discussions on the nature of love, the attempts to analyze the tender passion, and the eulogies of noted Spaniards, which Cervantes very loyally turns to the profit of the writers of the day. A conclusion to this work was promised, whether because it was the fashion so to do, or because Cervantes really meant it. But it never appeared, and *Galatea* slumbered on, practically unnoticed, for two centuries, almost to a year, when it was revived in French by the amiable Florian.

In the same decade with *Galatea*, other poorer pastorals, if possible, saw the light. Of a moral tendency, showing the sin of jealousy, was *Truth for the Jealous*, by Bartolomé Lopez de Enciso. The story is located on the banks of the Tagus, where a fight between two jealous shepherds is in progress. They are separated by third parties, and an assembly is formed to listen to songs. One singer mentions a certain Clarina, and her name brings out a story from Delanio, who tells how he had forsaken Florista for Clarina and the consequent rage of the former. Soon after this account the neglected one appears on the scene, and enters upon a long series of talks with the wise Laurenio on the nature of jealousy. New shepherds and fresh shepherdesses come in, love, and become jealous, while the wise shepherd calmly sits by and cites examples of the passion in antiquity. From these platitudes the reader is at last rescued by Enciso in person, who breaks into his pastoral with a description of the conventional palace, and eulogies of the royal family. After this broader digression the story is resumed for a while, finally closing with the usual promise of a sequel. But no one evidently cared for further moral advice on jealousy, and we hear no more of Enciso.

The next year, 1587, a shorter pastoral was published, having the avowed object of extolling Spanish scenery. It was called the *Nymphs and Shepherds of the Henares*, and its author signed himself Bernardo Gonçalez de Bovadilla, "student in the illustrious University of Salamanca." Like the others already cited, this new pastoral has a very slight plot. Its hero, Florino, is disdained by the beautiful Rosalia, and is consoled by the sympathetic Melampo. But Melampo soon receives his own sorrow, for Palanea will have none of him. Florino after a time is sent with his flock to the dales of the Tormes, and the nymphs are left to lament his absence, while Palanea also mourns over her desertion by Melampo. And so the story goes, enlivened —to look on the hopeful side of life—by many songs of ancient and mediæval love, and by chronicles of Danish history in verse. Finally, Florino is allowed to return to the Henares, and is there reconciled with the repentant Rosalia.

Another pastoral of limited fame, and unknown to modern readers, is mentioned by Cervantes under the title of *Shepherds of Iberia.* It was written by Bernardo de la Vega in 1591. The book seems to have disappeared, and we can give no extended analysis of it. There is no question that it was tedious even in its own time, and met with no success. The same thing is true of a religious imitation of *Diana,* and one or two secular pastorals of this closing decade of the century, though one redeeming book was published then, and one more writer, now illustrious, tried his hand at pastoral composition. This writer is none other than Lope de Vega himself, and his work bears the title of its Italian predecessor, the *Arcadia.*

Lope's story is distinguished from its fellows in that it maintains some connection between its several parts, and shows a little sense in its narrative. Its model was evidently Sannazaro's pastoral, and the locality chosen for the action is that of Greek Arcadia. But even with these traditional influences of mythology and classicism at work the actors in the new *Arcadia* are shepherds born on the banks of the Tagus, and many of its incidents recall the well-worn themes of the Spanish pastorals. Consequently Lope is always mixing up fabled antiquity with the Spain of Phillip II., and yet redeems such confusion in place and time by the merits of his poetry, the excellences of his style, and the fecundity of his erudition in the domain of ancient learning. The *Arcadia* begins as follows : The shepherdess Belisarda is wooed by many suitors and is won by Anfriso, though she has been betrothed by her parents to the unworthy Salicio. When the shepherds meet they complain of the lovers, and then proceed to discuss the essence of love. Afterward Menalca begins a story, in which a giant plays a part. Though she is frequently interrupted by outside happenings, and subordinate tales chosen from the fables of mythology, yet strong in the virtue of perseverance she holds on her way undaunted, whenever there is a momentary lull in this agitated rural existence. The secret affection of Anfriso and Belisarda becoming known, the shepherd is sent away from his village, and must trust his sighs to pen and ink. He visits Italy, is there tampered with by a magician, and at last is induced to abandon his mistress. Her anger and spite on learning of his fickleness throw her into the ever-open arms of Salicio, and only when she is firmly married do the lovers learn of their mutual mistake. Now, Anfriso has but one refuge—the intellectual one. The wise Polinesta takes him in charge, cures him of love by the allurements of learning, and makes out of a very shaky suitor a very solid student. Having reached this edifying goal through a sea of incidents and a forest of citations, the author concludes his book with a eulogy of the Duke of Alva, for whom the novel had been undertaken.

The amazing multiplicity of Lope's digressions, and the extent of his knowledge of the learning of all ages, might very well have discouraged any less completely equipped author from pursuing the line of pastoral composition after the appearance of the *Arcadia*. And it was indeed some years before the style was taken up again with any degree of success. Near the end of the first decade of the seventeenth century the Spanish pastoral was revived along the lines of free imitation of the Italians, as Lope had suggested, and some works of considerable literary value were the result of this second growth. But popular interest had declined, and the authors, who desired something more than a parlor public, turned their energies to other themes which contained a stronger element of novelty. The fact is that *Diana* had incorporated into its own self all the pastoral notions of the time, and the contents of its score of imitations in Spain produced nothing new of a genuine pastoral nature. Perhaps the best of all these later stories is the book of another Portuguese, written in the Portuguese idiom, the *Primavera* of Francisco de Lobo. In the successive pages of this novel, which appeared in parts during the first fifteen years of the seventeenth century, the landscape and rural manners of Portugal are eulogized with a fair degree of taste and vigor. But no successors were awakened by the *Primavera* in the western kingdom, and the days of the pastoral were felt to be numbered.

It had taken but six decades, two generations, to exhaust in western Europe the pastoral school of literature. The reason for this short life lies obviously in the artificiality of the kind. Its themes appealed only to a limited and fashionable circle, and with the change of the fashion it passed away. On account of these restrictions in interest and cultivation it is very difficult to estimate the real importance of the pastoral novel, and the amount of its direct influence. *Diana* had certainly a long and successful run. It went through many editions, both in the original and in translations. But apart from this pioneer, Lope de Vega's *Arcadia* seems to be the only pastoral which attracted any general attention, at least if we are to judge by the standard of successive editions, perhaps the only fair criterion. Even Cervantes' name could give his *Galatea* nothing but the honor of foreign renderings. A general survey of the field would bring us, then to the conclusion that the excellence of the *Diana* and the tone of its thought started a literary fashion, of which various writers tried to take advantage, whose works, however, had not sufficient merit to find a welcome outside of the family circles of the patrons to whom they were dedicated. For the only echo of their existence to be found in other Spanish fiction of the times would seem to be confined to that disturbing episode in the first part of *Don Quixote*, where Grisostomo languishes and dies for love of the hard-hearted Marcella. The pastoral element in the drama of Spain held true to the tradition of the eclogue and the *auto*, and it never produced those elaborate spectacular plays which placed before the theater-goers of France entire episodes, dramatized bodily from the pastoral novels of the day.

But when we consider the effect of *Diana* on the development of the modern novel, we must assign it a place second in importance in the history of fiction to *Amadis of Gaul* alone. For in its two hundred pages of poetry and prose are found the germs of many novelistic notions, suggestions of emotions or situations, which have been elaborated in later times and in other lands by authors of the ideal school, who in the majority of cases were not aware of the source of their inspiration. Still it was not its pastoral disguise which gave *Diana* so wide a circle of influence, but rather the sentimentality of the book, the modern feeling of sadness, and the modern view of nature's sympathy with man, which is its most distinguishing characteristic. To appreciate the tone of *Diana* and its effect on the minds of its public, we have only to compare it with the Greek pastoral of *Daphnis and Chloe*, which the translation of Amyot made accessible to the literary men of France the same year that bore witness in Spain to the popularity of Montemayor's story. The novel of Longus, in spite of the attention it received from humanists and admirers of classical antiquity, did not modify at all in renascent Europe the trend of pastoral writing. It was too simple, too calm, too unromantic, to appeal to the warriors of Henry IV. or the navigators of Queen Elizabeth. Their adventuresome spirit longed for reflections of active life, for the joy and the melancholy of emotional shepherds, while their curiosity in the real identity of the fictitious characters of the modern pastoral made the loves and disdains of these characters the more attractive to them.

In the matter of emphasizing passion and emotion the Italian and Spanish pastoral authors had worked together. Boccaccio had shown the way to the more modern sentiment of Sannazaro, while in Tasso and Guarini it is the human heart as it beat in Italy of the decadence, which sings of its deceptions in love. The Spaniards of the sixteenth century had no tradition of antiquity to struggle against. They presented only the modern side of individual feeling from the very beginning of their pastoral work. So in the combined result of the two literatures on the tendency of their French imitations, the Italian and Spanish were united in the warmth of their emotion as contrasted with the cold analysis of the Greek rhetoricians. But when it came to the style of their work and its plan the moderns fell apart. The lack of a definite central idea in the *Arcadia* rendered it powerless as a literary model among the logical writers of France. Its plot was not sufficiently developed and its episodes were held together only by the merest thread. On the other hand, *Diana*, with all its faults, was a story which had some necessary connection between its parts ; and by the merits of its literary structure its deficiencies of style, when compared with the brilliant periods of the *Arcadia*, were in great measure atoned for. Accordingly, when both pastoral schools appealed to the favor of a foreign public, it was the more disciplined product of the Spanish mind, which secured the literary primacy.

The great medium through which the novelistic elements of *Diana* were conveyed to our latter-day authors was the celebrated novel of Honoré D'Urfé, the *Astrée*. The plan, tone, and make-up of the *Astrée* are practically the same as those of *Diana*, and many of the situations and notions of the Frenchman are openly borrowed from his Spanish master. And when we take into consideration that the *Astrée* not only set free the great stream of French fiction in the seventeenth century, but that its melancholy shepherds and disdainful shepherdesses controlled the drama of France for a time, and set the social fashion of the most influential European capital for fifty years and more, we may gain some slight idea of the extent of Montemayor's importance in the history of modern literature.

For it did not stop with the career of Corneille and the life of Mlle. de Scudéry. The popularity of literary productions in France based on the laws of reason thrust back indeed the oncoming tide of sentimentalism, but only for a time. And when, after two generations of Cartesianism and skepticism, the emotional soul of Jean Jacques Rousseau was aroused to action by the kindred sentimentality which went out to meet him from the pages of the *Astrée*, the true career of the Spanish pastoral had at last begun. Changes in place and changes in social surroundings came in for their share, to be sure. Yet after all due allowance has been made for different times and different circumstances, it is clear, as a matter of literary heredity, that the sentimentality of *Diana* has developed into the sensibility of *La Nouvelle Héloise*, and that the appeal to romantic passion, which was sounded from the Tagus to the banks of the Lignon, found its lasting echoes among the hills which shut in the blue waters of Lake Geneva. The melancholy of Sireno, who loved the wife of another, is repeated in the longings of St. Preux and in the despair of Werther. While all the heroes of the romantic school in literature renew, in their complaints, the refrain which wooed in vain the cruel beauties who pastured their flocks by the pleasant brooks which watered the tablelands of Leon and Castile.

CHAPTER X.

THE novelists of the nineteenth century have made the
public of to-day tolerably familiar with the composition of
realistic fiction. Since the days of Walter Scott and beginning with the decline of the romantic school, there is hardly
a story-writer to be found who is not more or less in harmony with this prevailing fashion. Nor are the reasons for
this predilection at all obscure. Realism in literature was
born into the present civilization under the pressure of social
unrest, and hostility of the lower born toward the former
ruling classes, as well as from the desire to be true to nature
and render a literal counterpart of contemporary manners.
It is to be lamented that caste prejudice has had to do with
a school of such wide-reaching influence ; for realism, as it
now stands, is hardly different from pessimism. It is no
longer a protest against the aristocratic or unreal, but is
rather a delineation of human helplessness in the conflict of
mankind with the vices of its surroundings and the certain
goal of its temporal existence. Hence the rise and progress
of the school called naturalist, and the striving after the exact
reproduction in literature of man's physiological environment.

There can be very little doubt, however, that these scientific divagations of fiction afford for a time a pleasing
variation from the novelistic reduplication of such exploits
as are performed by Amadis' descendants, and from the
constant wailings of the disciples of Sireno and Felismena.

Yet there are limits set to the charms of realism, as well as to the allurements of fantasy, and in the long run the latter seems to endure better than its rival. For the world is not so generously responsive to its children who demand from it both living and recreation, as to induce them to while away their leisure hours in reviewing their own struggles here below, and reflecting that the end thereof is physical death. The school in fiction which dwells on the hardships of humanity may gain, by its talent and art, a comparatively abiding welcome with that portion of the public which possesses an educated taste, but it will never succeed, even in the height of its celebrity, in winning to itself the majority of novel readers. The crowd demands pleasure from its books, and when the authors who can rightly lay claim to style and composition fail to bring on oblivion of its daily routine, it turns without any compunction to second-rate compilers. The content and not the form is the essential thing to the great majority. Or more correctly it is the spirit of the content. We are therefore at all times confronted with the fact that the sales of novels furnish a reliable indication of the true feeling of humanity. And they show that the people at large is always hopeful, believes in itself always, and in its own progress, and that discouragement in regard to the present, or despair for the future, is ever confined to a limited circle of the select few.

For this vital reason the ideal novel has always been both the pioneer and the favorite type of fiction. Walter Scott appeals to a wider circle than Thackeray, and not for his theme alone, but for the manner of treating his theme. And if we go back to our own particular province, and compare the relative popularity of the various kinds of novels in the sixteenth century, we can easily understand the lasting supremacy of the romance of chivalry over its rivals. It alone was hopeful. The most successful of the pastorals was sad in tone, if ideal in conception, and when the writers of the pastoral related events taken from life they became realistic, however perfect their rustic disguise might be. So their works soon passed away, and left vacant places to be quickly filled by the avowed tales of actual experience.

The wonderful creative energy of the Spanish mind had not been wholly exhausted, then, by the formation of the romance of chivalry and the pastoral novel. It still retained of its great capacity for romancing sufficient force to produce perhaps its most important invention. For the story it tells of the struggles for existence of the impoverished descendants of the warriors of Ferdinand, or the companions of Pizarro, has lived longer than all its accounts of glory or despairing love. The hero of the new episode is not a knight but a plebeian. His morals are those of a rogue or sharper, and from his Spanish title of *picaro* the term "*picaresco*" has been applied to the narrative of his achievements. These were mainly in the line of his getting on in the world, his knavery or villainy, his attempts to cheat or steal, his cringing and bullying, until after years of hardship and mental exertion he has acquired a sufficient competency or position in the community to be able to repose from his cares, and find leisure to intrust to the world the account of his successful devices.

It is therefore evident that the first purely realistic novel was ushered into existence under the most untoward auspices. It did not profess from the start to describe life in its general relations, but only the rascally side of life. It was a novel of character perhaps, or rather of the deceit which can be made to predominate in a low character, and it was also a novel of manners in its description of the various classes of people through which our rogue threaded his devious way. It is something like the pastoral in its directness of appeal, but it is openly autobiographical, instead of being transparently so. In its material, however, it is much more original than its predecessors, and is wholly and entirely Spanish, though of course Renaissance rascals were by no means confined to Spain. It did not go outside of the peninsula into the literature of other nations to seek for the contents of its plot. It relied on observation for its subject-matter, and it discarded whatever could not come into the field of ordinary existence. There is no element of magic or the supernatural in the *picaresco* novel, even in such a small dose as the personal pastoral itself allowed.

The invention of the *picaresco* novel pleases our idea of symmetry, for it completed the circle of novelistic action. Following the imaginative stories of an ideal society based on feudalism, and accompanying the half allegorical, half real narratives of pastoral life which verged closely on the portrayal of real events, there was still a place for a series of fictitious events, which should be the direct reflection, or the exact impression, of the occurrences taking place in hard, practical, every-day existence. Unfortunately, however, these reflections and imprints were colored by personal and class feeling, and conveyed to the public, which found itself concerned in them, only a partial representation of the actual surroundings. The *picaresco* novel sees only the life which the more discontented and ambitious members of the middle classes saw ; the struggle to rise in a period of general decline, the fight to get on in the world, to gain wealth, or to keep it when once acquired. These first examples of realistic writing marked out the way to be followed by the subsequent productions of the school ; and it is the evil in the world which forms the principal theme of the continental Le Sages, Balzacs, and Tolstois. In England alone with Fielding and with Thackeray—the truly realistic novelist— do we find a fairly complete picture of the triumphs as well as the trials of humanity.

But from the very fact that the realistic authors of Spain in the sixteenth century forced on their readers the painful side of human experience, their works did not become numerous or popular in the usual sense of the word.   It was only the unfortunate in ambition, those who were conscious of being defrauded by society, that defended a literature of discouragement.   The upper classes of the social structure, whose wealth remained an occasion of continual self-satisfaction to themselves, or those whose birth, though not attended by riches, was exalted enough to receive the adulation of plebeian prosperity, these happy beings never lent a willing ear to the laments of the poor and the restless.   On the other hand the great majority of mankind, without social aspirations, intent alone on inexpensive pleasures, is rarely, if ever, affected by the bitterness which periodically pervades the class between the people and the aristocracy.   The masses of a nation do not believe in man's defeat in his conflict with nature.   Hope never leaves them ; even when in a time of national decadence the whole social fabric above them is wrapped in gloom.   Consequently, a literature of despair is never found in chapbooks, and the descriptions of failures, without final rewards here below, have no market with what wecall the people and with the trading class which has sprung from the people.

Still we are aware that the history of fiction testifies to a steady demand for what is termed realistic writing.   That demand is not dependent on fashion like the pastoral novel, for it has a lasting body of supporters ; but it nevertheless increases in extent, or decreases, according as the class which sees in it the reflection of its feelings, absorbs the upper stratum of society, as in a time of general unrest, or shrinks to the restricted numbers of those who are perennially discontented.   This last was the state of the case in Spain under Philip II.   The combination of the disappointed had become strong enough to make itself heard, but it had not, as in the seventeenth century, won over to its ranks the larger part of the educated and refined.   Therefore two *picaresco* novels only come within the scope of this history.

The origin of the *picaresco* novel appears to be the same as that of satire in general. It was evidently a protest against the prevailing style of literature, which in the romances of chivalry showed an utter disregard for the real condition of the Spanish nation, by celebrating only the deeds of the one class in feudal society, the nobility. In the career of the *picaro*, the despised third estate avenged itself for the successes of Amadis and Palmerin. The appearance of *Lazarillo de Tormes* was a direct challenge to the eulogists of vanished knight-errantry. Instead of a hero urged on by love and loyalty to win fame by the strength of his arm and the generosity of his mind, the Spanish public was invited to compare such a career with the actual adventures of any rascal taken from among the common herd, while personal observation was appealed to in the question of deciding which life was borne out by the facts, and which was not. In other words the *picaresco* novel was not only a study of a rascal, but it was, besides, a protest against the predominance in literature of the aristocratic type. In carrying its hostility to the romances of chivalry so far as an entire forgetfulness of their spirit, the insurgent went to the other extreme, and busied itself with portraying the exact opposite of the manners and ideals of a true and perfect knight. And undoubtedly this feeling of revenge and irony made the heroes of realism from the very start the embodiment of all that is mean and crafty.

But there is also in these presentations of the people's cause a more noble sentiment than that of mere revenge. It is the sense of indignation, which must have moved just hearts at the blindness of the popular literature for the true condition of the country, at the endless repetition of jousts and campaigns in which geographical Spain even was hardly ever in question. True patriotism might have inspired a wholesome delineation of the virtues and vices of the nation, its misfortunes, and the elements out of which regeneration should come. But in the bitterness of class resentment the virtues were strikingly absent, and the vices occupy the foreground of the picture ; and so, by insisting on the characteristics of the dark side of life, and in holding up before man the reflection of his sorrows without a corresponding view of his happinesses, the realistic novel failed to fulfill its true mission. It satirized, to be sure, the disdain of the romances of chivalry for the actual condition of Spanish life, but in its championship of the weak and suffering it omitted to defend the nobler instincts of man, and therefore it has remained in the history of literature as an exponent of but half the truth, and that half the less inspiring portion of the whole.

The example thus set by the *picaresco* novelist has been only too often followed by the realistic authors of all later fiction, though the claim that half the truth in art is better than no truth at all is amply borne out by the fact, that the two *picaresco* novels of the sixteenth century are the only examples of all the many romances of that time which can be read at the present day for themselves alone. For they are sketches of human nature, not fanciful outlines of a non-existent society. And through this quality they appeal to our lasting sympathy.

The causes which produced the *picaresco* novel have already been suggested as connected with the circumstances of the Spanish people at the end of the reign of Charles V. Long before the appearance of realistic fiction the social conditions necessary to its existence had all been evolved. The fifteenth century saw the decline of the nobility in France, and the rise of the third estate and the monarchy, its natural ally. But in Spain the forays against the Moors had kept alive the institutions of feudalism long after they had passed away in the other countries of Europe. The political unity of the nation, completed by the fall of Granada, the sudden accession of wealth gained by the discovery of America and the plunder of its treasures, speedily changed the relations which had hitherto been preserved in the society of the peninsula, and assimilated them to those prevailing elsewhere. It was on the eve of this sudden transformation that the glorification of feudalism, which had so long lingered among the traditions of the people, took on a literary form. The romances of chivalry dwelt wholly on idealized memories, and drew their material from a state of affairs which had definitely passed away. Yet the brilliant achievements of the Spanish soldier and navigator, the exploits of Gonsalvo de Cordova in Italy, and the extension of Spanish rule under the great emperor who represented, in his generous character and chivalrous spirit, the true notion of a paladin, rather added to the favor which the eulogies of knight-errantry had already obtained, and prolonged their popularity for another generation. Not until these temporal glories had faded, and the last of the knights-errant had prepared himself to own to the world his own disappointment by a romantic abdication of all his sovereignty, did those whose eyes were not blinded by this outward display of power and prosperity venture to challenge in fiction the magnifiers of feudalism, and oppose to the gallantry of an impossible nobility the complaints and misery of the despairing inhabitants of contemporaneous Spain.

It is in studying the history of the country under its most brilliant monarch that we may easily trace the genesis of the *pícaro*. The reign of Charles had begun shortly after the nation had tasted the pleasures of foreign conquests. The extent and location of his possessions added greatly to the territory to be defended by Spanish arms, while also increasing the renown of the Spanish name. In the changes of European warfare induced by the increasing employment of firearms, the relative importance of the foot soldier to the horseman had rapidly grown, and had opened the door to promotion in the ranks. As soon as the opportunities of the meanest private to win fame and gain riches became known to the Spanish people, the whole male population of the peninsula swarmed into the armies. The success across the ocean of Cortez and Pizarro, and the magnificence and power they displayed before their astonished countrymen, aroused the cupidity of the humblest peasant. It was to be expected that the sight of such rewards for valor and boldness, placed with little regard to birth or rank within the reach of the persevering and audacious, should upturn the whole social fabric of the nation. The poorest laborer saw in a military career the way to social advancement, and the basest deckhand beheld in the Spanish Main the pathway to fortune. As a consequence of these enticements the ordinary callings of peaceful life were abandoned by their followers. Toil, so slow to be recompensed, was despised, and even the walks of industry were neglected for the more especial development of maritime commerce.

The effects of such a universal withdrawal from the shop and the farm were soon felt in the scarcity of the comforts and even the necessaries of life. But the results were not appreciated so long as the armies and the fleets continued to absorb all the able-bodied men of both city and country. It was only when the wars in Europe grew less frequent, and exploration in East and West had garnered its best harvests, that the conditions of life at home became evident to the returning warrior and mariner. Not so much that they found nothing to do, but that they had become unwilling to do it. His active life in camp and on sea had weaned the average man of all interest in more settled pursuits. Manual labor these conquerors of the world despised, and the country therefore was filled with idlers—drawn from the petty nobility as well as from the third estate—who had not acquired in their career abroad the means of future support. Still they had to live, and the only resource left to them by their pride was their wits. Thus we find in Spain in the closing years of Charles V. a class of sharpers by no means few in numbers, who, by flattery of the rich and deception of the stupid, sought to gain by mental effort alone a sufficient livelihood. In no country, perhaps, at least in modern times, have been seen so many parasites and rascals as in Castile at the middle of the sixteenth century. Their perseverance in vagabondage, and their ingenuity in wheedling, well merited to be handed down to posterity in the most popular form of fiction. But from taking cognizance of such rabble, surely the romance of chivalry and the pastoral story may plead to be excused.

The wars abroad and the marauding expeditions by sea had not only unfitted the poorer classes of the Spanish nation for humdrum labor, but had also demanded for their maintenance a continual drain on the national wealth. To make headway against this demand, the people relied not on a corresponding development of home industries, but on the vast amounts of gold and silver which were being poured so freely into the country from its possessions in America. Yet such accession of currency soon raised the price of the necessaries of life without contributing in any way to their increase. To meet the growing expenses of the government taxes were planned, which meant in those days a forced levy on the peasants and farmers. These cultivators of the soil, being unable, from the nature of their occupation, to escape the eye of the collector, found themselves wholly at the mercy of the assessor, and were often forced to hand over the assumed value of their crops before the latter were even harvested. So a first consequence of this new departure in Spain was deserted farms. To add to these conditions of material distress, a shortsighted administration established between the individual provinces a system of tariffs, which completed the ruin of husbandry, and ended in the surrender of whole districts to the more merciful protection of nature. .And in the Spain of the Empire, that favored country oppressed with glory and filled with gold, famine stalked abroad relentless. Bread became more precious than jewels, and hunger is the main thought of *Lazarillo de Tormes.*

To this lack of the common necessities of life the sense of the insecurity of person was a further aggravation. The Inquisition, which at first had been used as a power against the Moorish infidels, had been kept by the government as a useful civil auxiliary, and was now turned loose upon the loyal subjects of the realm. Its methods of secrecy in arrest, trial, and imprisonment gradually undermined in the minds of the common citizen all notions of law and justice. Spies were everywhere, and the daily evidences of their subtle activity gave each man good reason to look upon his neighbor as a possible informer against him. Thus the foundations of friendship were destroyed by mutual suspicion and each man lived unto himself. It behooved everyone to look closely to his own interests, to disregard the claims of others, to show to misfortune no pity, and to suffering no charity, under penalty of incurring the vengeance of his unknown masters, whose victim he might be thus aiding. That this statement is no exaggeration the legislative enactments of these decades survive as a living testimony. It is on record that assistance for the poor and unfortunate was furnished only by the lowest classes of the community, who alone had nothing to fear for themselves either in property or in person. The results of this repression of the sympathetic side of man were seen in the proportionate development of hardheartedness and cruelty, and in the manifold manifestation of these vices. Indifference to the common ties of humanity went hand in hand with fatalism in religion. To souls, which were steeled against all compassion for their fellow-beings, laughter and tears had no meaning, or meant one and the same thing. Every man for himself became the motto of Spain in the highest period of her military greatness, and every man for himself is the spirit of the *picaresco* novel. The struggle for existence is no recent theme for literature.

It is possible that this new kind of fiction was also a vent for the bitterness of discontent, which a despotic administration would not allow to be expressed in other and more active ways. And if so, then allowances must be made for this repression, which would only accentuate the evil traits of the picture which it draws. Yet after all due reservations, enough is still left in the *picaresco* novels to give us a good idea of the existence they pretend to portray. They must have been true in the main, else they would not have outlived the contempt of their public. They professedly rely for their material on observation of their surroundings and the study of contemporaneous manners, and they do not appeal in any way to the traditions of the people or the favor of an imported literary fashion. They are original and they are indigenous, and previous novelistic accumulations have very little to do with their make-up. Grant the *picaresco* writer his theme, the material on which he works must be of his own finding. This would not, of course, preclude all suggestions which the novelist may have obtained from outside sources, but it would oblige him to adapt any such suggestions to the situation which he is intent upon describing.

It is probable, with these conditions in view, that the first *picaresco* novel, *Lazarillo de Tormes*, was influenced in certain episodes by antecedent literature, and that its opening chapters may furnish us with a clew as to the kind of literature which was thus laid under contribution. The subject of these chapters is a description of the practical jokes which a boy guide plays on his blind master, and the various punishments he receives for his labors. Similar themes were no strangers to the literature of Europe from its earliest origins, and the tricks of young Lazarillo were invented long before his time by the purveyors to the popular amusements of the Middle Ages.

For in that golden age of romantic literature human infirmities, and particularly deformities of the body, were looked upon as punishments decreed from on high for sin. And this view of man's physical weaknesses lasted through the whole period of the Renaissance down to the eighteenth century. Therefore, to our forefathers the conclusion was obvious, that those persons upon whom Heaven had set a seal of condemnation should not receive the pity and charity natural to true believers, but that the divine judgments should be ratified on earth by the ridicule and cruelty of the faithful. In obedience to this pious sentiment the lame and the blind became in literature, as well as in real life, the legitimate objects of derision. Especially was this the case with the most popular literature, the drama. The mediæval stage of France, which set the fashion for the secular playwrights of Europe previous to the revival of learning, developed a whole series of plays in verse, based on the mental and bodily shortcomings of its characters. These plays were known by the name of *farces*. Many of them were merely samples of buffoonery and coarseness, resembling very strongly the tavern anecdotes of the present day. Not a few, however, showed genuine wit, though not of the most refined type, and a degree of literary merit which has preserved them from the general destruction experienced by their fellows. All of these survivals belong to the fifteenth century, with one exception. And it is a curious fact that this exception, a French *farce*, played at Tournai, not far from the year 1277, should have the same subject as the first episode of *Lazarillo de Tormes*. The preservation of this piece furnishes quite a conclusive proof of the popularity of its subject, and its appearance in

Spanish fiction 275 years later testifies to the universality of its application.

This old Flemish story of *The Boy and the Blind Man* begins with an appeal of the beggar to the passers-by, and the invocation of blessings on the heads of those who make substantial responses to this appeal. But the blind man has as yet no guide, so laments for his helplessness follow close on his benedictions. As he moves along he wanders from the way, and only after some inconvenience to himself is he brought back into the road by a boy who happens to meet him. This kind attention results in an offer from the beggar to hire the boy to lead him to Tournai and help him beg in that town. After some parleying the boy agrees to a bargain, and they unite their efforts to get alms by singing. But music has no charms for the charitable people of that region, and the boy, growing weary of his task, suddenly finds an imperative reason for a short absence. When he comes back, however, he steals up behind his blind master and deals him a staggering thwack, without awakening his suspicion. A few minutes later the boy reveals his presence, and the beggar complains to him about the blow he had received. Further dialogue between the two conspirators leads to a commission given the boy to buy food. For this purpose the blind man hands over his purse to his able assistant ; but when the rogue has it once safely in his grasp he reviles the beggar in the choicest terms of his vocabulary, and makes off with the money, to the undoubted delectation and approval of the honest burghers of Flanders. The scene ends with the promise to the boy of a sound thrashing if his master ever catches him again.

Belgium and Spain were farther apart in the thirteenth century than they are to-day, but there was nothing to prevent the cross-road jugglers from peddling their tricks, and such simple plays as they chose, all over Europe. And though we have no evidence of the presence of *farces* in the Spanish literature of the Middle Ages, it is probable that this little drama, and many others like it, were being performed in the peninsula daily without ever rising to the dignity of a literary mention. At all events, the union of Spain with the Netherlands at the accession of Charles V., and the inroads of Spanish soldiers and traders into the latter country, must have made many of the invaders familiar with the scenic amusements of the market-places of the North. And the rapidity of the literary communication between the two countries is evident from the publication of *Lazarillo de Tormes* itself, which for a long time was attributed to the presses of Antwerp, although it is now quite certain that a printer of Burgos, in Spain, first issued it. Yet, the Antwerp publisher lagged behind him a few months only.

The origin of the opening incidents of our novel cannot be limited to the popularity of the one *farce* cited, since many others must have treated the same subject, varied the tricks of the boy, and narrated the revenge of the blind man. While there is no direct evidence in literature that such was the case, an interesting piece of indirect testimony has recently come to light in connection with a Latin manuscript preserved in the British Museum. The margins of this manuscript were filled up with sketches of scenes taken from the popular literature of the time, the larger part of which were made in England. Among them are several illustrations of the boy and blind beggar cycle of plays, thus testifying to the existence of more than one *farce* dealing with the subject, and also the widespread favor which they had attained. These particular drawings belong to the first part of the fourteenth century, and already anticipate some of the stratagems of the Spanish *picaro* of the sixteenth, as well as the floggings which reward his ingenuity. The most celebrated is perhaps the scene where the boy, standing near his master, is busily sucking the wine from the latter's jar through a hollow reed, a trick which *Lazarillo de Tormes* has absorbed bodily. Seeing, then, that the material of the first few chapters of the novel resembles so strongly certain episodes of previous *farces*, we are quite safe in drawing the conclusion, that the author of this first prose narrative of actual life had borrowed from the stage certain incidents adaptable to the general trend of his plan, and which had the further advantage of being familiar to his readers. So, after all, a moderate amount of foreign matter, and more exactly some elements of French invention, entered into the composition of the *picaresco* novel of Spain.

Lazarillo de Tormes is anonymous. For some time its authorship was assigned to the great noble, Hurtado de Mendoza, but there is nothing to show he had anything to do with its contents. On the contrary, the spirit of the book would point to some discontented member of the middle class, who did not sign his work, either through fear of the Inquisition or because he looked on it as of no literary import. The latter theory might receive support from the extent of the novel, which is of ridiculous size compared with its rivals of the Amadis and Palmerin family. The experience of little Lazarus fills, indeed, hardly fifty pages of ordinary print, and might therefore be more appropriately termed a story than a novel, were it not for its great significance in the history of fiction. But it proved to be a David among Goliaths. At the first stone from its satirical sling the gigantic shapes of the knights-errant staggered and fell, to rise no more.

The date of the publication of *Lazarillo de Tormes* is undoubtedly the year 1554, hard on the approaching abdication of Charles. In that year it went through two editions in Spain, and one, at least, in Flanders. Whether it had existed previously in manuscript for any length of time is not known. But probably not, since the state of affairs it depicts could hardly have developed in the early years of the great emperor, and even after they had become general some time must have elapsed before the Spanish public would have allowed them to be openly disclosed to the world.

The novel, being short, contains only four detailed episodes. The incident of the boy and the blind beggar we have already cited. The second episode is Lazaro's experience with a priest, the third his service with a decayed nobleman, and the fourth his connection with a seller of indulgences. Thus all classes of Spain, but the commercial, were levied on, and their traits faithfully handed down to posterity. The *bourgeoisie* was spared, perhaps out of the caste feeling of our anonymous observer, for his successors do not hesitate to hold the merchants and traders up to derision, together with the clergy, nobility, and common people. Another reservation also as to the complete originality of the novel, and its independence of outside influences, may be made in the matter of the last episode mentioned, which had been told before in Masuccio's collection of Italian stories, *Il Novellino*, in that division where the roguery and the mishaps of monks are narrated. But the remaining two adventures of the youthful *picaro* are wholly Spanish, and are exact reproductions of the manners and condition of the upper classes, and of their continual struggle against hunger, the " evil of Spain."

The story of *Lazarillo de Tormes* is told in the first person by the hero, and runs as follows : He was born in a mill on the river Tormes, near Salamanca. His early life was eventful, in that his father did not long escape the gallows, and his mother was compelled to earn her livelihood in Salamanca, where she first boarded students, who attended the university in that town, and took in washing. In this career she did not prosper overmuch, and was finally forced to enter domestic service. At this crisis she surrenders her boy,

Lazaro, now entering on the tenth year of his age, to a blind beggar, in search of a guide, who promises to be a father to the child. With him our hero makes his start in active life, and begins his getting of worldly wisdom. For at the very instant of their leaving the town, as the blind man and his guide are passing over the bridge, which was ornamented with the figure of a stone bull, Lazaro takes his first lesson in human experience :

" ' Lazaro,' said my master to me, ' put your ear against this bull and you will hear within a great noise.' In my simplicity I approached, thinking it to be as he said, and when he felt that I had my head close to the stone he put strength into his hand and gave me a great thump against the devilish bull, so that the pain of the bunting lasted me for more than three days. And then he said to me : ' Dunce, learn that the servant of a blind man must give points to the Devil.' And he laughed heartily at his great joke. And at that instant it seemed to me that I awoke from the innocence in which, as a child, I had been sleeping, and I said to myself : ' He speaks the truth, and it behooves me to keep my eyes open and to plan, since I am alone, how I may get on in the world.' " And wide open his eyes were ever after.

Lazaro and the beggar, than whom " since God created the world no one was more astute and shrewd," wandered over Spain, getting their living as best they could. The blind man knew by heart a hundred prayers and made the churches resound with them, " having an humble and devout countenance, which was well composed when he prayed, not making gestures or faces or screwing up his mouth or eyes, as others are wont to do." He was also a soothsayer and knew many charms and incantations, and in the matter of medicine, " Galen did not know the half he did." His remedies were simple and fitted to all troubles : " Do this, do that, gather such an herb, dig up such a root," rarely failed to work a cure, and the women looked on him as all-wise. But notwithstanding the rewards which such talents obtained, Lazaro got very little for his share of the spoil. An empty stomach was his lot until it kindly sharpened his wits, without which, he says, "I had many times died of hunger; for with all his skill and cunning, I countermined him in such a manner that always, or most often, I got the greater and the better share." The blind man kept his provisions in a canvas bag, securely locked, but hunger showed the boy how to rip a seam and thus obtain not only bread but also "many good bits, ham and sausage." From attacking his master's larder the want of food drove Lazaro to intercept his income : " All the money I could beg or steal I changed into half-pieces of silver, and when he was asked to pray, and they would give him a whole piece, because he was devoid of sight he did not seem to notice me when I threw it into my mouth and had the half ready. And suddenly, when he extended his hand, his money went into it, diminished by my change to half its real worth." However, the blind man suspected his guide of cutting off his revenue, but yet could revenge himself only by giving to his clients half the quantity of prayers.

In the same way Lazaro invented devices for satisfying his thirst. Finding that his wine diminished while he was eating (Lazaro sucking it up through a straw as in the illustration in the manuscript), the beggar held the jar between his legs. But now the boy lay down and tapped the bottom of the vessel, thus causing the liquid to drop slowly into his mouth. The hole made in this way he filled up every time with wax. But the crafty beggar had his suspicions and awaited his vengeance. One day, while the boy is gulping down the precious fluid drop by drop, the earthen jar is dashed down violently into his face, breaking his teeth, knocking him senseless, and filling his flesh with the broken scales of its glazed surface. From this moment war is openly declared. The boy plots revenge and the master loads him with blows. When bystanders remonstrate, they are gained over to the beggar's side by the story of the wine. Yet the boy is still the guide and he leads his master through the roughest paths, where he stumbles and is bruised ; and so the honors of deceit and violence remain about evenly divided. One day, for instance, an overripe bunch of grapes was given the beggar, and he proposed to eat it one grape for another with Lazaro, to which the latter agreed : "But straightway at the second turn the traitor changed his intention, and began to pick them two by two, thinking I would do the same. Since I saw him break the bargain I did not stop with picking the same number as he, but I picked two by two, three by three, as fast as I could eat. The bunch finished he remained a moment with the stem in his hand, and shaking his head said : 'Lazaro, you have deceived me. I will swear that you have eaten the grapes three by three.' 'I did not,' said I, 'but why do you suspect it ?' This most amusing blind man answered : 'Do you know how I perceive that you ate them three by three? Because I ate them two by two and you said nothing.'"

But Lazaro's initiation into the struggle for existence was nearing its end. One day he stole from his master's plate a sausage, leaving in its place a turnip. The substitution was too evident, and the beggar, seizing the boy, forced open his mouth and endeavored to scent the sausage. Overcome by the pain, Lazaro vomits his meal into the blind man's face, as did Sancho Panza afterward while investigating the loss of Don Quixote's teeth. Infuriated by this contumely, the beggar pounds and beats the boy most savagely, and his life is saved only by the arrival of people attracted by the noise. After careful nursing Lazaro comes back to his bondage again, but his torn scalp and lacerated flesh serve to strengthen his resolution to first pay back his master and then make good his escape.

One day they had been begging under a gateway, and when night came on the beggar wished to return to the inn. But they had to cross a brook which had been swollen by steady rains. Under pretext of finding a place where they may jump the stream, Lazaro leads his charge into the public square, places him in front of a stone post, and saying that here the brook was narrow, bids him jump, leaping forward first himself. The blind man retreated a step to gather headway, and then threw himself with all his might, and dashed his head against the post, which resounded as loudly as though it had been hit with a big gourd, and fell back half dead and with his head split open ! " ' How did you smell the sausage and not the post? Smell! smell!' said I to him, and I left him in the hands of the crowd which was running up to his assistance. . . . Never did I know what God did with him, nor did I wish to know."

With this last act of revolting cruelty the first episode of *Lazarillo de Tormes* is brought to an end. Of course it would be unjust to consider the reciprocal brutality of the beggar and his guide a fair picture of the humanity of the age and people. Their vengeances were undoubtedly extreme examples, such as all realistic fiction since their day seems bound to select. Yet the spirit which animates the actors in these scenes, the utter selfishness, the entire absence of pity, and the vices excited in man by the fierce gnawings of hunger, may be taken as fairly illustrative of the attitude of the Spanish nation in its period of distress. When we admit that our first and overpowering instinct is the one of self-preservation, we cannot wonder greatly at its activity among the lower classes of an impoverished people.

How far this necessity of self-preservation extended under the pressure of the extreme want of the nation, is seen in the next picture of our novel, which presents, in a way, scenes from clerical life. When Lazaro escapes from his first master he turns beggar himself without meeting with any considerable success. So after a while he hires out to a priest as acolyte, on the theory that priests live well, and their attendants must therefore be above suffering. But famine had entered the service of the Church before Lazaro, and the boy soon finds that nothing has been gained by his change of employers : " For the blind man, in comparison with this one, was an Alexander the Great [who was the mediæval type of liberality] compared with avarice itself." All eatables in the clergy-house were kept in a strong box, under lock and key, and were doled out so sparingly that Lazaro found an onion once in four days was to be his *pièce de résistance.* When the priest dined he generously threw the bones of his meat to the boy, saying to him, "'Take, eat, triumph, for the earth is yours ; you fare better than the Pope.'"

After three weeks of such nourishment the bodily strength of the acolyte was at a low ebb. His very knees hardly supported him as he stood. To steal the alms of the devout from the plate at the offertory was impossible under the scrutiny of his watchful master, "whose eyes danced in his skull like quicksilver." And the wine which remained from communion lasted this prudent householder a week. These saving habits would soon have convinced our hero that the jolly monks of old feasted only in song, had not weddings and funerals intervened to prove that the traditional spirit of the priesthood was kept in abeyance only by the constant menaces of famine. On such occasions Lazaro was also permitted to relax from his forced abstinence. "God pardon me," he says regretfully, "for never was I an enemy of the human race excepting at that time in my life, and then the reason was because we ate well and I stuffed myself. For then I desired and even prayed to God that each day might have its victim. And when we administered the sacrament to the sick, especially when we gave extreme unction, . . . I asked the Lord with all my heart and will . . . that he would take them from the world. When anyone of them escaped—God pardon me for it—but I gave him to the devil a thousand times, while he who died received from me the more abundant blessings." But twenty deaths in six months, and the consequent funeral feasts, barely kept the young acolyte from utter starvation, while the severity of his continual fasting became all the more sensible after these occasional banquets. Still he had no desire to leave this new position of his, not only because he had become too weak to walk any distance, but also because he feared he might fall into even worse hands.

Yet his hunger must be relieved, and he soon hit upon an expedient to that end. By wheedling a carpenter he obtained a second key to the blessed bread-box, and now could satisfy, though sparingly, his supreme cravings. In spite of his self-denial, however, the priest began to miss his loaves, and Lazaro found himself reduced to the consolation of an optical meal, by "unlocking the chest and gazing on that 'face of God,' as the children say." And so he fasted until Heaven suggested to this pious rascal a new device, which in its turn finally betrayed him, and the priest in anger discharged his assistant, who was thus launched again on the sea of adventure.

He journeys toward Toledo, that pride of old Spain, and looks about him, as he goes, in quest of a new employer. One day his diligent search is rewarded, and in the streets of the noble town our *picaro* meets with a Spanish squire, "who was going along the way, respectably dressed, well-combed, his gait and bearing correct. He looked at me and I at him and he said : 'Boy, are you looking for a master ?' I said to him : 'Yes, sir,' 'Then come behind me,' he replied, 'for God has shown you grace in meeting me ; you have surely prayed some good prayer to-day.'"

It was early in the morning and the squire continued his walk, followed by his new domestic. At eleven o'clock they entered a church and took part in the service. At its close, with the same measured step and proud carriage, the hidalgo again took up his promenade about the town. But in passing the markets never a purchase did he make. At the stroke of one he returned home, took off his cape, folded it carefully, and sitting down on a stone bench, after blowing the dust from it, he began to question Lazaro, who was now nearly famished. The house was silent, without furniture. Lazaro looked in vain for a kitchen or a cook, and after a long agony the squire told his valet that as he had breakfasted he would not dine. Driven to his last ditch our poor hero now sorrowfully drew from his bosom some morsels of bread, the largest of which his master noticed and appropriated, after a few courteous remarks. When night came on the squire concluded that, on account of thieves and the darkness, he would not go out to get provisions. Morning dawned. The nobleman arose, dressed himself carefully, girded on his sword with many boastings, "and with easy step and erect body, making with it and with his head many graceful movements, letting the hood of his cape fall on his shoulder, and at times on his arm, and placing his right hand on his hip, he went out," a genuine Spanish hidalgo, who, though driven to the wall by hunger, would not derogate from the habits of his class one iota, but kept up before the crowd the appearances of rank and wealth, while suffering continually the keenest of all bodily distresses. And he was no exception in the brilliant Spain of Charles V. In that devoted land many lords and ladies, clad in silks and velvets, sat solitary in their ancestral castles and worshiped "God's face," on which they so rarely gazed. But they saved their honor, though their body starved.

Outcast Lazaro had no honor, he. Begging to him was far better than starving. Yet he really respected his fam-

ished master, whom he realized to be of finer mold than himself and never was able to resist the pleadings of his hungry
eyes. And so the servant became the provider for the
household, and Lazaro, instead of receiving the support he
had anticipated, had merely added another empty stomach
to his own. His diligence in begging was incited by this
double duty, and for a time he earned the whole fare. But
a new misfortune came to vex him. The authorities of
Toledo were forced by the increasing destitution of the community to issue a decree against the presence of beggars
coming from other provinces, and death by starvation men-
aced the helpless strangers. The charity of some poor silk-
spinners, who, in contrast with the indifference of the well-
to-do, divided their scanty earnings with their neighbors,
saved the valet, but how the spark of life was kept in the
gaunt body of the master none but himself knew. Every
day he dressed himself as usual, and promenaded the streets
of the town, manfully supporting "the curse they call
honor,"—which Lazaro could not understand, yet nevertheless esteemed,—and picking his teeth with one of the few
straws that still remained in his lodging. But the final
catastrophe could not be long avoided. One day the land-
lord came to collect his rent, for the noble also was not a
citizen of Toledo. The squire has too large a coin for the
payment. He steps out to change it and never returns.

It would seem from the style and general tone of these
three episodes that the object of our novel was already
attained. It had now placed in detail before its readers
the wretchedness of those whose physical defects make
them constant pensioners on the community, together with
the want of the clergy and the smaller nobility. Care and
attention had been bestowed by the author upon these
descriptions in order to make them vivid and lifelike ; and
after this task was performed his interest in his work
declined. He had intended to follow up these studies of

types with scenes of a more individual nature, but he himself has become weary of dwelling on the distress of the
country, and the sketches which are added are made hur-
riedly, and only in outline. They continue the portrayal of
the contemporaneous conditions of Spanish life, but they
lean more and more toward the personal side, being mainly
concerned with Lazaro's rise in the ways of the world. After
the disappearance of the squire he took service with a monk,
who wore him out with his many foragings. Next he assisted
a seller of indulgences, who testified to the poverty of the
land, by offering as bribes to the country curates a pear or
a head of lettuce. This sharper hired a judge to fall into
convulsions in a church during the service, and then, by
pretending to cure the supposed invalid, got no small amount
of money out of the sick people of that place.—This scene
is probably not original with the author of *Lazarillo de
Tormes*, but is borrowed, most likely, from Masuccio's collection of stories.

From the seller of indulgences Lazaro went over to a
painter, for whom he mixed colors. Afterward he obtained
a position as a public water-carrier, a job he sub-let from a
chaplain. In this occupation he finally began to earn a
little money, and after several years' labor had saved enough
to buy some good clothes for himself in which he became,
as he quotes, a " respectable citizen." His next step up the
ladder was to rise to the grade of a constable, but this calling he soon found too dangerous for his liking, and accordingly he bent his energies to obtain a government office,
still the height of popular ambition in Spain. As Lazaro
says : " No one gets along excepting him who has one."
He succeeded in his effort, and was made a public crier.
So money and esteem were finally his. His connection
with the ruling authority gained him the respect of mankind, and he clinched his good fortune by a subservient
marriage with the rather discredited housekeeper of the

archpriest of San Salvador. Peace and plenty are the reward of his matrimonial complacency. He gets his food from the archpriest, his clothes come from the archpriest, his abode is near the archpriest's, and nothing but the evil tongue of slanderers can disturb his repose. And when the archpriest condescends to notice these malignant spirits, and cautions his man with the worldly maxim that "' he who hearkens to evil-speaking will never prosper,'" Lazaro shows the result of his great change of heart in the reply : "'Sir, I have made up my mind to attach myself to the good.'" Thereupon he proceeds to rebuke his meddlesome companions, and finds in his virtuous action the recompense of never-diminishing comforts, until the curtain drops on his satisfied repose.

It is hardly necessary to dwell on the cynicism of this conclusion to the *picaro's* career, nor do we feel obliged to expatiate on that philosophy of life which made a full stomach the happy goal of earthly existence. This is rather a subject for sociology than literature, and, as a matter of fact, has not continued to be the moral of the realistic novel, but rather passed away with the "evil of Spain," which occasioned it. The subsequent writers of the school have put in its place a struggle for existence, to be sure, but yet for a higher type of existence, the end of which should be rather social and political power than mere bodily comfort.

Under a despotic monarchy, or a government by the aristocracy, there was little hope for the rise of plebeians in public affairs. Consequently it was mainly a struggle with nature which characterized the existence of the lower classes. Now that the doors to power and authority have been thrown open to all kinds and conditions of men, we witness a fight for the supremacy of man over man. In this way the field of literary observation has been broadened, and the writers on realism have adapted their tone to the spirit of their surroundings. Yet, it is undisputed that this first short sketch of the ills of humanity, as represented by Spain of the sixteenth century, gave to realistic fiction both its methods and its standpoints of view, and these have lasted down to the present day. No better proof could be given of the fidelity of *Lazarillo de Tormes* to the true observation of human nature.

The immediate influence of this Spanish story was considerable, in spite of the cruelty of its descriptions and the national shame which it so plainly advertised. Besides the editions in the mother country and in Flanders, translations into other languages spread its popularity abroad. It was done into French in 1561, and into English by 1586 at the latest, while both in France and England editions of these versions followed close on one another. The Inquisition opposed the book as being hostile to clerical influence, and in 1559 bestowed upon it the honor of a place in the Index. Still, the secular arm could not suppress the favor with which it was received outside of the peninsula. The printing presses of Italy and Belgium supplied it to all who could purchase, and in Spain itself the ban was removed in 1573, in return for the omission of the objectionable parts.

As was the case with the romances of chivalry and the pastorals the success of the first *picaresco* novel called out sequels. An anonymous continuation appeared in 1555, and is somewhat longer than the original story. It tells how Lazaro, in spite of all his precautions to lead a peaceful life, fell in with a gay crowd, and how they reveled and sported in Toledo. Among these new friends were some strangers from Germany. When they had left town and life became somewhat tame to our hero, he was persuaded to enlist in the war against Algiers. And so he forsook his easy and comfortable existence, and tried the hazards of the sea. Hardly was he out of sight of land when a storm arose, his ship was wrecked, and Lazaro sank to the bottom of the sea, only to metamorphose into a tunny. Among the finny tribe he cut a great figure, contracted an advantageous marriage, and yet at last, going the way of all fish, was taken in a net. As he was being hauled to the surface nature interfered again in his behalf, and changed him into a merman. Accordingly he was kept as a curiosity, was carried to Seville, and there placed on exhibition. But the sight-seers of Andalusia possessed all the vices and virtues of their class in other lands. They so pulled and punched our merman that they very soon stripped off his scaly coat and brought him back again to human form. However, he was so changed by his watery sojourn that his best friends no longer knew him, and it was only with the greatest difficulty that he succeeded in rehabilitating himself in his former citizenship. When this was accomplished he had lost his desire for family life, and found his chief delight in confounding with his subtle arguments the learned doctors of Salamanca.

This sequel to *Lazarillo de Tormes* has certainly nothing in common with the original work, and cannot be reckoned in the same category of fiction. From the time that Lazaro left Toledo the story of his adventures is an extravaganza pure and simple, the moral of which is not apparent to posterity. In this absurd account there is hardly a trace of the observation of real life, while the connecting thread of the narrative seems to be the satire which underlies it. Yet this sequel did a good work. It effectually discouraged for a time all other continuations of the novel, and it was not until the year 1620 that any further attempts in that direction were made. By that time the original idea of picturing the manners of the day had been swallowed up wholly in narrating the adventures of an individual. This is true, at least, of the sequel written at Paris by the Spaniard Juan de Luna, who dwelt mainly on the anti-clerical side of his story, while drawing some of his material from the old drama, *Celestina.*

All indications derived from contemporaneous references and successive editions go to show that the first *picaresco* novel was heartily welcomed in the land of its birth, and that its influence penetrated into all but the lowest classes of society. And therefore it seems rather singular that its popularity did not immediately arouse the emulation of other authors to achieve distinction along the same line of romancing. Perhaps the action of the civil authorities in placing the book so soon on the Index deterred ambitious realists from risking a similar fate. But more likely the favor of the romances of chivalry among the populace, so deep-seated and enduring, and the craze for pastoral novels among the courtiers and their dependents, left the ungracious portrayals of every-day facts without a sufficient number of adherents among the reading public. The people loved the aristocratic tone and the optimism of the tales of feudalism, and sought in them a diversion from their hard and humdrum existence. Those of the educated classes who prided themselves on their literary taste, found æsthetic enjoyment in the refined style and ingenious developments of the pastorals, and thus gave this school a disproportionately long career. Even Cervantes, whose great work is based on the happenings of ordinary life, and who is clearly indebted for some of his inspiration to the experience of young Lazaro, tried his hand first at the pastorals, and in later years did not disdain heroic fiction. We cannot, therefore, marvel greatly that a kind of novel which was hostile alike to feudalism and to pretended rusticity, which depended for its power on exactness of observation and delineation of customs and manners really existing, should have found itself without an avowed circle of defenders when it fell under the ban of the Inquisition. It took many years more of individual disappointments and national decline to create a public which was willing to face the reproduction in literature of its actual surroundings. And it was only when the romance of chivalry and the pastoral had worn out their traditional themes that the romance of plebeian doings ventured to claim again its due share of attention.

Forty-five years after the appearance of *Lazarillo de Tormes*, and perhaps in the very year which saw the beginning of *Don Quixote*, a second *picaresco* novel appealed to the suffrages of the Spanish people. It was not anonymous. Mateo Aleman, a native of Seville, and a government official, was, like so many of his class in more recent times, an occasional author. Of the other works from his pen nothing has survived, but the manner in which he tells the story of his rascal proves him to have been a man of parts, a keen observer, a good narrator, and an excellent student of society. The first part of his work, called after the name of its hero, *Guzman de Alfarache*, was published in 1599. The narrative is autobiographical, like the story of its predecessor.

Guzman was a native of Seville, of illegitimate birth, though claiming nevertheless in his make-up the inheritance of certain traits from his father, a Genoese merchant and something of a thief. His abandoned mother brought him up until he left her at an early period and wandered over the country, attended by several idle companions. The adventures of this band, the experiences its members undergo, especially in the filthy inns of the smaller towns, the stories they tell, and the jokes they play on their greedy hosts, form the first series of the episodes in the novel. The vivacity and wit of the account redeem to some extent the ugliness of its facts, and temper the ponderous moral reflections, in which the author at times loses himself. All the stories are not of a low order, and one among them is particularly pleasing and romantic, possibly belonging to the inexhaustible stock of Moorish tales. It tells how two lovers of Granada, Osmin and Daraja, were separated shortly after their marriage by the capture of the latter. Osmin left Granada in search of his wife, but was also taken prisoner and carried to Seville. There he has the good fortune to get a glimpse of Daraja, which prompts him to devise some stratagem for meeting her face to face. He disguises himself first as a mason, and afterward as a gardener, gains thus ready access to her master's house, and obtains frequent interviews with her. After various vicissitudes, in which Osmin changes his part many times, wins renown in bull-fights and joustings, is mobbed by the populace, "which is always hostile to nobles," and narrowly escapes being hanged, the lovers are once more united, and all ends well.

This episode, with others, is inserted into the main narrative with the evident intention of varying the subject and holding the attention of the reader. Returning now to the principal theme we read of Guzman's struggles with poverty, his career at Madrid as a domestic, and his sufferings from hunger. One result of his practical experience he freely confesses to be the disappearance of his sense of shame. Under the pressure of circumstances he enlists at last in the noble army of *picaros*, but still bestows on his audience abundant moral advice. He enters an inn as scullion, is soon dismissed for stealing, yet manages to profit by his release to accumulate by various tricks enough money and clothes, to set up at Toledo after a while as a man of property. But there he becomes in his turn the prey of dissolute associates, loses all his money, and finally takes service for the Italian campaign. On his way to Genoa the captain of the ship makes a confidant of Guzman. When he reaches that town he is apparently welcomed by his father's family, and is induced to take up his abode with them. But the very first night he is scared away from their roof by an apparition, and begins his career all over again.

He learns the beggar's trade, which Italy practiced at that time, describes the factories which prepared cripples for the market by early mutilation (as in Hugo's *l'Homme qui rit*), and in a long satire on Italy and Italian customs awards that country the palm for downright cruelty. After a while he reaches Rome, where a cardinal receives him and makes him his page. Guzman shows his gratitude for this honor by turning the house upside down with his practical jokes, until his passion for gambling drives him again out of doors. Afterward he enters the service of the French. ambassador, where he prospers for a while, and hears the tragic tale of Dorido and Clorinia, which he repeats to us as illustrative of Italian manners and Italian character.

Dorido is in love with Clorinia, but in his confidence of her affection toward him he agrees to cede her to his friend Horatio, provided she prefers the latter. Clorinia proves faithful to her lover's trust and rejects Horatio's suit. But the latter is only angered by her fidelity. In his madness he stabs her to the heart, and then succumbs to Dorido's vengeance, who cuts off the hands of his faithless friend and hangs up his body at his mistress' casement. The recital of this cheerful incident brings the first part of *Guzman de Alfarache* to a close.

Thus far in the second novel of the *picaresco* group we have what may be loosely termed an expansion or revision of the first. And in some respects this revision is for the worse. We miss in Aleman's story that clearness and definiteness of presentation which the fewer episodes and the absence of digressions made possible in *Lazarillo de Tormes*. On the other hand the adventures of Guzman reveal more completely the various sides of contemporaneous Spanish life, by the very fact that they are so varied and introduce so many characters. In these respects the novel is more like the English romances of Smollett or Fielding, following man through his different circumstances—neglecting of course his best instincts—and aiming to portray the leading features of the average existence. In comparison with

Guzman we might say that the author of *Lazarillo* had a
proposition to defend, while Aleman concerns himself only
with a reproduction of what a wanderer might see and experience. Consequently, from the standpoint of fiction,
Aleman's book is much more of a literary composition than
the narrative of his anonymous predecessor, and far surpasses the latter, both in the development of its successive
situations and in the style peculiar to a romance. One
might say that *Lazarillo de Tormes* is a drama divided into
well-marked acts, or that it is a serial painting of the *genre*
type comprising so many distinct subjects. And indeed it
does bring to mind some of the street scenes which Murillo
has handed down to our admiration.

Yet we do not mean to imply that, while *Guzman de
Alfarache* is the better novel, it does not lose, by the multiplicity of its incidents, something of the force and directness of its model. Certainly its pious reflections are far
inferior, in their verbosity, to the short and pungent morals
of *Lazarillo de Tormes*. Yet Aleman is not so bitter. His
introduction of stories foreign to the main idea tempers
agreeably the prevailing satire of human kind, and the
socialistic views which pervade it—bringing in frequently
the contrast between the sympathy of the poor and the
charity of the rich—are not so unyielding as the stern
struggle for a livelihood which animates the whole spirit of
the older novel.

The popularity of *Guzman de Alfarache* was immediate
and widespread. The very next year, 1600, it was done
into French, while at home it succeeded—where *Lazarillo*
had failed—in drawing the attention of literary men toward
this hitherto neglected department of novel-writing.
Indeed Aleman may be called the second founder of the
realistic novel, for with him it first started into active life.
So much so that before he himself was ready to print his
second part, already in manuscript, his own thunder was

stolen by a literary pirate, who marketed, in 1603, a sequel to *Guzman* which pretended to be the authentic one. This thief's real name was Juan Marti, but in his book he took the pseudonym of Mateo Lujan de Sayavedra. From Aleman's remarks on his attempted deception it would seem as though Marti had obtained access to the unfinished pages of the real second part.

However that may be, Marti starts off with Guzman in Rome at the French embassy. But he soon falls in with two Spaniards, who join him in sneak-thieving and afterward make him their dupe. He therefore leaves Rome and goes to Naples, indulging in many moralizings on the way. At Naples he becomes the servant of a priest, and gains an idea of life in that town. Next we find him as a steward and a great personage, though when suspected of theft his station does not save him from the jail. Pardoned after a time he enters the viceroy's service as a menial to his cook, and finally returns to Spain with the viceroy. On reaching Barcelona he comes across old friends among the beggars of the town. So he concludes not to remain there, but goes to Alcalà to matriculate in the university and enjoy student life. After some time spent in educational pursuits, he takes up again his wanderings, arrives at Valencia, and enters Heredia's company as an actor. He is not long, of course, in falling in love with the leading lady. Now Margaret of Austria makes her triumphal entry into the city, and Guzman, plying his old trade during the festivals given in her honor, is caught and sent to the galleys. Here Marti suddenly breaks off his narrative with the conventional promise of a continuation at some future time.

But the falsifier was too ambitious for his own reputation, and he would have fared better with posterity not to have connected his story with the novel of Aleman, since he is far inferior to him both in invention and composition.

Instead of expending what talent he possessed on the study of human nature, and on general observations on society, Marti fills out his plan with anecdotes, superstitions, the details of trades and professions. He rejoices likewise in his own erudition and makes labored efforts to vary his task with stories from outside sources, as Aleman did. In following the whims of his model, as well as his plot, Marti also attempts to convey morals to his readers, and pushed this fault of Aleman to a wearying extreme. The result of the whole imitation was the complete failure of his venture in literature ; and his notoriety to-day is due, not to his own struggles after fame, but to the lashings which he received from the scourge of the enraged novelist, whose sequel he had so clumsily tried to forestall.

The genuine continuation was published in 1605, prefaced with a prologue on Marti's forgery, a subject which does not fail to stir up the author at every turn of the ensuing story. For here Aleman is more openly satirical than in the first part. He has also conceived the notion of beginning each chapter with some virtuous counsel, and then following it up with a rascally adventure. We find Guzman still in Rome, and acting as the go-between in the amorous intrigues of his French master. The account of these amours is varied with the recital of many anecdotes, and the insertion of not a few fables; and one episode, which may well be omitted here, is taken from Masuccio's collection of tales. But though the ambassador may be fortunate in love, the flunky is not, and after being victimized several times by the women to whom he is attached, Guzman incurs his employer's displeasure and leaves Rome. In so doing he jumps from the frying-pan into the fire, for he soon runs across Sayavedra, and is exposed from now on to the deceit and treachery of that archrogue. Together they pass through Siena and Florence, which the author describes at some length, and by the aid of money they had

fleeced from a greenhorn they reach Milan.   Here Sayavedra, who had already robbed his companion, and then
obtained his pardon, plans a forgery on a merchant by
enlisting in the project the latter's clerk.   They succeed in
defrauding their man, and once more in funds, turn their
faces toward Genoa.   There Guzman's relatives, who had
driven him off when poor, receive him now with open arms,
supposing him to be rich.   He accepts their hospitality
most effusively, and when the opportune moment comes,
takes his revenge by robbing them and immediately
decamping for Spain.   No voyage in the old-time novels
ever escaped a storm.   During the one which now
threatens the destruction of their craft Sayavedra drowns
himself, and receives a good riddance from his companion.
The rest of the passage is enlivened by the rather weak
yarns of the captain of the boat.

The ship lands its passengers at Barcelona, where the
adventures of our hero multiply.   He makes the tour of
Spain, as he had already done of Italy.   In Saragossa he falls
in love with a blooming widow.   In Alcalà he admires the
streets and the learning, and when he reaches Madrid, after
getting into difficulties with the police and undergoing
arrest, he marries a woman of property for the sake of her
comfortable dowry.   Yet life even now did not resemble a
bed of roses.   His better-half proved exceedingly fractious,
and her ill-temper drove our *picaro* to the abject extremity
of seeking consolation for his marital woes in the perusal
of pastoral novels and romances of chivalry.   Finally the
death of his wife affords his wounded sensibilities a respite.
But with the aggravation he entombs also the balm, for her
dowry dies with her.   Forced to enter active life again, he
enrolls himself in the list of the candidates for orders at
Alcalà, but soon falls in love and marries a second time.
His new heart's delight is not a scold nor a prude.   In fact
Guzman's establishment is supported by the money which

his wife's lovers pay to her, and the surplus above the necessary expenses Guzman applies to the amusement of gambling.

Naturally, such a household does not long keep itself out of the clutches of the law. Adversity smites it, and the couple flee to Seville, where Guzman visits once more his aged mother. He is rid of his wife by her elopement with a sea-captain, and he himself is now at liberty to return to his old pursuit of thieving. He gets employment as a steward, robs his mistress, is caught, and sentenced to the galleys for six years. The description of his new surroundings, the dress and manners of the galley-slaves, now occupies no small space. His companions can give him points in rascality, and succeed in robbing him of what he still possessed. But he wins the favor of the overseer, excites thereby the envy of his mates, and, when the opportunity presents itself, is accused by one of them of stealing his master's plate. For this offense Guzman is well flogged. But the treachery toward him has aroused his anger. He watches for an occasion of taking vengeance on the convicts, and when their plans of escape are brought to his ears he betrays them to the authorities. Thus he regains his liberty, and concludes the story of his adventures with the promise of still another sequel.

The second part of *Guzman de Alfarache* is somewhat longer than the amount first published, and rivaled it in popularity. Its appearance was the signal for many editions, both of the whole novel and of the parts separately, and for translations into every language of western Europe, and even into Latin. To account for the extraordinary favor with which it was received we may very well suppose a general reaction against the novels of pure imagination, and in behalf of a more real view of humanity and its conditions. Aleman was shrewd enough to profit by this change among the reading public, and by his wit and talent placed himself easily in the front rank of the authors of his day. For he handles well his pen, writes correctly and fluently, while his observations are bold, keen, satirical, and founded on what was actually before his eyes. And it is not one of the least of the attractions of the book that its hero believed thoroughly in himself. His rascalities were his character. His disposition was a compound of deceit and avarice, and in his composition the sense of shame had been omitted, albeit he is one of the most pious of all the rogues of fiction. Such a pure type of a low-lived villain excites our interest by the very subjection of all ideals to the most ignoble ends. Guzman balances Amadis, and the *picaro* affords, at times, a not unwelcome foil to the true and perfect knight.

The posterity of Aleman's novel is legion. Supplanting the memory of *Lazarillo de Tormes* by its extent and variety, it started the *picaresco* story on a career of prosperity, which lasted in Spain for a full half a century and was signalized by the appearance of many brilliant productions. Nor did its influence cease with its progeny in the mother country. In France, in the last years of Louis XIV., the spirit of Spanish realistic fiction aroused the emulation of Le Sage. Modified and adapted to other surroundings of race and time by his genius, the transformed novel soon made its way across the Channel, to receive a fresh infusion of vigorous Anglo-Saxon blood which should preserve its life for another century. And the realist novelists of the present day, the Balzacs and Thackerays—to cite the chiefs —are as surely the disciples of Fielding and Le Sage as Gil Blas was a relative of Guzman de Alfarache and a descendant of little Lazaro, who first saw the light in an old mill by the side of the river Tormes.

CHAPTER XI.

AFTER their great creations in the line of both ideal and
realistic fiction, and after the founding of the three kinds
of novels on which all future romances were to be patterned, the Spanish story-tellers of the Renaissance might
very well have been excused from further obligations to
modern readers.   Yet in the midst of so busy a production
of all these kinds, which especially appealed to the taste
of the times and were in fashion, it is not surprising
that other species than the principal ones should be sought
after by isolated authors, and that embryos of what have
later become full-fledged types should be discovered among
the mass of novels written in the peninsula during the sixteenth century.

The attempt to derive the religious novel from the
romances of chivalry has already been noticed, and examples of the results attained have been submitted to inspec-
tion.   And akin to the pastoral novels, aside from the
didactic element, there was to be found a fair amount of
stories in which allegory played a leading part, though
none of these stories reach the stage of complete romances.
Furthermore, starting from the love sophistries of mediæval lyric, there are echos also of what might almost be called
society novels.   An instance of this kind is offered by the
Question de Amor, assigned to Diego de San Pedro, and
belonging to the year 1512.   Here the question as to
whether he is the greater sufferer who has loved and lost

or he who loves in vain is varied and prolonged by descriptions of court life, and of social customs in Naples and other Italian cities.   But San Pedro's book does not possess enough plan to be ranked higher than a half-serious, half-amusing narrative, and it did not incite any further efforts to realize that type of composition which it more than vaguely hints at.

With better success, from the modern standpoint, at least, was the novel of travel undertaken by a certain Jeronimo de Contreras.   His story, the *Selva de Aventuras*, which appeared in 1573, contains a plot in the shape of a love affair, which is the thread connecting the different journeys the hero makes.   The reason that the traveler, Luzman by name, leaves his native Seville to visit foreign shores, is because his suit had been rejected by the beautiful Arbolea, and like so many lovers of more recent date he sought for healing balm in the distractions of travel. When his lady dismisses him he follows the example of Amadis, and remains for some time under the pious consolation of a Spanish hermit.   Afterward he passes into Italy, the land of sightseeing in those days.   He visits Venice, runs across in the mountains of the North a princess of Ferrara, whom disappointment in love had led to assume a hunting costume, explores Milan, meets with a second unhappy swain, and leisurely drags his melancholy up and down the whole peninsula, describing the cities he enters and the events which attract his notice.   At last captured by pirates he breathes out his sorrows in a prison of Algiers, until he is free once more to return to his fatherland and the abode of his mistress.   But during his prolonged absence Arbolea in sheer desperation had become a nun.   Nothing now is left for Luzman but to imitate her example, and to turn hermit, which he does straightway.

It is plain that the *Selva de Aventuras* is before all a book of travel, and that the love story in it is only the setting, a pretense to hold the reader's interest. And though the author tried to re-enforce his meager plot by multiplying the accounts of blighted affections which obtained among the chance acquaintances of his hero (a clear trace of the influence of the pastorals), the narrative of Italian journeys and hardships among the infidels proves a much more attractive subject than the memory of a suit rejected. For in this story there is no necessary connection between the two themes. But some thirty years later, at the beginning of the seventeenth century, when the plot and the incidents of travel were more intimately combined by a writer of talent, the Spanish public was treated to a genuine novel of adventure in the *Viaje Entretenido* of Agostino de Rojas. Still in many respects, and particularly in their selection of material, the novels of travel resemble the *picaresco* stories, though the spirit of the two kinds is entirely distinct.

De Rojas had a follower in Scarron and his *Roman comique*, and the nineteenth century has abounded in successors to the latter and to writers of his ilk. But it cannot be claimed that the Spanish novel of travel has directly produced any important type of fiction. Other influences came in from the realists and from the writers of antiquity to obscure the genealogy of the direct descendants of this school ; and to-day stories of adventure, which are held together by a plot, have deserted the matter-of-fact descriptions of Contreras and De Rojas for the imaginative school of Antonius Diogenes, and Cyrano de Bergerac.

There is a second type of these independent attempts at novels in the Spain of the sixteenth century which deserves mention, a type which may be said to be an outgrowth of the romances of chivalry. It is a novel of erotic adventure placed in a definite locality and period—an historical novel, in other words. To begin the series of historical novels the country was prepared not only by its evolution of the stories of feudalism, but also by the great events which had taken place upon its own soil. For many generations the tablelands of the center and the mountain ranges of the south had borne the long burden of civil strife and wars of religion, which had found a responsive echo in the ballad poetry of the country ; while on the other side of the frontier, in Seville and Granada, the endless struggles between infidel and believer, and among the infidels themselves, had been no less fertile in the production of subjects for popular song. In the fifteenth century these romances of the Moors had already begun to reach the ears of their hereditary foes, and by their peculiar tenderness and the sweetness of their melodies had excited the admiration of the chivalrous Crusaders. The discovery of the New World, and the voyages of exploration which that event incited, might reasonably have been expected to furnish historical novelists with abundant and appropriate material—and did indeed supply Camoens with the facts necessary to his epic poem. And yet neither they nor the purely national traditions of the Spanish people had a more definite effect on literature than the romances of chivalry would indicate. So it was the Moors, and the Moors of Granada, who supplied the Castilian author with the characters and the plot of his tentative historical fiction.

This author was Gines Perez de Hita, and his work goes under the name of *The Civil Wars of Granada*, a book which is partly true as to its facts, and partly fictitious. The latter element especially prevails in the first division of the narrative, which was published in 1595. Here the author follows the same method of composition that was carried out so well in more modern times by Walter Scott, and places in an historical framework the imagined careers of private individuals. The years which he chooses for the setting of his story are those immediately preceding the downfall of Granada, and the story he tells concerns the famous feud between the family of the Zegris and the race of the Abencerrages. Hita claims, as Cervantes did soon after him, that his narrative is simply a translation from a Moorish writer, but its whole spirit is Christian, and the standpoint of view is entirely Spanish. So we are obliged to reject the testimony of our scribe and assign the merits of the whole account to the credit of his inventive powers. And it is a curious fact that this romance, with its partiality for the Abencerrages and its contempt for Boabdil, has penetrated the popular sentiment of western Europe and turned it forever against the enemies of its hero—and against the unfortunate monarch who lived to see the last Moorish kingdom in Spain sink under the weight of his throne.

The Civil Wars begins with a short sketch of the founding of Granada, and a description of the city and the factions which desolated its streets during the last years of Moslem rule. The ground having been prepared in this manner, the particular actors of the story are then introduced, and we are apprized of Muza's fortunes, who is loved by Fatima, but who loves Daraja, who in turn loves Abenamar, one of the Abencerrages—a situation of conflicting affections which was very likely borrowed from the pastorals. But besides love-making there is plenty of chivalry. Muza, as champion of the Moors, fights to a draw with Calatrava, the champion of the Spaniards, in a duel that strikingly resembles the prolonged combats in *Amadis of Gaul.* A banquet and ball in the beleaguered city followed this combat. During the festivities Muza presented a bouquet to Daraja, who later gave it to an Abencerrage. When Muza found his flowers in the possession of the latter his anger broke out in insulting words, and the ancient feud of the Zegris and the Abencerrages was once more revived. But peace is temporarily restored by the king, and everybody gives himself up to the pastimes of the court.

Now Hita begins to vary the prose of his work with occasional ballads he pretends to have taken from the Moors, and which very likely were sung by the minstrels of the border. To each of these romances he appends a long explanation, developing their subjects in prose, and thus narrates as many episodes of love and adventure as there are poems. The first series of ballads relates the wooing of Zaida by the knight Zaide, the opposition of the maiden's parents to the suit, and the jealousy of Zaide's friend, Tarfe. One day the lady sent to her lover a tress of her hair, and he in his joy unbosomed himself to Tarfe. The anger of the rejected swain overcame his sense of knightly honor. He finds occasion soon to tell Zaida that Zaide is boasting of the favors she bestows on him. Her shame and wrath are not long concealed from her distressed lover, and at her rebuke he revenges himself by the death of Tarfe. Now the Zegris gather to take vengeance on Zaide, but Boabdil appears again as peacemaker and marries the knight to his lady-love.

While the quarrels of the rival houses continue in the city in spite of the presence of the common enemy without the walls, the crowd seeks distraction from its impending doom in the pleasures of bull-fights and tournaments. But family hatred disturbs even the very amusements. In the jousts Fatima's father treacherously arms himself with an iron-tipped lance and, by wounding his opponent with it, embitters still more the hostility of the clans. Another challenge is brought from the besieging Christians, this time in the name of Ponce de Leon. It is accepted by Malique Alabez, and the combat between the champions again results in a draw. St. John's Day now approaches bringing its usual number of festivals. In the joustings of that day Abenamar defends the portrait of Fatima, as in *Palmerin of England* the knights protected the likeness of Miraguarda. After many brilliant deeds at arms Fatima's champion adds to her picture the face of Galiana, whose lover had fallen before his onset. In the midst of these scenes of chivalry there are long descriptions of the dresses of the ladies and the trappings of the cavaliers. Street parades take place, and in the make-up of the floats the rival families try to outdo each other in magnificence. But the Zegris have not been idle in the meantime. They have agreed on the destruction of the Abencerrages, and now accuse them to the king of disloyalty. After these incidents the tournaments are renewed, and Abenamar continues to gather in the portraits of other beauties, until his career is cut short by the arrival of Calatrava.

It cannot be said that our author is especially versed in the Moorish religion, whatever may be his acquaintance with the history and customs of his neighbors. For he makes the faithful of Granada address their supplicating prayers to a "golden Mahomet," in very much the same fashion that the French mediæval epic was wont to describe the idolatrous adorations of the Arabs. But Mahomet is deaf to the entreaties of his worshipers. That evening Albayaldos accepts Calatrava's defiance, but is mortally wounded by the Spanish hero, is suddenly converted to Christianity. and expires (after being duly baptized) with many pious admonitions to Muza on his lips. This conversion is the signal for another dispute between the two factions of the infidels.

And so the story winds its way in and out of the romances which now form the greater part of the narrative. Abenamar marries Fatima. The Zegris, at their wits' end for an accusation against their rivals, maliciously slander the queen to Boabdil, and with the outburst of his wrath gain at last his alliance. The execution of the Abencerrages is decided upon. Boabdil posts the Zegris in the royal palace, sends for the devoted family one by one, and has them beheaded in the famous Court of the Lions. However, one of their pages escapes to alarm the city. A great uproar ensues, in the midst of which Muza enters the town on his return from a foray against the Spaniards. He hears the news and summons the people to his standard. They storm the Alhambra and recover the bodies of the slain. Now the royal family itself takes sides, and the constant warfare in the public streets places the whole city under a genuine reign of terror. At last, tired of civil strife and indignant at the treachery practiced upon them, the Abencerrages and their adherents determine to go over to the Christian camp and be converted to the true faith. They accordingly put themselves in communication with Ferdinand, abandon Granada, are baptized, and enter the ranks of the Spanish host. Finally the Moorish queen herself is seized with the prevailing desire to change one's creed ; and when she is publicly accused of the crimes invented by the Zegris, four Christians, disguised as Turks, appear to champion her innocence against her four assailants. The victory of the believers naturally follows, the queen is freed, the Alhambra is taken by the Crusaders, and finally, after many more incidents and additional apostasies, the city itself falls into the hands of the Spanish rulers.

We have chosen to look on *Las Guerras Civiles de Granada* as a romance rather than as an historical treatise, and the reception which it met among the contemporaries of its author seems to sustain our position. For no sooner had the first part appeared than editions of it began to multiply, thus testifying to a popularity such as no mere chronicle of events could have enjoyed in that age. Such favor must also be wholly credited to the romantic sentiment of the book, since when we come to look on it as a piece of literature, we find it woefully lacking. Unity of action it possesses through the general nature of its subject, the history of the Abencerrages. But the tone of the work is plainly false, excepting, perhaps, to the most bigoted and credulous ; its style is of very inferior quality, and the scenes in it that are really well described are few and far between. In view of these defects, at a time when art in literature was being more and more sought after under the influence of the revival of learning, we have no recourse but to ascribe the welcome which Hita's invention received to the prose expansions of the ballads containing the amorous adventures of as many loving pairs, as well as to the beauty of the ballads themselves. We may recall that in Montemayor's *Diana*, the episode of the Abencerrage and his mistress is easily the best of the volume, and from the frequent presence in Spanish literature of such traditions concerning the Moors and their courtships, it is clear that the Christians of Spain had long been accustomed to the recital of similar legends, and found pleasure in the music of the songs out of which they undoubtedly had grown. Hita was shrewd enough to make a collection of these erotic tales and join them together by the general idea of a great final national disaster, a notion which reveals a man of talent who well deserved the success he obtained.

His story, like the other prominent Spanish narratives of the century, spread beyond the territorial boundaries of its native land, and, following the example of the romances of chivalry, entered on a new career in the novels of France in the seventeenth century. It did not, however, create the European historical novel as might have been expected. On foreign soil the affectations of the Hôtel de Rambouillet perverted the literary spirit of Hita's new departure in fiction, and drew from it the same results as had been drawn from *Amadis of Gaul*. *The Civil Wars of Granada* sank back therefore to the grade of the heroic-gallant novel from which it had tried in vain to separate itself, and was reproduced in such compositions of French fiction as *Almahide* of Madeleine de Scudéry and *Zayde* of Mme. de La Fayette. Romantic, rather than historical, these novels in turn appealed to the sentimentality of Florian and the melancholy of Chateaubriand, and their influence in literature finally died away at the very time when the true historical novel was being created. This was the end of Hita's attempt to substitute for the insipid romances of chivalry the love and valor of the imaginary actors of a definite historical epoch. Like the author of *Lazarillo de Tormes*, he may be said to have been ahead of his times, but in his case the anticipation is to be reckoned by centuries and not by decades.

He himself may have suspected this fact, in spite of the success which his first volume experienced, for in the second part of his narrative, which appeared in 1604, he cut loose entirely from the first, and related the Morisco rebellion of 1568 in very much the style of a lean and matter-of-fact chronicle. To be sure, he introduces a few ballads of his own manufacture, "so," as he says, "not to break with the style of the first part," and tells one or two interesting stories about the lovers who opposed so daringly in the Sierra Nevada the power of Philip II. Yet these are merely wanderings from the main road, and affect but little the historical tendency of the book.

With Perez de Hita the long line of Spanish inventors in the field of fiction comes to an end. For fifty years and more down into the seventeenth century, the models of their ingenuity continued to be reproduced by their countrymen in many creditable works. But new discoveries in romancing were no longer to be made in the peninsula. From now on the tokens of novelistic primacy pass to other lands, to France first and then to England. Yet whatever may be the improvement in the quality or construction of novels since the loss of the Armada, we must not forget that the novels which came forth from Spain of the sixteenth century set the example for all those, countless in number, which the other nations of Europe have accumulated down to the present day. The novels of the East, and more especially the stories of the Alexandrian age, entered into modern literature only in the way of suggestions and incidents. Of the same nature, and no greater, was the influence on subsequent writers of Italian fiction, heroic, realistic, or pastoral. But Spain gave to foreign novelists not only the mold in which to cast their matter, -but also the spirit which was to animate it. And when we trace out the ancestry of all the various kinds of that prose romancing which has become the distinctive literary feature of the nineteenth century, we shall find that they descend in near or remote relationship from the inventive geniuses of Portugal and Castile.

This fact is all the more apparent when we come to consider the literatures of the other peoples of western Europe precedent to the seventeenth century, and endeavor to discover among them even suggestions of perfect novels. The writers of Italy concerned themselves with the productions of pastorals only, and never persevered in the full development of even this their favorite kind of fiction. The *novella* in prose, and in poetry the great creations of Dante and the romantic epic, under the influence of the Renaissance, seemed to supply the bulk of the demand for other novelistic reading. Novels, to be sure, were appreciated in Italy, but the public was satisfied with translations from the Greek and the Spanish, and made no claim on the imagination or observation of native authors. This neglect of the longer works of prose fiction on the part of Italian writers is difficult to explain, especially when we take into consideration their taste for lyric-narrative poetry and their talent for writing short stories.

Though Italy in her literary history has never shown much aptitude for the making of novels, and therefore may be readily excused for her shortcomings in this respect previous to the sixteenth century, she yet shines by contrast with her Romance neighbor of the Northwest during the period in question. For after the wave of mediæval romancing had died away, France did not originate any kind of fictitious narrative until the great outburst of that school which began her classical era in literature. It was perhaps too much to expect that there should be any literary growth on her soil during the devastations of the Hundred Years' War; and when the monarchy had brought peace to' the land under Louis XII. and Francis I., the contemporaneous inroad of the vigorous literatures of the South occupied for a while the attention of her literary men, while the revival of learning, which reached her so tardily, carried the aspirations of the educated back to the imitation of antiquity.

Yet there are a few traces of that assimilation and modification of foreign material which has ever distinguished the genius of the French, and has given them their lasting hold on the artistic life of other nations. The romances of chivalry were adapted to French taste, and were continued, with certain changes in tone and sentiment, through many sequels. And in the matter of the pastorals, *Les Bergeries de Juliette* bears witness to an improvement in plan over its Italian models, and already argues a new departure in novelistic composition, which the *Astrée* justified later on. The French translations of the Greek novels were also more elegant and lasting than anything of the sort which Italy had undertaken. And so by the end of the sixteenth century we find all the known kinds of foreign fiction, ancient and modern, excepting the *picaresco* novel, fully naturalized on the soil of France.

Under Louis XIII. France performed an important service to the Germanic nations, in transmitting to them the versions she had made of the fiction of Spain and Italy. But in the sixteenth century, at least so far as Germany and Holland are concerned, this process had not as yet begun.

In those countries the native renderings of the old French epic romances were still at the height of their popularity, and formed, with very inconsiderable exceptions, the whole stock of light reading within reach of their inhabitants. The idea of originating similar stories, or of picturing their own life and surroundings, did not make itself felt with the deliberate Teutons until the seventeenth century was well under way. What is true of Holland and Germany is still more true of the Scandinavian nations. They followed their more civilized kindred at a respectful distance.

But England, which in the eighteenth century was to repeat Spain of the sixteenth, had already begun to bestir herself in regard to the composition of genuine novels. In the two decades previous to the year 1600 several of her leading authors, and more particularly her dramatists, had exercised their pen on subjects which exceeded the limits of the ordinary story. This movement was various in its manifestations, and cannot be traced to any one source. It was probably in the air, as it seems to have been in France, but in England it took shape earlier in consequence of the greater mental stimulus of the Elizabethan era. It was clearly fostered by the translations of Spanish novels through their French versions, and by the southern travels of the venturesome spirits who occasionally abandoned their favorite taverns in the British capital. Among the wealthier and more educated class it was no doubt quickened by contact with the literary men of the social circles of the Continent.

Such at least is the lesson drawn from a general survey of the material which was used by the English novel-writers— if they may be properly dignified by that term—of the time. Their subjects were clearly suggested by the Italian *novelle* and by the French renderings of Greek and Spanish novels ; and a direct communication with Spanish literature is not at all apparent in these works of fiction. Still the avenues of approach were so numerous, and the literary activity of the period so intense, that it is not safe, with our present uncertain light on the subject, to assert absolutely that among the English story-tellers there may not be one or more who may have come into actual contact with the ready writers of the Spanish peninsula.

The honor of being the first Englishman to raise fiction above the level of a mere tale must undoubtedly be assigned to Lyly, although the term novel can hardly be applied to his *Euphues*. It is too plainly a hand-book of etiquette, made a little more palatable to the public by the employ- ment of a hero and by a few indications of the trend of the hero's affections, to be treated under any other head than that of didactic fiction. This is not saying that novels may not be moral, political, or social arguments, but in this case Lyly was too much concerned with the ways of polite society, and too little with his plot or characters to be openly admitted to the sacred pale of novelists. Yet he very likely paved the way for more ambitious successors, and set in motion narratives which did not err, so far as his had done, in the didactic direction.

While Lyly was intent on initiating his countrymen into the mysteries of the fashionable world his contemporary, a man of fashion himself, Sir Philip Sidney, was employing his leisure moments in the composition of a genuine romance of chivalry. At least we must suppose he had in mind a novel of the heroic type, since the general outline of his *Arcadia* resembles so closely the conventional plan of that school. Sidney, however, was no imitator. He wished to be original in all respects, and partly perhaps through this desire, and partly also because he was writing for the amusement of his beloved sister, he varied his story of valor and knightly adventures with episodes after the manner of the Italian pastoral and romantic epic, and with incidents which were suggested possibly by the Greek novels, in that day so widely read. Thus the result of his literary effort in the domain of fiction is another composite, which endeavored to unite too many different elements to be a success. For there is in his *Arcadia* a mixture of the noble and the buffoon, which smacks strongly of Italian influence, like the sentiment underlying *Orlando Furioso*. In its verse he copies the forms of Italian poetry, though it may be remembered that these forms had already been imitated by the pastoral writers of Spain, and that Sidney pays no more attention to them than he does to the meters of classical prosody, which appear by their side in his romance.

Why Sidney called his work by a name which must have suggested to every educated man of his time the pastoral of Sannazaro is not clear, unless indeed he intended by the loan to emphasize the poetical portions of the novel. To be sure he very likely gave it no title at all, since he left it incomplete at his death, and in manuscript, and the editors may have called it after the country which is the scene of the action. Yet in choosing that country for his background the author must have realized the discord he would create, in departing so far from the traditional conception of Arcadian life, and in placing in its peaceful midst his episodes of feudalism and erotic adventure. The most original part of his book is, confessedly, the development of the comic element in the history of Dametas and his family, and the taste of a genuine Shaksperian public is reflected in the rough jokes and buffooneries of this country clown.

In enumerating the various sources, Spanish, Italian, French, or Greek, which were drawn upon to supply material for the *Arcadia*, we must not forget the occasional flashes of independent observation and the views of real life, which from time to time unconsciously obtrude on the assumed ideality of the romance. For a romance it is, in its present form, an incongruous pastime of daily recreations, but which—had the author foreseen its publication

—might have been molded into the shape of a regular novel and have been to English fiction what the *Astrée* was to French—a starting point for a new departure. But the departure was never made, and later stories show slight traces of its presence, while Greene's *Arcadia*, published three years before Sidney's, is a pastoral pure and simple, and in no way belies the name it bears.

If Sidney had no followers in the line of ideal fiction, he had at least a rival with the novel readers of the time in the person of Thomas Lodge. The latter's *Rosalind*, which appeared about the same time as the *Arcadia*, resembles the latter in its essence, being an attempt to fuse in one narrative the best features of the heroic and pastoral school of fiction. It is possible that Lodge may have received some useful hints from the efforts of Sidney, but at all events his story is more compact, more logical, and consequently more readable. Certain situations of the romances of chivalry are here repeated and the pastoral notion of the heroine's disguise in man's dress plays a prominent part in the plot.

All of these works of English literature—which form what may be called the imaginative fiction of their day—have been too often analyzed and commentated to require any further mention now and here. But there existed along with them another style of insular romancing which has not been so frequently enlarged upon by modern writers. It is true this style is not so important as the former, since it in no way asserted any originality in intention, nor aspired to be the beginning of a new school. We refer to the appearance in England of stories of adventure containing a very strong flavor of the *picaresco* tales of Spain. One of these stories, a tract or pamphlet, by Chettle, published in 1595, to which he gave the name of *Piers Plainnes Seaven Yere's Prentiship*, is an unmistakable witness to the presence of *Lazarillo de Tormes*. After the manner of the Spanish rogue, Chettle's hero was bound out for seven years, in Crete and Thrace, to a courtier, a money-lender, and a miser successively.

Less apparent, however, are the forerunners of Thomas Nash's *Unfortunate Traveller, or, The Life of Jack Walton*, which was printed in 1594. Very likely much of the credit for its peculiar tone is to be given to Nash himself, and not to any special literary fashion with which he may have been acquainted. He must have read, with Chettle, the English translation of *Lazarillo de Tormes*, published in 1586, and in his *Anatomie of Absurditie*, in 1589, he shows his literary animus in denouncing most vigorously the popular romances, which perpetuated in prose the fantastic deeds of the mediæval heroes of France. Accordingly, a few years later, he was all equipped to bring out what he would claim was a true romance, and show up by its pictures of true life the ridiculous travesties of the chapbooks of chivalry. Yet while the spirit of *Lazarillo de Tormes* no doubt counted for something in his reform of fiction, his plan and incidents have a strange likeness to *Guzman de Alfarache*, the junior of *Jack Walton* by five years.

This same Jack Walton begins his life-work in the genuine *picaro* style by playing practical jokes on various victims. But he has in his temperament much more of humor than of the spirit of revenge, and his wits are not sharpened, like those of his Spanish colleague, by the grinding of hunger. After a while this happy-go-lucky youth enters the service of the Earl of Surrey, and accompanies that nobleman in his travels on the Continent. They vary the tour usually followed at that time, and make for their goal, Italy, through Holland and Germany. Here some of the customs of the people furnish amusement to our Britons, who are especially entertained by the beer-drinking and the Latin speeches which form a part of the social receptions in the Fatherland. Finally they reach Venice and the

real rascality of the story begins.   Jack changes places
with his master, and passes himself off for the earl.   But
he soon runs into the meshes of the law, is arrested as a
counterfeiter, and clapped into prison.   There he finds a
woman, a fellow-captive, makes love to her and, after their
release, travels with her as far as Florence, where they meet
the true earl.   The latter has grown weary of his wanderings and soon leaves for England, while Jack sets out for
Rome.

The imperial city does not awe our scamp in the least.
Its manners and even its monuments appear to him highly
ridiculous, and he avails himself of every chance to make
fun of them.   Suddenly, however, he is made an involun-
tary witness of a most blood-curdling scene of violence
and crime, and is seized by the police as being the real
criminal.   But an English exile saves his innocent neck
from the halter, and our *picaro* seizes the occasion to
deliver a set oration against the allurements of foreign
travel.   Now some Jews make him a prisoner, but a hanger-
on of the Papal court obtains his liberty from them and
reduces him to even a worse slavery.   From this he escapes
with his female friend, who has found him again, and sets
out once more with her for the North.   At Bologna they
come upon the real murderer in the affray at Rome and
hear him confess his guilt, a scene which calls out a few
moral reflections on murder, while inducing the couple to
profit by this example and by their experience.   So they are
formally married at last, and proceed on their way to join
the English army in Flanders.

Nash's notion was clearly to write a *picaresco* story, and
to make his Jack its hero.   He has kept to the subject
well, and has handled his matter with as much skill as his
rivals of the South.   But he failed to attract the attention
they did, for reasons which pertain to style, fashion, and
locality.   The Spaniards had more taste than Nash.   They

painted their pictures of rough life with more care and with a better shading. They were thus better artists than he, and art had become the watchword of the later Renaissance. English literature also was neither esteemed nor much known on the Continent, and consequently did not often receive the honor of translation. The current of civilization continued to set wholly from the South to the North long after Nash and his ilk had passed away, and no considerable reflux made itself felt until the days of Pope and De Foe. Should there ever arise, however, the question of priority in the description of Italian travel, or in satire of that land at the time of her decadence, the Englishman must be awarded the palm, for *Jack Walton* was published half a decade before *Guzman de Alfarache*. Still it may be questioned in view of this coincidence in the general theme of the two novels, whether there were not in existence, by the last quarter of the sixteenth century, *picaresco* tales, either in Italian or Spanish, which may have suggested their plan to both Nash and Aleman, since after making only a moderate estimate of the popularity of *Lazarillo de Tormes*, it seems almost impossible that its idea and adventures were not imitated for two score years by any writer in all Europe.

There is another interesting point to be noticed in regard to this outbreak of the *picaresco* novel in England. The hero of the Spanish stories was a self-conscious sharper, a hypocrite who proposed to get his living out of the evil side of human nature. Not so with the English *picaro*. He was an adventurer, to be sure, but an adventurer for the sake of adventure, like his contemporaries on the sea, Frobisher and Hawkins. He had no enmity toward his fellow-man, he had no revenge to take on society. He did not feel oppressed, and forced back on his own cunning to win his daily bread from the objects of his contempt or envy. He plays jokes on greenhorns, but the jokes do not entail suffering.　He laughs at the world, but his laugh is loud and hearty, too boisterous to end in a sneer.　And then he shows true indignation at vice, provided the vice is not his own, and fires the gallery with his exordiums on virtue illustrated by contrast.

In short we have in Jack Walton and his race that type of the rollicking, rough Englishman of the lower class, who delighted in life for the fun it afforded him, and took a hearty interest equally in clownish horse-play or perilous adventures.　At the bottom he is a solid, sound, uncorrupted Anglo-Saxon, whose sins are the result of his ungoverned temperament, and not of his perverted moral judgment.　Contrast Jack Walton with little Lazaro or Guzman, more famous than he, and the fidelity of his creator to his own insular type of rascal and jester is altogether evident.　By this study of his own race, and the independent conclusions he draws from his observations, Nash attained the honor of the originator of a literary type ; for Tom Jones could never have descended in direct line of ancestry from a pimp of Toledo or a sneak-thief of Seville.

Of such an amount is the novelistic baggage of England previous to the seventeenth century—one court story, two mixtures of the chivalrous and the pastoral, one *picaresco* of the English stripe.　With the consideration of these four specimens our review of the novel in the period of time which was allotted to this history properly ends.　The ancestors of the later European novel have been named and visited, and their family relations have been approximately indicated.　Yet it may not be unacceptable to the diligent reader to find in this true narrative the account also of the only other movement in novel writing, which is known to have existed previous to the year 1600.　At least such an account will have the merit of brevity, even if in itself it may lack attractiveness.

The Occidentals have been sufficiently humiliated in recent years by the proofs of their inferiority in inventions and discoveries to the great nation of the East, to bear with resignation the idea that the novel, as a completed form of fiction, was known to the Chinese before it was conceived in the West. From the thirteenth to the middle of the sixteenth century, or thereabouts, there was considerable activity in this department of literature in old Cathay, and the novels which were then written have been handed down to the present day in the same stage of development they reached three centuries ago. Their mission was clearly the didactic one. The great mass of Chinese fiction has always been addressed to the lowest social circles, and is still noted for its coarseness and indecency, rather than for its narrative qualities. So to offset the corrupting influence of such scenes the more serious disciples of Confucius produced a set of serious works, which were intended to act on the popular mind as so much moral instruction. Some few also were designed for imparting the facts of history.

The number of these learned or hortatory compositions is perhaps a dozen. Of the dozen some eight are known to Europeans, and have been accorded the honors of translation into French and English. The originals are anonymous, for fiction was not highly enough regarded among the ruling classes of Chinese society to be able to recommend to public esteem even those writers who acted as preachers against evil—the worthy Thsai-tsen, or " authors having genius." The purpose of these stories is distinctively edifying. They are divided into two classes—one designed to teach history, the other morals. The specimens of the first class are very crude from our standpoint of what fiction should be, because the fusion of romance and history in them is so imperfect. The manner of composing them was simply to take an historical background, to place in it the correct historical characters and events, and to fill in the gaps with incidents of romantic invention. In this way it was hoped to make chronological facts more toothsome to the rising generation of Nanking and Pekin. It may have done so, for tastes differ exceedingly as one makes the journey around the world, but to the Western palate these Oriental sweetmeats are both tough and acrid.

The second class, where moral edification is the object, is better appreciated among the barbarians of Europe. Our own literature occasionally strays into the field of exhortation, and we are often taught by shining examples in fiction that virtue and intelligence not only bring happiness to their fortunate possessors, but that they are also liable to be rewarded by advancement even in temporal affairs. So we are somewhat prepared for a few leading precepts from the antipodes, and have means for comparing them with the moral teachings of our own novelists. But the Thsai-tsen do not stop short with harangues to mankind to be good. They are too well stocked with knowledge for that, and into their ethical tracts they stuff such a wealth of learning about Chinese mythology, history, and folk-lore, that their pages often become too erudite for the ignorant commoner of European extraction. Still he can, by judicious omissions, easily follow the plot of the story, and appreciate the details concerning the life and customs of the country, which are incidentally presented in the allusions to the surroundings of the leading characters.

The Chinese novels which have been done into Occidental vernaculars, and which were probably the best samples of their kind inasmuch as they have won this attention, may be designated in general as novels of manners, rather than as character studies. Their tone is optimistic. The good prosper in them, and attain success by the employment of their higher mental endowments. The wicked may go on prosperously for a time, but at last they are brought low. One is distantly reminded of Dickens' procedure in these respects. In other words, the plan of a Chinese novel of this type is that of a melodrama. The three leading actors are the hero, heroine, and the heavy villain who persecutes them, but is baffled, as all heavy villains must be, by their final union. The triumph of the righteous, however, is obtained less by physical force than in the Western Hemisphere, for the basely calumniated Celestial conquers his enemies by the remarkable development of his intellectual fiber, and wins his bride by the steady pursuit of knowledge.

So we are not surprised to find that the story of *The Fortunate Union*, translated toward 1826 by Sir John Davis, celebrates the erudition of a young man of good family, who has passed an excellent civil service examination, and who is far-and-away the most upright and cultivated youth of his generation. For such a paragon it was naturally hard to find a fitting mate, but one at last is presented, whose literary abilities are second only to her moral virtues, if indeed they are not first. But the envious are busy ever, and the jealous intriguers of Mongolia exhaust all their almond-eyed stratagems to prevent the union of these embodiments of the true, the good, and the beautiful. For a while their tricks avail, thereby affording us of the Occident many interesting details of the life, manners, and sentiments of respectable people in China. At the end, of course the villains are foiled, and virtue appropriates to itself its temporal reward.

Perhaps a better known specimen of the Chinese novel is one of the latest, belonging, without much doubt, to the first half of the fifteenth century. It is called *The Two Educated Girls*, and was done into French in 1860 by Stanislas Julien. A nobleman of the imperial court rejoices in a daughter, Chan-taï, who, at the age of ten, robs the older poets of their laurels by her verses on the *White Swallows*.

This wonderful achievement reaches the ears of the emperor and prompts him to demand of her father her presence at the capital.   No sooner has Chan-taï reached that enchanting place, than the talents enshrined in her modesty gain for her the esteem and admiration of all its inhabitants.   In the poetical contests which invite her skill, her grace and learning inspire the good and frown down the arrogant.   The prizes are all hers.   The natural sequence of such continued triumph is the jealousy of the discomfited rivals.   They unite to slander her to their imperial master, but he only rails at their insinuations.

Now, the second maiden of learned parts arrives on the scene ; not another scion of a noble house, but a plebeian villager, whose erudition has broken out at the age of twelve.   This impassioned rustic is not, however, without the germs of tender emotions.   The literary compositions of Ping, a young man renowned for his prose style, ensnare her budding affections, while her lines make no less an impression on his melting heart.   In this state of rapture our enamored village genius is summoned to court, where Chan-taï welcomes her, protects her, and forms with her what is destined to prove a lasting friendship.   So the narrative proceeds to develop the accomplishments of its heroes, and decry the envy of their detractors ; and after it has devoted two-thirds of its length to this task, another wonder of the masculine gender meets Chan-taï by accident. He is her fate and she his.   A poetical courtship ensues, and the parchments suffer, until a general wedding unites the couples of the virtuous and learned, and all live happy ever after.

It will be seen that the Eastern predecessor of *Les Femmes savantes* indulges its readers more in a description of manners and literature than it does in the elaboration of a plot. Others of the Chinese novels possess more of this latter requisite ; or, if not more, the plot appears earlier at least in the romance. Thus, in *The Two Cousins*, which belongs to the middle of the fifteenth century, and which de Rémusat turned into French in 1826, there are more incidents and a greater excitation of the sympathy. For the jealous and those who persecute the good invent a larger number of schemes to baffle the righteous cause, and force true love to triumph over an increased list of obstacles before it reaches the desired union.

In other novels of this class the domestic life of the upper ten plays a greater part, and we listen to the account of the fortunes of aspiring young men who seek to win fame in the state examinations, through which the best minds of the nation rise to the highest places in the government of the country. The works of this kind have a greater interest for us, because of the glimpses they afford of the real spirit of the great people of the East, but very likely they were not any more attractive on this account to the public for which they were written. Yet it is noticeable that whatever the theme or the incidents of the novel, the connecting thread, love, which gives it its plot, is not the passion with which we are familiar in our own works of fiction. It may grow, to be sure, into something more intimate and tender, but at first the mutual affection of hero and heroine, as pictured in the romances of Confucian China, is born of esteem for character and of admiration for literary gifts.

It is hardly worth while to comment longer on this style of Oriental fiction, for it adds nothing to our conception of novelistic composition. The construction of the works which represent it, is, indeed, most elementary, resembling in that respect the earlier plebeian examples of Greco-Roman fiction. Like the story of *Clitophon and Leucippe*, or the *Babylonica* of Jamblichus, the narrative of *The Fortunate Union*, or *The Two Educated Girls*, consists of a series of adventures in private and public life, which have borrowed the skeleton of a love story, not only to make themselves interesting, but also in the case of the Chinese novels to render more agreeable their moral instructions. The principal motive power in the action of the story is also the same in the fiction of the Sophists and the followers of Confucius, namely, the persecution of the lovers. In Greece, however, their arch-enemy was Fate; in China, this evil spirit is personified in a man. For this reason there seem to be plausible grounds on which to base the theory that the Chinese novel is a melodrama in a lengthened form, and that the ultimate origins of it are to be found in the popular theater of the nation. The fiction which these serious tales displaced was coarse and vulgar, and very like such plays as our own mediæval *farces*—the supposed starting-point of the Spanish realistic stories—in both subject and manner. Like both the Greek and the Spanish tales of individual experience there is in the Chinese novel no notion of psychological study. They are simply descriptions of customs and events. They are earlier in time than our European novels of the Renaissance, but, as they shared in the life of all other creations of that motionless empire, when once created they never progressed, and Chinese fiction, together with Chinese art and Chinese thought, remains stationary, fixed at the very point it reached five hundred years ago.

NOTES.

CHAPTER I.

The definition of novel given here was derived from Rhode's book on the Greek novel, where it is assumed that a plot is essential to this particular kind of prose fiction. The more recent dictionaries of the English language, including the Imperial and Century, also recognize the essential elements which distinguish the novel from its fellows in fiction.

CHAPTERS II.–III.

For a general history of the subject of these chapters, see E. Rhode's *Der griechische Roman und seine Vorläufer*. Leipzig, 1876.

For the *Nimrod* fragment, see the scientific periodical *Hermes*, vol. xxviii, pp. 161–193.

For further bibliography and other analyses of the novels see Dunlop's *History of Fiction*, revised by Henry Wilson, Bohn's Standard Library. London, 1888. For English translations of Heliodorus, Tatius, and Longus, see Rowland Smith's *Greek Romances* in Bohn's Library. The selections given here are from Smith's rendering. For Xenophon of Ephesus there is no English translation, but a German version may be found in G. A. Bürger's *Sämmtliche Werke*, vol. ii. pp. 436 *seq*. Göttingen, 1844.

The remaining Greek novels and fragments are not available to modern readers outside of their Latin form, excepting the story of *Apollonius of Tyre* in the *Gesta Romanorum* in Bohn's Library.

For the imitations of the Byzantine period, see Karl Krumbacher's *Geschichte der byzantinischen Literatur*. Munich, 1891.

Consult also *Archiv für das Studium der neueren Sprachen*, vol. l. pp. 1 *seq.* In the *Contemporary Review*, vol. xxx. pp. 858 *seq.*, is an article on the early Christian romances.

The influence of Greek novels on mediæval French literature is, discussed in G. Paris' *La Littérature française au moyen âge*, ch. 3, and Bibliography, 2d ed. Paris, 1890.

For Boccaccio's sources see M. Landau's *Quellen des Decameron*, 2d ed. Stuttgart, 1884. Stories ii. 6 and v. 3 do not seem to me to be of Greek origin. The activity of the Greek novel at the Renaissance is treated in Dunlop, and in H. Körting's *Geschichte des französischen Romans im xvii. Jahrhundert*, vol. i. pt. i. ch. 2. Oppeln, 1891.

Chapter IV. -

For the bibliography in this chapter see the one in G. Paris' *La Littérature française au moyen âge*, already cited.

Analyses of the Breton prose romances, of *Perceforest*, and of the prose versions of some of the heroic epic poetry are also given in Dunlop.

Chapter V.

A general account of the Spanish romances of chivalry is to be found in Ticknor's *History of Spanish Literature*. See Index.

On the origin of *Amadis de Gaula* see Th. Braga's *Historia da Litteratura Portugueza—Amadis de Gaula*, Oporto, 1873, and L. Braunfel's *Kritischer Versuch über den Roman Amadis von Gallien*. Leipzig, 1876.

The work of Joao Lobeira is discussed in the *Zeitschrift für romanische Philologie*, vol. iv. pp. 347 *seq.*, and in Gröber's *Grundriss der rom. Philologie*, vol. ii. pp. 167–190, 216–226.

The text of Montalvo's *Amadis de Gaula* is printed in the *Biblioteca de Autores Españoles*, vol. xl. *Libros de Caballerias*. The introduction to this volume, by Pascual de Gayangos, contains a study of the history of the romances of Spain, and a list of them extending down to the year 1800.

The best English translation of *Amadis*, considerably abridged, is that of Robert Southey. London, 1803.

CHAPTER VI.

See Ticknor in the German translation by Julius, with supplement by Wolf, and Gayangos in the *Biblioteca*, for bibliography of this chapter. Dunlop gives a meager analysis of *Amadis* proper, but is quite full for the sequels, the *Palmerins* and *Tirante the White*.

Brunet's *Manuel du Libraire* furnishes notes for the foreign translations under the different titles.

The Ticknor collection of books preserved in the Boston Public Library is the best collection of Spanish books accessible to Americans. I failed, however, to find in it *Lepolemo*, which Ticknor states explicitly was in his library.

The best English rendering of *Palmerin de Inglaterra* is Southey's. London, 1807.

CHAPTER VII.

For a general view of the subject consult A. Gaspary's *Geschichte der italienischen Literatur*, preferably in Zingarelli and Rossi's Italian translation. Turin, 1887–91. It contains also an abundant bibliography. See also J. A. Symonds' *Renaissance in Italy*.

On the eclogue in mediæval literature consult F. Macri-Leone's *La Bucolica latina, nel xiv*. 1889. G. Körting's *Boccaccio's Leben und Werke* is the authority on that writer.

Sannazaro's *Arcadia* is critically edited by M. Scherillo. Turin, 1888. Compare also F. Torraco's *La Materia dell' Arcadia*. Città di Castello, 1888. Symonds gives excellent translations from the *Arcadia* in vol. ii. of his *Italian Literature*.

Poliziano's drama is well described in Symonds. Symonds' *Catholic Reaction* contains a long study of Tasso.

For Guarini see V. Rossi's *Battista Guarini ed Il Pastor Fido*, Turin, 1886 ; also Symonds' *Catholic Reaction*.

The opening episode of the *Pastor Fido* is given by Pausanias, book viii. ch. 21. See Bohn's edition.

For the novelistic ideas and influence of these works see Körting's *Geschichte, etc.*, vol. i. pt. i. ch. 4, and Index. Dunlop analyzes only the *Arcadia* and, unsatisfactorily, the *Ameto*.

Chapter VIII.

For the authors mentioned in this chapter see Ticknor's *History of Spanish Literature*, Th. Braga's *Historia da Litteratura Portugueza*, Oporto, 1870; Grober's *Grundriss*, vol. ii. pp. 287–304. For Ribeiro see in Braga's series, *Bernardim Ribeiro e os Bucolistas*. Oporto, 1872.

For Montemayor, see J. G. Schönherr's *Jorge de Montemayor*. Halle, 1886. This is a Leipzig dissertation.

The most available edition of *Menina e Moça* is in the *Obras de Bernardim Ribeiro*. Lisbon, 1852.

Diana is published in the series *Biblioteca cldsica española*. Barcelona, 1886.

A more complete analysis of *Diana* is to be found in Dunlop's *History of Fiction*.

Chapter IX.

For the influence of *Diana* in France, see Körting's *Geschichte des franz. Romans im xvii Jahr.*, vol. i. Index. Compare also Schönherr.

For the other novels named in the chapter, see Ticknor's *History of Spanish Literature*, Index, and Supplement by Wolf. Always the German edition. Most of the novels mentioned are to be found in the Ticknor Library. I was not able to find, however, Bernardo de la Vega's *El Pastor de Iberia*.

My doubts as to the actual popularity of the Spanish pastoral after *Diana* were suggested by the fact that the copy of Bovadilla's *Nimphas y Pastores de Henares* in the Ticknor Library was never read. The copy was printed in 1587, and I had the honor of cutting some of its opening leaves in June, 1890.

Chapter X.

See Ticknor's *History of Spanish Literature*, Index; also H. Körting's *Geschichte des franz. Romans*, vol. i. pt. i. ch. 3.

For the farce *Le Garçon et l'Aveugle* see *Jahrbuch für rom. und eng. Litteratur*, vol. vi. (1865) pp. 163–172. The manuscript illustrations are mentioned in a letter by J. J. Jusserand to *The Athenæum* for 1888, p. 883.

For *Lazarillo de Tormes* see A. Morel-Fatio's *Études sur l'Espagne*, Première Série.   Paris, 1888.   The text for *Lazarillo* and *Guzman* is given in the *Biblioteca de Autores Españoles*, vol. iii.   A study of *Lazarillo* from the sociological standpoint appeared in *La Revue des Deux Mondes*, vol. lxxxvi. pp. 870 *seq.*

Dunlop's analysis of *Guzman* may be compared to the one given here.

CHAPTER XI.

For the Spanish novels cited see Ticknor's *History*, Index.

For the English novel see J. J. Jusserand's *The English Novel in the Time of Shakespeare*.   London, 1890.

For analyses of the novels mentioned see their authors' works, Dunlop's *History of Fiction*, and Bayard Tuckerman's *A History of English Prose Fiction*, ch. 3.   New York, 1882.

For the Chinese novels see the prefaces of the translations mentioned: *Les Deux Cousines*, by Rémusat, Paris, 1826; *Deux jeunes filles lettrés*, by S. Julien, Paris, 1860; and *La Revue contemporaine* for 1860.

INDEX.

THE END.